William

William Holden

A Biography

MICHELANGELO CAPUA

McFarland & Company, Inc., Publishers

Jefferson, North Carolina, and London

Library of Congress Cataloguing-in-Publication Data

Capua, Michelangelo, 1966–
    William Holden : A Biography / Michelangelo Capua.
        p.   cm.
    Includes bibliographical references and index.
    Includes filmography.

    ISBN 978-0-7864-4440-3
    softcover : 50# alkaline paper ∞

    1. Holden, William, 1918–1981.   2. Motion picture actors
and actresses — United States — Biography.   I. Title.
PN2287.H58C37   2010
791.4302' 8092 — dc22   2009037836
[B]

British Library cataloguing data are available

On the cover: publicity photograph of William Holden from the
early 1950s; background ©2010 Shutterstock

Manufactured in the United States of America

McFarland & Company, Inc., Publishers
    Box 611, Jefferson, North Carolina 28640
    www.mcfarlandpub.com

To Leonardo

Table of Contents

Preface

William Holden was one of Hollywood's most enduring stars, a true leading man with a career that spanned more than 40 years and included over 70 films and three Academy Award nominations. Charming, handsome and gifted, Bill (as Holden was called) was the archetypal all–American youth with a strong open face, a disarming smile and a strong, pleasant voice. He came along with absolutely no experience and charmed audiences with his affable personality and handsome look. He won an Oscar as the cynical sergeant in Billy Wilder's *Stalag 17*. Yet most filmgoers tend to remember him best as either the gigolo-writer in Billy Wilder's *Sunset Blvd.* or the restless hunk in Joshua Logan's *Picnic*. "Golden Holden" he was called when in the late '50s he was so powerful at the box office that nearly every important script went through his agent. Bill's life was also a tornado of international adventures and romances with such glamorous film stars as Audrey Hepburn and Grace Kelly. His story, though, is one of a complex, tortured personality, as he suffered from alcoholism and depression. A mature Holden re-emerged as an outlaw in *The Wild Bunch* and as a symbol of cynical decency in *Network* and *S.O.B.* Nevertheless, Bill wanted to be remembered not only as a Hollywood superstar but also as a cosmopolitan gentleman with a deep commitment toward the preservation of African wildlife. Today the William Holden Wildlife Foundation, established after his tragic death by his friend, actress Stefanie Powers, still carries out Bill's unfinished work.

I have benefited from the help of many informants and institutions, and from the assistance and support of friends without whom the completion of this project would have been impossible. I would like to thank Yaakov Perry, Alessandro Bigazzi, the fantastic staff of the British Film

Institute in London, the staff of Bobst Library, New York University, the staff of the New York Public Library for the Performing Arts at Lincoln Center, the Museum of Television and Radio of New York, the staff of the British Library's Humanities Reading Room, St. Pancras, London, Bob Thomas (author of *Golden Boy: The Untold Story of William Holden*) and Jerry Ohlinger's Movie Material Store, New York.

Finally I offer my great gratitude to my editor Stuart T. Williams for his invaluable help and patience with my English translation.

Introduction

Medical Examiner Case No. 81-14582: Accidental death from blood loss.
Reading like a file from an episode of television's *CSI*, it is a real case filed
on November 16, 1981, by Los Angeles County Coroner Thomas T. Noguchi. Noguchi supervised the autopsy of William Holden at the Forensic
Science Center where he established extreme blood loss as the cause of the
actor's death.

Oddly, the event paralleled the opening scene of *Sunset Blvd.*, the
film which made William Holden a top star. The scene features the corpse
of gigolo Joe Gillis, played by Holden, found by police floating face-down
in a Hollywood mansion swimming pool. In reality, one of the most
beloved stars from Hollywood's Golden Era was tragically gone. Holden
was an actor whose masculinity appealed as much to men as his all–American looks appealed to women. Yet, his rich, handsome, and famous exterior hid a lonely, misunderstood alcoholic.

Bill, as everybody called him, bled to death from a deep head wound
caused by a drunken fall. At the age of 63, the solitary Holden was not
aware how severe his injury was, trying to staunch the bleeding with tissues rather than calling for help. According to the coroner's report, his
blood alcohol content was 0.22 percent, meaning that he consumed at
least eight to ten drinks in short order prior to the accident. An empty
quart size vodka bottle was found in his kitchen trash and another half-
empty bottle in a cupboard. Noguchi estimated that Bill was conscious
for only five or ten minutes after the fall and died in a half-hour.

The accident occurred in Holden's fifth-floor luxury condo bedroom,
located on Ocean Avenue in Santa Monica's Shorecliff Towers. According
to the coroner's report, Bill tripped over a throw rug and hit his head on

3

the sharp edge of a teak nightstand. The wound on the right side of Bill's forehead was over two inches long, penetrating to the skull. He had banged his head into the furniture with such force that the nightstand slid into the wall, leaving an indentation. Bill reclined on the bed for a few minutes, trying to stop the flow of the blood before rolling onto the floor in agony, where he quickly died. Strangely, the telephone, less than an arm's length away on the nightstand, had a few drops of blood on it, but remained untouched. When his body was found by a police officer who broke into the condo, Bill was lying to the right of his bed, supine, with his arms at his sides, wearing only a pajama top. The bedclothes and the carpet under him were blood-drenched, the television was on, and a movie script, which he was apparently reading, was nearby. The condo was carefully inspected and dusted for fingerprints but no sign of foul play was found: The door of the apartment was locked, and nothing had been stolen. Everything pointed to a terrible accident. The police sent the body to the Forensic Science Center for an autopsy, which ruled out the possibility of an assault or any other criminal act. The body temperature and decomposition, cloudy eyes and a greenish abdomen indicated to Noguchi that Bill had been dead for at least four days before he was found.

Bill's body was found thanks to an intimate friend, Pat Stauffer, who had not heard from him in almost two weeks and was more worried than usual. The woman asked Brian Keating, Holden's butler at his Palm Springs house, to drive from the desert to the Santa Monica condo used by Bill when he was in Los Angeles on business. Once Keating arrived, Shorecliff Towers' manager Bill Martin would not admit him. The Santa Monica Police Department was called and on-duty Sergeant Dick Tapia was dispatched. The policeman asked that Martin be allowed to enter Bill's condo, using a spare set of keys. On entering the residence, Tapia discovered Bill's lifeless body and immediately notified the precinct, which sent two police cars and an ambulance. In a couple of hours the tragic news had leaked to the media and the whole world learned about the death of William Holden.

Friend Billy Wilder, who directed Holden in four films including *Sunset Blvd.* and *Stalag 17*, commented, "He was such a secret person. He would not open up — even with his close friends — or ask for help or someone to listen to him."

1

Wild Boy

••

"I wanted to be the best motion picture actor in the world. My heroes were Fredric March and Spencer Tracy. They were my ideals." — William Holden

••

The Beedle family had been living in America for four generations. They emigrated from England at the beginning of the 19th century, settling in Ohio, known among American immigrants for its fertile land. Dissatisfied with his farm, Joseph Beedle moved in 1812 to O'Fallon, a small, quiet, rural town in Southeastern Illinois. There, Beedle bought a large piece of land where he established a big farm. With his first profits, Joseph built a house in downtown O'Fallon at 319 North Cherry Road, where William Franklin Beedle was born in 1892. In his early days in school, Bill proved to be a promising athlete, winning any sort of sport competition, especially decathlons. Young Bill was also an excellent student and a member of the local Baptist church choir. He majored in chemistry at McKendree College in Lebanon, Illinois, where he met a pretty, spirited fellow student, Mary Ball from Litchfield. The couple was engaged after a few months of dating. The very religious Mary was proud that her family was related to Martha Ball, George Washington's mother, while Mary's father was cousin to Senator Warren G. Harding, who later became the twenty-ninth president of United States in 1921.

"The Beedles are a cocktail of Irish, British and German blood mixed in an American shaker.... I am the great-great son of one of the founders of our fatherland," proudly admitted William Holden years later about his ancestors.[1]

In the spring of 1917, Bill Beedle and Mary Ball graduated from McKendree College a few days before their wedding was announced. The ceremony was held in the parlor of Bill's house on Cherry Street and followed by a modest reception. On April 17, 1918, Mary gave birth to a healthy, lively boy she named William Franklin, Jr., and called Billy to distinguish him from his namesake.

Billy's father Bill was still a strong, athletic man despite suffering from a chronic lung condition, pneumosilicosis. Doctors strongly advised that he leave the harsh weather of Illinois and move to a warmer place to avoid any irreversible consequences. In the meantime, Mary gave birth to her second son, Robert (Bob) Westfield Beedle, in 1921. The following year, Bill quit his job as a druggist and moved his family to Monrovia, a small rural town twenty miles east from Los Angeles. There he had accepted a position as industrial chemist at the George W. Gooch Laboratories.

Eighteen months after settling into their new bungalow, Mary gave birth to her third boy, Richard (Dick) Porter Beedle. Mary interrupted her teaching career after giving birth to Billy to be a full-time mother, taking care of the house and accompanying the children to school. On Sunday, she brought them to the Oneonta Congregational Church, teaching them good manners and nurturing their faith by reading to them from the Bible. Bill worked long, hard days at the labs and in his spare time used his talent as a former amateur gymnast to teach his three sons, especially Billy the eldest, tumbling, physical training and boxing.

The strict upbringing had only a mild influence on little Billy, who at five insisted on being called Bill like his father. The child was very vivacious and outgoing, gifted with a strong curiosity that left little time for his studies, forcing Mary to enroll him in Sunday school at the Oneonta Congregational Church.

In an article written years later, Mrs. Beedle remembered one Sunday morning when Bill showed for breakfast in jeans and a t-shirt, announcing that he was not going to Sunday school. He had a new bicycle, it was a beautiful day, and he could see no reason not to enjoy it. Mary calmly reminded him of the inseparable link between privilege and responsibility. It would be okay to skip Sunday school if Bill were willing to give up going to the movies the following Saturday. Needless to say, he went to Sunday school. Another time, when he was ten, Bill burst with excitement when Ray Schalk, popular catcher for the Chicago White Sox and a family friend, offered to take him out to watch a training session. Being

Bill Beedle on a boat at twelve (1930).

mad about baseball and a big fan of Schalk, he wanted that day with the team more than everything else. But since Bill had shown signs of being allergic to school work, Mary disapproved of him missing a school day. "But I may never get a chance like this again," Bill told his mother. "I know. It's really too bad," she replied. At that moment Mary thought Bill was about to cry. But he just stood there looking in his mother's eyes before walking over to call Schalk, saying, "I'm awfully sorry, I'd give anything to go. But I'm in a jam at school and I can't."[2]

At the end of 1929, the Great Depression took hold of the American economy and millions of Americans suddenly lost their jobs. Like all other businesses, the Gooch Laboratories went through hard times, facing the possibility of bankruptcy, and the Beedles feared for their financial stability. In a desperate effort to overcome crisis, Bill and Mary decided to merge their savings to take ownership of the laboratories. Two years later, their efforts were rewarded: Under Bill's management, Gooch Laboratories again prospered, allowing his family to move twenty miles south to the affluent neighborhood of South Pasadena.

Moving changed little Bill's personality, Mary explained many years later in an interview: Her son had always behaved politely and kindly like "an angel," and then suddenly after changing residence he transformed into a reckless and rebellious boy, getting into dangerous situations with his friends.[3] According to schoolmate Richard Steele, Bill's undisciplined behavior was not merely an effort to prove his masculinity, but simply a reaction of being snubbed by the local rich, bourgeois kids, who excluded him from their parties.

Nevertheless, Steele remembered Bill as a very happy, outgoing kid with a subtle sense of humor and extraordinary athletic skills, which allowed him to walk on his hands and tumble in the air like a professional gymnast. Stamped in Steele's memory was the contradictory image of Bill in his teens, being still and serious in the Episcopal Church, singing hymns in the choir. As soon as the service ended, he jumped on his secondhand motorcycle (bought by his father) and performed stunts for the exiting crowds. Besides doing impromptu stunts for church crowds, Bill also used his reckless behavior to make pocket money. Boys would bet him to do things such as jump a nearly five-foot fence of iron spikes from a standing position or walk along the outer rail of Pasadena's "suicide bridge" on his hands.

One day his mother looked out the window and saw him coming down the street on his motorcycle, standing in the saddle, both hands aloft. She didn't dare scream at him, but waited until the exhibition was over before collaring him and reading him the maternal riot act. Bill insisted there was nothing to it.

"If that's so," she demanded, "why were the boys betting on you?"

"They didn't think I could do it."

"Doesn't that prove it's dangerous?"

"No. They just never tried it."

"But why don't they try it, if it's not dangerous?"

"Because I won't let 'em. It's my motorcycle, ain't it?"[4] There was no way for Mary to win an argument with him. Eventually she would punish him, forbidding him from going to the movies.

Only by luck did Bill avoid a dangerous accident when he hit a car driven by a local farmer who had suddenly swerved. The damages were minor, but Bill was so afraid of his parents' punishment, he asked the farmer to take him home to personally explain that Bill was not responsible for the accident.

One night Bill and a friend threw a straw dummy onto a highway in front of a speeding car. The vehicle was being driven by two highway patrolmen who caught the two kids hiding in the bushes, roaring with laughter. As punishment, the two youngsters spent the next six weeks at a neighborhood station learning state traffic regulations.

In his teens, Bill became one of the most popular students at the South Pasadena High School. Girls were crazy about his clear blue eyes, sexy smile and hyper-masculine, reckless behavior. Boys envied his athletic body, his sports trophies, and the adoring girls around him. His only limitation was being a bad dancer, but girls seldom realized it when caught by his charm on the dance floor.

Bill always found the time to practice the clarinet, the drums and the piano, and to sing in the boys school choir, play football and basketball. This left very little room in his schedule for his studies. Because of his poor grades, he was forced to attend summer school in order to graduate from junior high.

During summer vacation in 1936, and upon Bill's graduation from South Pasadena High School, Bill Sr. forced his three sons to help out in the laboratory with the hope that one day the boys might follow in his footsteps. Bob and Dick did not mind, but Bill hated the processing of fertilizer. He used every excuse to avoid it, forcing his disappointed father to make him a Gooch Labs delivery boy. Bill picked up and delivered supplies with his motorcycle all over the town. Nevertheless, when the time came, Bill appeased his dad by enrolling in Pasadena Junior College as a chemistry major. Before classes started, Bill took a long cross-country auto trip, from California to New York City. It was his first real adventure away

Bill at fourteen in South Pasadena in 1932.

from Pasadena. He visited many places he had only heard or read about, but it was New York that fascinated him the most with his cosmopolitan allure — the Empire State Building and, of course, the lighted marquees of Broadway. He watched so many plays and Broadway shows that he became stage struck. Once he returned to the Pasadena Junior College, he took a course in radio drama and was selected to act in several radio plays for the local station KECA. During his sophomore year, while Bill was singing in the college's *a cappella* choir, Robert Ben Ali, a local amateur director, noticed his bass-baritone and asked him if he was interested in a small role in *Manya*, a play he had written, produced and directed. The play was about the Curie family of Paris, whose daughter Marie (Manya was her nickname) accidentally discovered radium. Ali wanted to use Bill as the show's narrator. Ali was so impressed by the narration that he asked Bill to take over a small acting role in the show (that of Eugène Curie, Marie's 80-year-old father-in-law) when the actor originally cast was suddenly indisposed. The only previous stage experience Bill had was at age of ten when he played the lead in *Rip Van Winkle* in his school's annual sixth-grade play. Bill loved new challenges; despite his lack of experience, he accepted immediately.

The rehearsals took place at the Pasadena Workshop Theatre and the performances began the following spring. To look the part of the 80-year-old man, Bill had to go through long, heavy makeup sessions where a white beard and wig were applied, while he practiced speaking in a lower, slower tone. Gilmore Brown, impresario of the prestigious Pasadena Community Playhouse, was so impressed by the cast's professionalism that he invited them to extend the run for ten extra days in the larger Playbox Theatre. On opening night at the Playbox, Milton Lewis, assistant to Paramount's head of talent Arthur Jacobson, was seated in the first row, looking for fresh new faces. Lewis liked Bill's voice and his manner intrigued him, even though he (Lewis) was unable to judge his features under the baggy clothes and heavy makeup. Later the talent scout went backstage to talk with Bill and invited him to drop by Paramount Studios the following day to meet with his boss for a screen test. Strangely unimpressed, Bill declined the invitation since he had a chemistry test and could not miss it. "I don't need the business," Bill told Lewis. "I just did it for fun."[5] "Opportunity knocks only once, Beedle," replied Lewis.

"This time, it'll have to knock twice," said Bill.[6]

Lewis reported the story to Jacobson, who was amused by "the little chemist" and asked Lewis to contact him again and invite him for a screen test the day *after* the exam. A few days later, in the spring of 1938, Bill Beedle arrived on his motorbike at Paramount Studios where he was expected for his first screen test. Jacobson was personally in charge of the audition.

First, Lewis handed him a script from the film *The Bride Comes Home* and invited him to read it aloud. The talent scout listened carefully and agreed to send it to his boss' office, where Jacobson asked Bill to improvise from *Manya*. After a few seconds of concentration, Bill hunched over and started delivering the lines, imitating the voice of old Eugène Curie.

Bill's theatrical mannerisms did not appeal to Jacobson, who suddenly stopped him, inviting him to tell a joke. Bill was caught off guard and delivered a flat, unconvincing story. Nevertheless, the head of the talent department gave him a script to take home and study. A few days later, Bill returned to Paramount ready to face the "fish bowl" test required of all candidates for acting contracts. They were directed to audition on a bright stage before a large glass screen, behind which sat Paramount executives, producers and directors in the dark, judging the actors. Bill auditioned together with a young actress, Rebecca Wassman. Although the judges were not overly impressed with his performance, he managed to pass the test. Paramount offered him the standard six-month contract at $50 per week, with the option to revise his contract every six months for seven years and the possibility of increasing his salary up to $750 per week at the end of the term. Not bad for a twenty-year-old schoolkid with no experience. More difficult than the "fish bowl" test was the task of convincing his parents of his intention to drop out of college to pursue a career in the film industry. (Because he was not yet twenty-one, Bill's parents' consent was required.) Bill promised that if he wouldn't make it as an actor in a year, he would go back to college and finish his studies.

Bill soon realized that Paramount was in no hurry to exploit their new faces. Arthur Hornblow, Jr., one of the most powerful Hollywood producers, saw Bill's screen test and wrote in a note, "How can you waste your money making tests of this kid? He's got fishy eyes and under slung jaw."[7]

When Bill arrived at the studio on his first day after the contract was signed, he had a fight with a security guard who refused him admittance because his name was not on the list. After Jacobson's office was called, he was admitted. Jacobson took him to Terry DeLapp, head of Paramount publicity, who looked him over and said, "Beedle, huh? That won't do. Sounds too much like an insect or like a toothpaste. You need a new name."

"True," replied Bill, amused. "In school, kids used to call me Bugs!"

Bill proposed a long list of potential names, among them Washington, as an homage to his illustrious ancestor. DeLapp suddenly remembered he had just hung up the telephone with a friend, *Los Angeles Times* editor William Holden. He instantly called the journalist and asked to borrow his name for a new actor. Holden did not mind and William Franklin Beedle, Jr., became William Holden.

The Paramount's Golden Circle on a personal appearance tour for Cecil B. DeMille's *Union Pacific* (1939). Top row, left to right: Louise Campbell, Betty Field, Joseph Allen, Ellen Drew and Judith Barrett; center row: Robert Preston, Patricia Morison, Susan Hayward, William Henry; bottom row: Joyce Matthews, Janice Logan, William Holden and Evelyn Keyes.

On February 21, 1939, the *Los Angeles Times* published a short article which mentioned that a young actor named William Beedle had changed his name to William Holden and been cast in the upcoming film *What a Life* starring Jackie Cooper.[8] Although Bill was pleasantly surprised to learn from the press that he would finally make his screen debut, DeLapp told him that the news was untrue. It was just a publicity stunt to have a title of one of the upcoming Paramount films printed in the paper.

Every day for many months, including weekends, Bill reported to Paramount, filling all his available time with acting and speech classes, being photographed for promotion, taking part in any sort of publicity in order to be noticed by someone and finally get a part. When he was free from all the engagements, he would wander onto all the sets asking the technicians questions, eager to learn every aspect of the film industry.

One day Bill was invited to a formal lunch along with twelve of Paramount's other promising young players, and it was announced that they now all belonged to "The Golden Circle," a new publicity stunt from Paramount to promote the studio's future stars. The group included Ellen Drew, Louise Campbell, Betty Field, Judith Barrett, Joseph Allen, William Henry, Joyce Matthews, Janice Logan, Susan Hayward, Evelyn Keyes, Robert Preston and Patricia Morison. Of these twelve new faces, only Bill and Susan Hayward emerged in time as stars. The group was sent out on personal appearance tours, including one for Cecil B. DeMille's *Union Pacific*.

"I wanted to be the best motion picture actor in the world. My heroes were Fredric March and Spencer Tracy. They were my ideals. I used them as a kind of goal for myself. I had enough of the extrovert in me to want that kind of recognition," Bill reminisced many years later about the beginning of his career.[9]

Finally he worked as an extra in two films: *Prison Farm*, where he appeared with some prisoners sledgehammering rocks, and *Million Dollar Legs*, a musical starring Betty Grable and Donald O'Connor where he delivered his first two-word line, "Thank you," along with ninety-nine other diploma recipients in a graduation scene.

2

Golden Boy

••

"When I went to the opening of *Golden Boy* and saw my name on the marquee ... I suddenly knew that it didn't mean a damn thing to me." — William Holden

••

In 1939, Columbia Pictures purchased the screen rights to Clifford Odets' play *Golden Boy*, for the then-incredible amount of $75,000. Only two years earlier it had been produced with great success at the Belasco Theatre on Broadway, starring Frances Farmer and Luther Adler. Rouben Mamoulian was assigned to direct the movie, and wanted Odets to adapt his own work. With the playwright unavailable, Mamoulian found two fledgling writers, Daniel Taradash and Lewis Meltzer. The two re-adapted the entire story for the screen and molded the tragic finale into a happier, albeit banal, "traditional Hollywood" ending.

A first-draft screenplay was sent to Harry Cohn, president of Columbia Pictures, who liked it and forwarded it to the Production Code Administration for pre-production clearance. Joseph Breen, the conservative head of the PCA, replied that the adulterous relationship between two major characters and a sexual affair between one of the two and another character had to be changed. Further, a series of lines of dialogue were to be eliminated. The script went back to the writers for revision and approved only after a third draft was delivered.

Cohn wanted Luther Adler, the magnificent Golden Boy on stage, to play the role again on screen, but the actor was unavailable. Second choice John Garfield was stymied by a feud between Cohn and Garfield's boss at Warner Bros., Jack L. Warner. Tyrone Power was Cohn's third

15

choice, but Twentieth Century–Fox refused to lend one of its biggest stars out to play the role. The role called for someone with a boxer's physique, who could actually box, play the violin and, above all, act. Beauty was not a specific requirement, but the lead had to be a tall, dark twenty-one-year old.

"How about going for an unknown, Harry?" producer William Perlberg prodded. "We could have a search for Golden Boy, like Selznick did for Scarlett O'Hara."[1]

Columbia launched a campaign to find a new face for *Golden Boy*. Elia Kazan, Robert Taylor, Henry Fonda, Robert Cummings, Robert Wilcox and Richard Carlson contended for the part. Budding actor Alan Ladd showed up at an audition with his blond hair dyed black, as the role of Golden Boy Joe Bonaparte required.

Ladd recalled the nightmare: "It was one of the hottest days of the year. While reading the test scene I began to feel a dripping down the back of my neck. I was taking a shower in black ink. Thanks to Mamoulian's tact, he pretended not to notice it."[2]

Only 65 of the nearly 5000 faces seen by the staff of Columbia's casting office made it to test with Mamoulian in those few months. Every test cost $300, ending in costly disappointment. In the meantime, Cohn set April 1 as the starting date for the film and Mamoulian had to begin casting the other roles. He signed Barbara Stanwyck as Lorna Moon, Adolphe Menjou as Golden Boy's manager and Lee J. Cobb as the father. Mamoulian asked the studio to round up Italian-looking girls as possibilities for the role of Anna, Bonaparte's sister. The studio gathered together five tests and Mamoulian and Perlberg went into a projection room to look them over. The first test, coming from Paramount, had a girl doing a scene with a boy they had never laid eyes on before. They had been on the screen only a minute when Mamoulian suddenly yelled: "Lights!" "Lights!" echoed an assistant.

"Anything wrong?" a subordinate asked.

"Wrong my eye!" exploded the director. "The kid in that test is our Golden Boy. He's not slick or sure of himself. But he has everything else. Fetch him."[3]

The director and producer run the test three more times before grabbing a telephone to find out his name and background. A few hours later, the mystery boy had a name — William Holden. Olive Long, from Paramount casting, had deliberately forwarded a test showing Holden together with Margaret Young, a possible candidate for Anna. If she hadn't, Bill would not have been offered the lead in *Golden Boy*.

Cohn immediately scheduled a test for Bill, to be made in front of Mamoulian, Perlberg and himself. The president of Columbia Pictures using his usual arrogant attitude asked him: "Can you act?" "I'm not sure," Bill admitted. "Can you box?" "No." "Can you play the violin?" "No." "Then what the hell are you doing here?" "Because you sent for me." "In that case," Cohn said, "we'd better make a test and find out why I sent for you."[4]

Bill's candor and enthusiasm appealed to Cohn, and he assigned him a test with Joan Perry, who had made a few movies with Columbia. Gracefully helping Bill to overcome his nervousness, she cued him and pointed out camera angles until they began filming at five in the afternoon. The test lasted several hours. Cohn came on the set with his right hand man, Sam Brisk and Bill whispered to Perry, "I'd sure like to know what those two sons of bitches are thinking."

"They're thinking," she replied, "that you are going to be Golden Boy."[5]

At the end of the test, Bill invited Perry out for dinner but the actress declined, explaining she had a date. Moments later, Cohn approached Perry, apologizing that he could not have dinner with her until much later. Bill was stunned to learn that the girl he just asked out was dating the president of Columbia. Cohn and Perry married a few years later.

That same night, the part of Joe Bonaparte was officially assigned to William Holden. He was ordered to move the following day, at Columbia's expense, to the Hollywood Athletic Club in order to avoid the long commute from Pasadena to the studio. In addition he would immediately start boxing training at night and violin lessons during the day. He was instructed to tell no one except his parents of the daily events. His parents were delighted but not particularly astonished since they knew little about Hollywood's star-making methods. Bill was so excited he couldn't keep the news to himself, calling an older school friend and telling him everything. In another burst of exuberance he jumped up and down on his bed which eventually collapsed.[6]

Nevertheless, Cohn was not completely sold on casting Bill in the lead, even though the idea that the young actor would cost him very little was very appealing. Paramount agreed to loan Bill to Columbia, accepting Cohn's weekly offer of $25 — half of his contractual salary — and no other extra expenses except his lodging at the Hollywood Athletic Club. The ensuing days were pretty hectic for Bill, who was hurried into preparation for his role. Hairdresser Helen Hunt dyed his hair dark brown and set it with seventy-five small rollers, curling it to make him look Italian. For a brief segment of the film his hair had to be straight, which meant she could not make the curling permanent. He went through the curling operation every day he had curly-haired scenes. Bill had eleven weeks to learn his lines, while learning to boxing and play violin. The whole film revolved around his character Joe Bonaparte, a young Italian-American torn between his passion for the boxing ring and his love for the violin. The violin was impressed on him by his father, who dreamed of him becoming a musician since childhood. Mamoulian knew that if he couldn't get a believable performance out of Bill, the movie was destined to be a dismal flop, and its star would return to obscurity.

Many years later someone asked the director why he risked handing the role to someone so inexperienced. He answered, "Holden wasn't like anyone else on the screen. He was essentially himself. He had freshness, charm, a certain attractive sincerity. He had a relaxed quality that made for naturalness. All those things were more important than acting finesse.... Bill had no experience, no technique, no foundation for reasoning out the part. I had to make the whole thing very personal to him, make him associate Golden Boy's thoughts and feelings with his own. First of all, I asked him to tell me all about himself, his past life. I was looking for some common psychological ground between Bill and Golden Boy. I discovered that Bill loves chemistry; his father is a chemist, and he started out to be one himself. But, in school, he discovered

Holden with curling, dyed black hair in a publicity shot for *Golden Boy* (1939).

that he wasn't getting along very fast or very far — which was why he switched to acting. I couldn't ask any better parallel than this. Golden Boy loves the violin, but picks up fighting as a short-cut to fame. After this discovery, I could make Bill believe in Golden Boy's constant battle with himself, feel it, act it out.... A part is like a suit of clothes. A man looks good in neither one, unless he fits it and it fits him. Up to a certain point an actor must fit a part; beyond that point, the part must be made to fit him. We made changes in *Golden Boy*, to fit Bill."[7]

On April 17, 1939, Bill's 21st birthday, *Golden Boy* went into production. On the first day of shooting, he arrived on the set pale and exhausted. His daily routines took their toll: boxing with veteran fighter Cannonball Green; violin lessons with concert violinist Julian Brodetsky; dialogue coaching with Hugh McMullan; and supervision from Mario, an Italian restaurateur hired by Mamoulian to supervise his Italian-American dialect and gestures. Barbara Stanwyck noticed Bill's tension and said, "Look, Bill, we all had to start in this business sometime, you are going to be terrific, I know you are. Just hold on, and if there's any way I can help, for God's sake let me know."[8] Everything progressed smoothly for the first three days, but on the fourth he suddenly found himself on a verge of a collapse and was forced to leave the set.

As he later admitted, "[It] was a dreadful period when I was going to be replaced any day. I not only had to act, but box and play a violin well. I was putting in 18-hour days, for I had to study violin an hour and a half every evening, and then report to the Hollywood Athletic Club for another hour and a half of training in the ring. I was going nuts from the intense strain, and it was evident in the daily screen rushes."

After one week, Cohn was ready to replace him. Stanwyck interceded on his behalf, when she realized Cohn meant what he said. She went to Perlberg and Cohn and yelled, "My God, he's only had a week. Leave him alone and he'll find himself. I don't know of any actor who could do it better. If you want youth, he's got it. If you want a fairly good boxer, he's it. He can't be a champion, because that's not the story. He's a very sensitive, intelligent young man. I don't know what other qualities you want. None of us can walk on water."[9] She also argued, "You haven't given him a chance. He's everything you want, but you won't leave him alone. I'll work with him every chance we get."[10] With Cohn convinced that Bill deserved another chance, Stanwyck began coaching him: Every night she read the next day's lines with him in her dressing room. Those evening

Holden with Barbara Stanwyck in *Golden Boy* (1939).

sessions continued throughout the production. Stanwyck was so involved in her mission that her fiancé, actor Robert Taylor, also helped Bill when he arrived to pick up Barbara.

"I don't think there's anyone who's done more for me in my career than Barbara Stanwyck," Bill said about his co-star years later. "Maybe ten percent of the actors you're fortunate enough to work with are real pros. They will do everything to cover and protect you. A lot of this has to do with integrity."[11]

Thanks to Mamoulian's sensibility and Stanwyck's assistance, Bill grew more assured and comfortable in front of the cameras. "I don't think anybody had so much determination and ambition as I had the day I started making this movie," Bill later admitted in an interview.[12]

Despite all the help, Bill remained very insecure and it appears that that was the main reason he started to drink. What began as a few sips in his dressing room to face the daily work increased into a habit, foreshadowing an addiction that would eventually ruin his life.

The shooting finished three days ahead of schedule. Mamoulian was more than satisfied with Bill's work and later commented, "Chemistry, looks, that mysterious quality, and iron determination, carried him through. Also the will to work and Barbara Stanwyck."[13]

According to the director, Stanwyck even let takes get printed that did not show her to best advantage if they happened to be the best takes Bill could achieve. Mamoulian and Cohn did not permit Bill to look at the daily rushes with Stanwyck and Menjou because they believed it would make him more self-conscious.

A few weeks before the opening of *Golden Boy*, Bill said to a *New York Times* writer, "Mr. Mamoulian was like a father to me. He was very patient and whenever I couldn't get the feel of the character he would take me aside and interpret it, as near as he could come, in terms of something that had happened to me."[14]

At the film's completion, Bill sent Stanwyck two dozen red roses as a token of gratitude for her invaluable help. It was a gesture of sincere appreciation that he repeated each year on April 1 (the anniversary of *Golden Boy*'s start of production date) until his death in 1981.

Golden Boy had its premiere at Radio City Music Hall in New York on September 15, 1939. Bill arrived in New York a couple of weeks earlier for promotion. "...I went to the opening of *Golden Boy* and saw my name on the marquee.... There was my name in lights. And I suddenly knew that it didn't mean a damn thing to me. It's been that way ever since."[15] This was an honest confession which proves Bill's great indifference toward the entertainment industry from the beginning of his career.

Golden Boy received lukewarm reviews from the critics who complained about the major changes made in adapting the original play. Nonetheless, many reviewers agreed that William Holden was a promising talent with all the qualities to become a star. The movie was moderately successful at the box office. Bill's parents expressed very little concern about their son's career, cautioning him about Hollywood's moral standards. Bill reassured his family and decided to go on with his career. He moved into a small house in the Hollywood hills together with his close friend and dialogue coach, Hugh McMullan. McMullan was a graduate of Williams College and Oxford University; before becoming a dialogue coach for Hollywood actors, he had been a teacher at Berkshire. He helped

Bill learn to appreciate music and art, advised him how to dress and recommended books from his substantial library. "[Hugh] made me appreciate many things I might otherwise have overlooked," Bill commented to the press.[16]

The most important thing McMullan did was introduce Bill to young actress Ardis Ankerson, known in Hollywood as Brenda Marshall. She would become Bill's first and only wife.

Following *Golden Boy*, Bill appeared in two productions made by Warner Bros. *Invisible Stripes'* superb cast was not enough to make the film more than a mediocre gangster flick. In the story, Bill was Sam Taylor, a good kid whose older brother, played by George Raft, was a gangster just released from prison. Raft ended up returning to his gang led by Humphrey Bogart.

In the early 1970s Bill was invited, along with Raft, on *The Tonight Show*, where they recalled their experiences while making *Invisible Stripes*. "I had only been in one film, *Golden Boy*, before I went to work in *Invisible Stripes*. I wasn't a very experienced actor, and besides I was pretty nervous working with two stars like Raft and Bogart. In one scene, I squared off with George in a fight because I resent his help. When we did the scene I must have been bobbing and weaving my fight scenes in *Golden Boy* because my head hit George's eye. I remember, when I saw the blood, thinking, 'Christ, it's George Raft. Now I'm going to really get it.' Well, he was as nice as could be even though his wound needed several stitches later at the hospital. He really was my big brother, in and out of the movie. In fact, if he had not helped me, I might have been thrown out of the picture. However it began, the director, Lloyd Bacon, was always yelling at me. I couldn't seem to get anything right — my lines or my movements. It was hell. Then George stepped in with the director and told him to go easy with me. The director finally lightened up on me because of George's insistence."[17]

Originally Bacon wanted Wayne Morris for the role of Sam Taylor, considering Bill inexperienced and unsuitable for it. To prove to the director that he could work well with Raft, Bill took a one-minute part in Raft's *Each Dawn I Die*, shot on a different set at Warner's simultaneously with *Invisible Stripes*. It was sufficient to convince Bacon, who first cast him in his film and later regretted it. Bill appeared very inexperienced. If the relationship with the director was not idyllic, working with Bogart was a nightmare. In *Invisible Stripes* Bogart took fourth billing to Raft, Jane

Bryan and even Bill, whom he considered a rookie. Bill proceeded to compound his co-star's resentment by his determination, in one scene, to drive a motorcycle with Bogart as a passenger in the sidecar. Bogart objected, "That S.O.B., he'll crack it up!" But Bill insisted. He promptly ran the bike into a wall.[18] No physical injuries were reported but a feud began between the two. It erupted again fourteen years later on the set of *Sabrina.*

Independent producer Sol Lesser cast Bill in *Our Town,* adapted from Thornton Wilder's Pulitzer Prize–winning play of the 1937-38 Broadway season. The director, Sam Wood, was able to recreate in a studio the same intimate atmosphere of the original drama, without that sense of claustrophobia typical of many films based on plays. Aaron Copland's excellent musical score and Bert Glennon's cinematography helped create the flavor of a typical small town in America's heartland. *Our Town* told of a young couple, George Gibb (William Holden), son of the local doctor, and Emily Webb (Martha Scott), his neighbor-turned-wife, and the friendships, victories, hopes and losses they experience in day-to-day living. The

Holden and Martha Scott as young lovers in *Our Town* (1940).

story traced their relationship as they grew and lived life in little Grover's Corners. It was Scott's first film experience, but she had played the part of Martha in the original theatrical production for over nine months. When the producers announced that she would work opposite Bill Holden, she expressed her skepticism about her colleague. Nevertheless, Bill's professionalism and long rehearsals of their dialogue for the following day made Scott quickly drop her prejudices.

"I adored that young man," revealed the actress in an interview. "I think everybody who ever worked with Bill early on, every young lady fell in love with him. I did too."[19]

A week before the film's general release in early May, the complete cast of *Our Town* enacted a one-hour abridged version of it on Cecil B. DeMille's CBS radio program, *Lux Radio Theatre*.

Bill's performance did not pass unnoticed. The *New York Times* critic Bosley Crowther wrote, "William Holden plays the boy with a clean and refreshing youthfulness,"[20] while *Time* magazine called *Our Town* "a cinema event." The film received six Academy Award nominations including Best Film and Best Actress and made big bucks thanks to a female audience that fell for the new–American boy, William Holden.

In 1940 after three films, Bill finally worked for the studio which first hired him: Paramount put him in the cast of *Those Were the Days!*, a trivial comedy set in an American college in 1904. It was based on the *Good Ole Siwash* stories by George Fitch about the fictional Midwest Siwash College. For the first time, Bill had top billing over the title like a real star. Nonetheless, the weak storyline was forgotten after only a few days of its release.

War pictures dominated the major studios in the summer of 1940. Paramount was developing a film about the Nazi takeover of Poland. Called *Polonaise* and written by William Brackett and Billy Wilder, it would tell the story of a young football star, played by Bill, who rescued his Polish grandmother after the Nazi invasion and brought her back to the United States. The project was postponed and later canceled after Bill was slated to do the western *Arizona* for Columbia instead.[21]

Arizona producer-director Wesley Ruggles wanted Gary Cooper in the role of Peter Muncie, a part tailored for him. Cooper declined and the role was given to Joel McCrea until more complications surfaced regarding the film's budget. Bill was finally cast at one-tenth the salary. Ruggles hoped the film would rival the success of his, Oscar-winning epic, *Cimarron* (1931), but it fell far short.

The bulk of *Arizona* was filmed on location a few miles from Tucson during the summer months of 1940. The cast and the crew faced extreme hardships, working in scorching temperatures approaching 130 degrees. Female lead Jean Arthur, then one of Columbia's biggest stars, arranged a deal with Cohn and Ruggles allowing her to begin work one hour earlier than the rest of the cast. When lunch arrived, she took two hours instead of the usual one, providing her the opportunity to shower, lunch and nap before afternoon shooting began.

When *Arizona* went into production, Arthur was terrified about appearing alongside Bill, eighteen years her junior. When she met him for the first time on location, she scanned him for few seconds and walked unceremoniously away without a word, leaving Bill perplexed and upset. Eventually they broke the ice and managed to generate enough screen chemistry.[22]

Arizona told the story of Phoebe Titus, the independent, tough-minded owner of a struggling freight line, determined to battle corruption and the plundering of her line. Titus, a sort of Calamity Jane, finds unexpected help and romance in Peter Muncie, a young cowboy from Missouri. Muncie heroically rescues her from Indians set upon her by a pair of villains.

Bill enjoyed riding horses and performing the chases and shootouts, insisting on doing all his stunts. Afraid of horses, he worked his way slowly from docile to wilder ones. He once overheard two new stunt men at the Columbia Ranch complaining about the soft life of Western film heroes. "We risk our necks, and they get all the credit," one of the men said.

Bill took off at a dead run for a nearby horse, vaulted to its back and had both guns drawn and blazing when he hit the saddle. He rode over to the two griping stunt men and pleasantly inquired, "You boys care to try it?" They didn't.[23]

The scorching weather delayed production, increasing costs by a third to $2,000,000. Harry Cohn considered Ruggles solely responsible for the loss of $500,000. The president of Columbia told the press that it was the irresponsible director's choice to film during the summer heat, generating the excess expense. He concluded that Ruggles was under contract to make more pictures for Columbia, and Cohn had no intention to fire him — only that he will never again be sent to Tucson to make a movie. The director replied that the picture was filmed in the early summer only because the studio had promised it by a certain date to the European distributors.[24]

Arizona premiered in Tucson on Christmas Day, 1940. It opened nationwide two months later to unfavorable reviews, which contributed to the film's disappointing box office reception. Many critics praised Bill's performance as "excellent" and "convincing," said *New York Times* scribe Theodore Strauss. In his review, Strauss quipped, "What Phoebe needs, obviously, is a strong man around — not exactly William Holden.... [He is not] sufficiently far from knee-pants to seem credible as her protective knight in armor."[25]

On August 23, 1940, immediately following the filming of *Arizona*, Bill was contracted to star in Paramount's *I Wanted Wings*. A quarrel erupted when Bill notified Paramount he would not report for filming, which was ready to begin. Contracted at $350 a week, Bill cited overwork and insufficient salary; the studio refused to negotiate. Four days later it was announced that Bill had agreed to make the film at his current, contracted salary. Charles Feldman, Bill's agent (whom Rouben Mamoulian had recommended to him during *Golden Boy*), publicly explained that his client did not wish to deprive the other participants in the picture of jobs by holding up production over the matter. In reality, Paramount placed Bill on suspension, under the terms of his contract, forcing him to report to work on *I Wanted Wings*.[26]

Filmed at Randolph Air Force Base near San Antonio, Texas, the picture was produced with the full cooperation of the government, eager to show to the world how American soldiers were trained — a sort of propaganda. The cast included Ray Milland, Wayne Morris, Constance Moore and seventeen-year-old Veronica Lake in her first starring role. *I Wanted Wings* was a tribute to the American peacetime Air Corps, depicting the lives of three air cadets. The director Ted Weeks insolently treated all the military officers and personnel like extras; he even complained that the noise of airplanes ruined the soundtrack and ordered a general to ground over 700 flights. He was fired two days later and replaced by Mitchell Leisen.

Milland and Morris, who both had pilot's licenses, flew their own aircraft in several scenes with military flight instructors on board yet hidden from the camera. The cast got along very well except for a few spats between Constance Moore and Veronica Lake. In an interview promoting the film, the director had many flattering words for Bill: "He is a very gentle, kind person, an excellent actor and very easy to work with. He is very timid about looking at the camera during a take, but we worked with him and got him over that."[27]

There were also set photographers always snapping publicity stills. One of them took a few photographs of Bill and Veronica Lake together, selling them to a tabloid with a fabricated love story. All the magazines reported the news of a presumed relationship between the co-stars who, in reality, barely talked to each other off the set. Bill was already sentimentally involved with Brenda Marshall and Lake was engaged to John Detlie, whom she married immediately after the picture was completed.

The fascination about war and the particular interest in airplanes by American youth made *I Wanted Wings* one of Paramount's major hits of the season, in spite of critics who described it as a flat-action "turkey" stuffed with boring, sentimental melodrama. Bombshell Veronica Lake stole the picture and became an overnight sensation thanks to a stray lock of her shoulder-length, blond hair during a publicity shoot. This "peek-a-boo" hairstyle, which hid one eye, became her trademark and was immediately widely imitated.

As a sequel to *I Wanted Wings*, Paramount planned a movie dealing with naval cadet training, *Tomorrow's Admiral*, starring Bill, Sterling Hayden and Betty Field. The project did not materialize and Bill returned to Columbia for his second western opposite Glenn Ford. Although *Texas* was Bill's seventh picture, he still received $125 per week. His agent was unable to get him a raise due to strict clauses in the contract that Bill signed two years earlier.

Glenn Ford was put under contract with Columbia at the same time as Bill. Before casting them each in suitable parts, Harry Cohn would say to Ford, "If Bill gives me any trouble you'll do the job, if you give me any trouble Bill will do the job." Cohn tried to have them compete for the press, always searching for a scoop, but as Ford explained, they were never in competition. "The more they tried to make us compete, the closer we became as friends. I don't think either Bill or I knew how to act, we only knew how to be ourselves."[28]

When they finally worked together in *Texas*, they showed both on- and off-screen chemistry that proved magnetic at the box office. The film was about two Virginians who witness a stagecoach robbery. They decide to rob the robbers and make off with the loot themselves. To avoid being caught, they split up. Years later, when they finally met up again, they find themselves on opposite sides of the law, one a rancher and one a bandit. Both were in love with the same woman (Claire Trevor). Only the good survives the final shootout. The plot, rich with typical elements of the

Western genre, included humor, greatly appreciated by the critics. Making *Texas* cemented Bill's friendship with Ford. They became inseparable, including sharing the pleasure of adventures with their female fans. When some reporters caught then in the company of two prostitutes, Cohn cautioned the actors to be more discreet to preserve their Hollywood image — a kingdom of fake puritanism. The president of Columbia gave them keys to a luxurious penthouse at the Chateau Marmont Hotel to use for their own discrete pleasures.

A few months earlier, Cohn summoned Bill to his office, remarking, "I hear you're going out with some dumb broad." Holden was baffled until Cohn mentioned the name of an actress he had been dating. Upset, Bill replied, "I think you're invading my private life. What I do after I leave the studio is my business." Cohn disagreed and argued, "That dame is poison. She's a dumb broad, and she's six years older than you are." Bill later discovered that the actress, in whom he had only a passing interest, had concealed a previous marriage and had been involved in a scandal.[29]

In an interview many years later he confirmed that episode, admitting, "When I was a young actor in Hollywood, I used to service actresses who were older than me."[30]

3

Love and War

"The army will toughen you up; put some character in that pretty face. When you come back to Columbia, you might be able to carry a picture by yourself, like Gable or Cooper." — Harry Cohn

Brenda Marshall, born Ardis Ankerson, was already a star when she met Bill. Ardis, as always Bill called her, was a pretty brunette, not very tall, with strong features. She was born on September 29, 1915, on the island of Negros in the Philippines, where her father Otto Peter Ankerson managed a large sugar plantation. She lost her mother when she was very young. (During World War II, her father was captured by the Japanese and held captive for many months, dying shortly after he was freed.) In the 1930s she and her sister moved to San Antonio, Texas, where they went to high school and later Texas State College. After college, she moved to New York and attended the School of Dramatic Art of Maria Ouspenskaya, where she met actor Richard Huston Gaines. The couple married in 1936 and two years later their daughter Virginia was born. After acting in several summer stock productions, Ardis appeared in 1937 on Broadway in *Wives of Tomorrow* and in the Federal Theatre's production of George Bernard Shaw's *On the Rocks*. After seeing Ardis, Arthur Jacobson, the talent scout who discovered Bill, arranged a screen test, but her high starting salary demands discouraged the executives at Paramount.[1] Jacobson released the test to other studios, and within forty-eight hours she was snapped up by Warner Bros. They changed her name to Brenda Marshall and she made her screen debut in *Espionage Agent* opposite Joel McCrea.

Later, she replaced Olivia de Havilland opposite Errol Flynn in *The Sea Hawk*, a role that briefly made her a star.

During a break on the set of *Invisible Stripes*, Hugh MacMullan introduced Bill to Ardis. Bill was immediately enchanted by her elegance, class and sense of humor. In September 1940, following several attempts thwarted by their very busy schedules, he had his first date with her. She then asked him to be her escort at the *Sea Hawk* premiere, and suddenly their romance hit the tabloids. At that time, Ardis was making about $750 a week—almost five times Bill's salary. She was in the middle of a nasty custody battle over her daughter Virginia while divorcing her husband. Bill, madly in love, remained a patient suitor, promising to marry her and adopt Virginia once she was single again.

In the summer of 1941, Bill was in Arizona working on the set of *The Remarkable Andrew* when Ardis' divorce was finalized. "To be patient is not my wife's first virtue," Bill explained years later to a French journalist. "One day she showed up with a suitcase on the set of my film in Arizona. She had come to marry me. Basically, she was just fed up to wait for me any longer."[2]

The couple did not waste any time preparing for a wedding in Las Vegas. Bill's parents were less than ecstatic about the marriage announcement—especially Mary, who considered Ardis a good-for-nothing (not only was she an *actress*, but a *divorcee* with a three-year-old baby). The Beedles firmly believed that Bill at twenty-three, and not fully mature, was not responsible enough to be a husband and a father all at once.

On the night of July 12, 1941, Bill chartered a small plane to Las Vegas where he planned to marry Ardis at

An early '40s publicity shot of Brenda Marshall (real name: Ardis Ankerson).

midnight. The couple was to be accompanied by Brian Donlevy and his wife Marjorie, their witnesses. Donlevy was in the cast of *The Remarkable Andrew* and had become a good friend of Bill off the set. Bill's plans got off on the wrong foot when the film's director, Stuart Heisler, forced the cast to work two extra hours that evening. Bill and Donlevy rushed to the airport still wearing their makeup. They finally met their women and boarded the airplane, which was forced to land at an uncompleted Army field when the commercial airport was closed due to bad weather. The four took a taxi into town, but the spa where they were to be married closed at 3 A.M. Bill woke the Reverend Charles Dunn and convinced him to marry them in a hotel room at 4 A.M. on July 13, 1941. The newlyweds enjoyed a champagne breakfast, leaving just enough time to go back to the airport and fly to Los Angeles for work.

Bill and Ardis purchased a new, small home on Toluca Lake in the San Fernando Valley. However, it was nearly three months before the couple was together under the same roof. Ardis had to fly to North Bay, Ontario, Canada, to shoot *Captains in the Clouds* on location. Bill returned to *The Remarkable Andrew* in Carson City, Nevada, to wrap up filming. Eleven days later, Bill was rushed to the hospital for an emergency appendectomy, and discharged after nine days. When Ardis arrived at the hospital to take him home, she complained of pains in the right side of her abdomen. Bill's doctor diagnosed her with appendicitis as well and she too underwent an appendectomy followed by a three-week recovery.

The Remarkable Andrew was an amusing comedy adapted by Dalton Trumbo from his novel of the same name. (Trumbo would later be blacklisted in Hollywood during Senator McCarthy's anti–Communism investigations.) Bill played Andrew Long, an honest bookkeeper falsely accused of diverting funds from the municipal books. The seven apparitions of America's founding fathers, including President Andrew Jackson (Donlevy), help him to clarify the financial misunderstanding. The critics generally liked Bill better than the film, which they found too frivolous in wartime.

With the ongoing world war, Bill's brother Bob decided to join the naval air corps. Bill felt that it was also his duty to volunteer for the army, but Paramount had already cast him in three more pictures. Withdrawing from his contract, even for a just cause, would have been impossible.

The first film was *The Fleet's In*, a remake of a 1935 Paramount musical. At the time he was cast, no one in the production expected him to be able to sing. Surprising everyone on the set, he used his experience as a former choir boy to display his consistent semi-baritone voice. However, his singing was eventually dubbed. Bill was very excited to work opposite Dorothy Lamour, already a star after working in several features with Bob Hope and Bing Crosby.

As Bill remembered, "I had a split contract with Columbia and Paramount, so I bicycled back and forth a lot. Whenever I did work at the [Paramount] lot and Lamour, Hope and Crosby were making a 'Road' picture, I always hung around their sets to watch those three work. My director would literally have to come and grab me by the collar and drag me back to my own set."[3]

The Fleet's In was the story of Casey Kirby, a timid sailor photographed kissing the Countess, a dance hall entertainer played by Lamour. The admiral's shy daughter demanded that Kirby persuade the Countess to attend a party she is throwing, and Bill's shipmates took bets on the outcome. The film ends with the two leads falling in love with each other.

"I was very pleased that Bill Holden was assigned to be my leading man in *The Fleet's In*," Lamour revealed in her autobiography. "Bill is not only charming, talented, and handsome, but also has a great sense of humor. Nobody knew how much he was going to need it; at the beginning everything went so well that none of us could have imagined all the troubles that were to follow. One of the first sequences involved Betty Hutton, Eddie Bracken, Bill, and myself. Betty and I share a house with about one hundred steps leading up to the front porch, and in an effort to impress us the boys decide to carry us up those stairs."

"Just before the picture started," Bill recalls, "I had had an emergency appendectomy. Today, with the modern surgical separation of the muscle tissue, you're up and walking around the day after the operation, and four days later you are out of the hospital and home. But in those days, with the McMerny incision where they cut *through* the muscles, the recovery period was much longer. You stayed in bed for a week and then — very slowly and very carefully — put one leg over the edge of the mattress to get up. My doctor, Dr. Neal, told me not to strain myself or else I'd pop open.

"I took one long look at those steps and another look at Dorothy. 'Well,' I thought, 'she doesn't weigh much, so what the hell?' I picked her up and climbed up seven steps before I felt the strain. Without thinking, I asked, 'How the hell much do you weigh?'

Eddie Bracken(left) and Holden "besieged" by beautiful girls in *The Fleet's In* (1942).

"'Cut!' the director called. 'You are aware, Mr. Holden, that we recorded that.' 'Dottie' [Lamour's nickname] only weighed about 125, and she looked a little put out until I explained that they had almost filmed their leading man's collapse. We ended up doing the scene in bits and pieces, and when they got to the long shots, doubles were called in."[4]

The Fleet's In did not help Bill's career but it increased his fan mail noticeably, especially from young girls who seemed to enjoy watching him in uniform.

Meet the Stewarts followed immediately. Based on Elizabeth Dunn's magazine stories of Candy and Mike Stewart, the film was a light comedy about an average American man married to a rich, spoiled girl, played by the lovely Frances Dee. Once again, Columbia cast Bill in a part any average all–American-looking actor could play. Bill did not worry about being typecast yet, since he needed the money. On the set, Dee, fresh from maternity leave, seemed unsure of herself. Director Al Green was about to replace her when Bill, smitten with her, asked Harry Cohn not to fire

Barbara Britton, Holden, James Brown and a set assistant on the set of _Young and Willing_ (1943).

her. Columbia's president reminded him that it was not Bill's job to interfere in the casting decisions. Nevertheless Bill's words convinced him.

"All right, all right." Cohn said impatiently, "You're wasting my money being away from the set. Get back there. And tell Al Green to go fuck himself."[5]

Meet the Stewarts opened in New York in May 1942 on the bottom of a double-bill. The few reviews were unfavorable and the picture was in theaters for only a week.

The same sorry fate awaited *Young and Willing*, filmed at the end of 1941 but not released until October 1943. *Young and Willing* was a low-budget production, entirely shot at Paramount, but later sold to United Artists. It was based on a successful play by Francis Swann called *Out of the Frying Pan* (which ran on Broadway years later and had among its players Montgomery Clift). The screenplay, however, lacked the effervescence of the original play, inspired by true experiences of the author's sister. Bill played Norman Reese, a young man living with five other struggling actors in an apartment upstairs from a Broadway producer. Susan Hayward was also in the cast and was clearly very attracted to Bill, whom she had known for three years when they were in Paramount's Golden Circle.

"Besides being handsome," she once said, "he was such a gentleman." They became close friends but never romantically involved. At the end of shooting, Bill gave her a clock with a mechanical, singing brass bird in a gilded cage, which she cherished all her life.[6]

Three days after his twenty-fourth birthday, Bill was sworn into the U.S. Army Air Corps at the Los Angeles recruiting station on Main Street. Before Bill left, Harry Cohn commented, "I hope this makes a man out of you.... The army will toughen you up, put some character in that pretty face. When you come back to Columbia, you might be able to carry a picture by yourself, like Gable or Cooper."[7]

After reporting to Fort MacArthur Reception Center, he was sent to the Army Air Corps Officers Candidate School in Miami Beach, Florida. Once he completed the program, he received his commission as a second lieutenant and was then shipped off to Tarrant Field Air Base near Fort Worth, Texas. Although Bill repeatedly requested combat duty, he was kept stateside and worked in public relations. Like many other Hollywood stars, he was asked to appear in training films and on several radio shows promoting the nation's war effort or war bond sales.

In his memoir, screenwriter Arthur Laurents remembers his first meeting with Bill in the army, sunbathing and reading on the roof at the Kaufman Astoria Studio, in Queens, New York. The Kaufman Astoria was an old studio used by the army to make training movies.

My serious drinking problems resumed with Bill Holden. To see a movie star reading *Gerontion* [a poem by T. S. Eliot] was intriguing enough to start a conversation. When I discovered he was unaware the poem was anti–Semitic, as was its author, I wondered whether Holden himself was anti–Semitic or just not very knowledgeable. I was glad to find it was the latter, not because he was so good-looking (I thought his good looks antiseptic) but because he was completely unaffected and eager to learn.... Holden just listened.

When I finished, he took a deep breath and said, "Why don't we have a drink?" which we did later.... That began our bonding ... very dry gin martinis. We ... began a competition to see who could drink the most. I won the last bout we had before we both left Astoria: fifteen dry gin martinis straight up. How did I do it?... The loser had to buy dinner.

The last time Bill chose the Bistro on Third Avenue under the el. As we walked in, I smelled mussels and said, "The floor is going to hit me in the face." It didn't, then or ever, but it did hit Bill. It isn't the amount consumed, it's not crossing the lines: first the dangerous line from social drinker to serious drinker, then the lethal line from heavy hitter to alcoholic. I never crossed the final line. Bill Holden died too early, an alcoholic.[8]

On July 26, 1942, Bill was heard on the radio in a program entitled *Dear Adolph*. It was the fifth of a series of six broadcasts written by Stephen Vincent Benet, consisting of six letters written to the German *führer* from six representatives of the American nation: a farmer, a mother, a businessman, a laborer and a soldier.

Bill was the soldier, whose letter informed Hitler, "We'll marry the girl we like — and the guy who makes a crack about her ancestry had better look out for his teeth."[9]

A few months later he was recruited to be part of *Wings Up*, a short recruiting film Clark Gable was putting together for the Defense Department. The boring film was narrated by Gable and included brief appearances by Bill and many other Hollywood personalities to publicize the need for new aviation officers.

While Bill was stationed at Tarrant, he corresponded frequently with his brother Bob, who was in Texas completing his training as a Naval Air Corps pilot. The two brothers couldn't get together because of their conflicting schedules. Bill often regretted this after Bob was killed in the Pacific the following January.

In Texas, baseball champion Hank Greenberg befriended Bill when they happened to share the same room. Greenberg recalled that they often had little more to do every day than face suffocating heat and blustery dust. He and Bill would go out and get drunk every night. In his autobiography, the baseball star remembered a curious episode that occurred while Bill was his roommate.

"One time I was away on a two-week trip and I returned home to Fort Worth very late at night, about two or three in the morning. I had the key in the door and I was trying to open it. Little did I know that Bill Holden was home, sitting up in bed. He had his revolver pulled out and had a bead on the door, thinking that he was being robbed. I burst through the door, and he flashed on the lights and said, 'Boy, are you lucky. I thought you were an intruder. I was ready to pull the trigger.'"[10]

If Greenberg was lucky that night, Bill was fortunate when a few days later fate saved his life. He was waiting at Salinas, Kansas, to board a B-24. His superstitious captain noted there were 13 passengers, so he refused to fly and ordered Bill to wait with him.

"I checked the 'chutes back at the flight office," Bill said. "The other men got on. Not long afterward, the plane crashed. Everybody on board was killed."[11]

Bill managed occasional leaves home to see Ardis, who had stopped working after she got pregnant. In May 1943 Bill legally changed his name to William Holden. On November 18, 1943, he returned home just a day before his son Peter Westfield Holden, named in part after Bill's younger brother Bob Westfield Beedle, was born. Bob wrote him to congratulate and to thank him for giving the baby his middle name. Before Bill could reply, Bob was sent on a military mission to the South Pacific.

On January 1, 1944, a terrible nightmare woke Bill in his quarters at Fort Worth. He immediately called Ardis to make sure she and the baby were fine. Then he called his parents to wish them a Happy New Year. Although he was reassured, he still felt a sense of anguish that lasted three days. On January 4, his mother called to tell him that Bob's Hell Cat fighter had been shot down by Japanese fire in a New Year's Day raid off the coast of Kavieng, in Papua New Guinea.

Broken up by the terrible news, Bill did not share his sorrow with anyone. He locked himself in his room and drank until he passed out. He regretted not trying harder to reunite with his brother when he was in Texas and felt guilty for not having combat duty. Feeling an emotional debt to Bob, Bill tried once again to be assigned to overseas duties, but the Air Force turned him down. Instead, he was ordered to appear at a series of war bond rallies and at shows to support troop morale.

One day Bill and Richard Webb, a friend and colleague from Paramount, were asked to report to the First Motion Picture Unit in the Hal Roach Studios, where the Army Air Force made training, morale and prop-

aganda films. Both went to the adjutant's office to present their creden-
tials. They had to stand at attention for almost half an hour while Captain Ronald Reagan recited all the regulations.

"That son of a bitch!" complained Bill, on leaving the premises, about
Reagan's strict behavior. He could not imagine that only a couple of years
later Reagan would become one of his closest friends and they would laugh
about that first meeting.

Despite his celebrity status, Bill refused to pull strings and get an early
discharge. He completed his military service in three years and eight
months. First Lt. William Holden was discharged in September 1945 and
immediately returned home, holding strong feelings of resentment toward
the Army that never allowed him to pursue a real military career like his
brother Bob.

All of a sudden the house on Toluca Lake was too small for the Holdens. Virginia, Ardis' daughter, was forced to sleep on a sofa in the dining
room since her bedroom had became the nursery of little Peter. Ardis was
also expecting her second child. Buying a new house was out of question
for Bill, who owed $18,000 in back income taxes and faced the fact that
Paramount and Columbia had almost forgotten him. His only resource
was the military salary which barely provided for the bare necessities. War
had changed Hollywood and the tastes of the American audience. Bill was
no longer the twenty-four-year-old boy but a twenty-seven-year-old man,
married, with kids.

On his first day back at Paramount, security guards did not recognize him and would not let him in. Bill immediately realized that the situation would be more difficult than he expected and this was confirmed
when the studio heads told him that he was forgotten and probably not
missed by his old fans. Some even insinuated that he now lacked the sex
appeal necessary and was no longer "the boy next door."

"I was short-tempered, moody, and depressed. I avoided all my
friends. I saw every movie I had missed. I read every available script at
Paramount. I worked around the house. Finally, after the Army, I had
expected there would be some adjustment requiring about a month at the
most. Well, for ten months, I was a fugitive from a psychoanalyst."[12]

For a time, he considered giving up the whole thing and going into
his father's chemical business. Despite being discouraged, Bill hired two
independent publicists, Jack Mulcahy and Larry Ginsberg, to revive his
image. Finally Paramount seemed to remember William Holden when

they purchased the rights to Norman Krasna's play *Dear Ruth*. It had been a Broadway hit in 1944, and Paramount intended to cast him as the soldier-lover in the screen version. Bill accepted the offer without hesitation. However, the project was delayed in pre-production; it finally started in October 1946.

On May 2, 1946, Ardis gave birth to Scott Porter. Shortly afterward, she announced giving up her acting career to be a full-time mother. Bill was still anxious about his financial situation since his work had not yet resumed. He feared a possible cancellation of *Dear Ruth* which made him extremely nervous and depressed.

About that difficult time in his life he later admitted, "I hit rock bottom. I was almost thirty and a wreck, a second-class actor in Hollywood ready to work for nothing just to support my family and ... to get drunk. If I hadn't had a family, I would not have found the strength to go on and hold out."[13]

4

Smiling Jim

....

"I'm the kind of guy, I guess, that any other ordinary man can identify himself with. If Holden can do it, the man thinks, then I can do it too." — William Holden

....

Paramount finally gave the green light to *Dear Ruth* in which Bill played an Air Force lieutenant who received love letters he believed were written by Joan Caulfield. However, Caulfield's teen sister, played by Mona Freeman, actually wrote and sent them along with Caulfield's photograph. On a two-day leave, the love-smitten lieutenant makes a surprise visit to Caulfield, prepared to propose to his supposed correspondent. When the deception is revealed, the older sister finds she is in love with him too. She breaks up with her fiancé and agrees to marry him. In desperate need of money, Bill sold his military uniform for $500 to the Paramount wardrobe department, which had budgeted $650 to acquire a lieutenant's uniform for his character.

Despite lukewarm reviews, *Dear Ruth* was a popular hit thanks to the funny but predictable script. Paramount made two sequels with the same cast except for Bill, who only returned for *Dear Wife*. On April 26, 1948, and again on December 5, 1949, Bill and Joan Caulfield recreated their roles in two *Lux Radio Theater* versions of *Dear Ruth*.

The first post-war Holden film to reach movie screens was *Blaze of Noon*, shot forty-three days after *Dear Ruth*, but opening four months earlier. Screenwriter Frank Wead personally called him to offer him the role. Bill's bleak financial situation left him little choice. He accepted the job with very little enthusiasm.

Blaze of Noon was based on Ernest K. Gann's novel about the early days of commercial aviation. Bill played one of four brothers who were pilot-pioneers in the air mail business. Anne Baxter, straight from an Academy Award for Best Supporting Actress in *The Razor's Edge*, was the female lead. The strong cast also included Sterling Hayden, William Bendix and Howard da Silva. Despite the strong players and spectacular cinematography of stunts flying in the primitive planes, critics panned the film, accusing director John Farrow of being too melodramatic.

Dear Ruth and *Blaze of Noon* earned Bill a "charity" salary of $10,000; Paramount agreed to pay him only after his agent turned on the pressure. Ardis realized that her husband's income was insufficient to support them. She decided to return to work, accepting a part in the Western *Whispering Smith* opposite Alan Ladd. Ardis' return to acting hurt Bill's ego, resulting in their first major conflict. Paramount studio photographer Irv Glaser believed that Bill and Barbara Stanwyck started an affair around that time. Whether the initiative was Bill's or Barbara's, they both needed a respite — he from his stalled career and she from her rocky marriage. Stanwyck never admitted to an affair, but she spoke affectionately of him.

"Bill and I go way, way back," she would simply say years later. "He's always been so grateful, simply because I helped him, in that I thought he would be a marvelous leading man."[1]

In early spring 1947, Bill made a brief song-and-dance appearance in Paramount's *Variety Girl*. The movie was a tribute to the Variety Clubs of America with a nonexistent plot that Paramount stuffed with nearly fifty guest stars appearing in dancing or singing acts. The star-studded cast also included Stanwyck, Veronica Lake, Ray Milland, Dorothy Lamour, Joan Caulfield, Gary Cooper, Alan Ladd and Burt Lancaster.

That summer, Bill was offered a $250,000 lead role by RKO producer Richard Berger in *Rachel and the Stranger*. Directed by Norman Foster, this Western was based on the frontier tale "Rachel" by Howard Fast. A former actor, Foster had married Claudette Colbert; to avoid competing with his more successful wife, he turned to directing mostly Charlie Chan pictures in the 1930s. Opposite Loretta Young, RKO cast Robert Mitchum, one of their most promising stars, as the second male lead. *Rachel and the Stranger* was filmed in the woods of Fox Hollow and along the Mackenzie River near Eugene, Oregon, where the cast moved for a six-week stay. Bill struck up an immediate friendship with Mitchum. They both would always speak favorably of each other as men and as actors.

"Bill and I had the strong suspicion that was a comedy. We played for comedy. We had a comedy fight in the picture," Mitchum explained years later in an interview.[2]

On the set, Bill was solitary, discontent with debilitating self-doubt regarding his own acting skills. When his presence was not required, he would retreat to his small house and drink alone. Conversely, Mitchum was very confident and did not do anything to hide it. He was a heavy drinker, too, but he did it loudly and around company.

Loretta Young was only few years older than her colleagues, but she had been a star for twenty years. She knew exactly how to move in front of the camera, aware of her best angles and of the importance of good lighting. Bill and Mitchum were often amused at her staging antics. She would often position her head before the camera rolled in order to have the perfect light on her face, and apologize for throwing one of them in a shadow during a take. Young immediately noticed Bill's insecurity when Mitchum was on the set. One day she said to him tactfully, "Why are you so nervous? You have the lead role. He doesn't get the girl, you do."

"I don't know what you mean."

"You know what I'm talking about. Bob Mitchum has gotten under your skin."

"You are crazy," said Bill, still showing his discomfort.[3]

To escape boredom, Young would invite some cast members for dinner at the small, middle-class house she had rented. One Saturday night she invited Bill and Mitchum who, to her surprise, drank nearly two bottles of whiskey between them and were, of course roaring drunk. She let it go — the first time. But when it happened again, she felt she needed to speak up. "You two are going to rot your stomachs!" she scolded them. "And what will happen to your wonderful talents then?"

Bill graciously agreed with her and thanked her for her concern. Mitchum had a different response. "Thin," he told her, "you worry too much. I've been on my own for most of my life, and I can take care of myself." ("Thin" was Mitchum's nickname for Young.)[4]

Loretta, a very religious Catholic, abhorred the use of curse words or any vulgarity in the workplace. She instituted a "curse box," requiring immediate charitable donations by any violators on the set. Many and varied stories have been printed about this peculiar money box, including one in which a set assistant explained the rates to Bob Mitchum: "It's fifty cents for *hell*, a dollar for a *damn*, a dollar fifty for *shit*—"

Mitchum, in a voice easily heard throughout Oregon, said, "What I want to know is, what does Miss Young charge for a *fuck*?"[5]

For Bill, the "curse box" was never a problem since he rarely cursed, especially around women.

Rachel and the Stranger was the story of widower Big Davey, played by Bill, who decides that his son needs a female to care for him. He buys indentured servant Rachel (Young), who becomes his housekeeper wife and whom he treats with indifference. When wandering hunter and longtime friend Jim Fairways pays a visit and flirts with Rachel, Big Davey realizes that Fairways is in love with his servant wife. After a fistfight, the two friends manage to protect themselves and Rachel from a brutal Indian attack.

Once completed, *Rachel and the Stranger* sat on the shelf for months. One reason for the delay was that Mitchum had been arrested and jailed for marijuana possession. Americans were shocked at a "drug-addicted" Hollywood star. The media described Mitchum as an evil, depraved and corrupting degenerate, whose career was over. But RKO used the event as a fantastic publicity stunt for the first Mitchum movie released after the "marijuana incident," and it worked. Thousands of people crowded the theaters to watch the film the "degenerate" Mitchum had made; *Rachel and the Stranger* was a big earner for RKO. It was nominated for Best Written American Western by the Writers Guild of America, and critics liked the movie. *Time* magazine called it "an engaging and unpretentious show [with] a skillful, comic, notably engaging performance by William Holden."[6] Bill later complained that he had been loaned by Paramount to RKO for $250,000, but received only $14,000.

Harry Cohn lined up Bill for *Lona Hanson*, a picture to be filmed in Mexico with Rita Hayworth, then at the peak of her career. However, she refused to report to work since she did not approve the script as specified in her contract with Cohn. Rita felt the part of a cattle ranch heiress had not been properly tailored for her, and would not show her in the best possible light. Incensed by her decision, and ready to roll, Cohn announced that he would stop paying her $5,000 weekly salary.[7] The project was postponed and Bill was loaned to 20th Century–Fox to play in *Apartment for Peggy*. It was Bill's first color feature and one of the best working experiences in his career. It marked the beginning of a long professional collaboration with director George Seaton, with whom he made three other films.

Seaton and Bill had briefly met at the studios, but were officially introduced by Seaton's wife Phyllis, who had coached Bill in the earliest days at Paramount. The director believed that Bill was perfect for the role of a returning soldier who with his pregnant wife (Jeanne Crain) rents the attic of a lonely old philosophy professor (Edmund Gwenn). Bill read the script and liked it, although he believed that the part was not big enough for him. He asked the director if the screenplay could be rewritten so that his part became a little more prominent.

"I can't do that," replied Seaton. "I think it's got the balance now that it should have; however, as we're making the film, if there's anything we can add along the way, anything I feel that will help the story, I'll write it in. However, I can't promise you that I can make this a bigger part at the moment."

Bill stood up, shook Seaton's hand, and said, "At least you're honest. Okay, you've got me."[8]

Although Bill, Crain and Gwenn had very different acting techniques, they all got along nicely with each other and with the director. Seaton later

Holden, Jeanne Crain and Edmund Gwenn in *Apartment for Peggy* (1948).

said that Crain had very slow delivery of her lines, and slow delivery on the screen was a deadly thing for the comedy. For this reason the director wrote her character "as someone who had diarrhea of the mouth." She had to talk rapidly. It became part of the characterization and it took Crain out of that deliberate delivery she had up to that point.[9] It was in perfect contrast to Bill's character, whose speech was slow and deliberate, and against Edmund Gwenn, who was a professor and spoke perfect Oxford English.

In late 1948, Bill also appeared in the psychological thriller *The Dark Past*. It seemed that producers were slowly realizing that Bill was perfectly capable of a wide range of complex characters.

In a long *Los Angeles Times* interview Bill sent out a very clear message to the Hollywood producers: "I'm getting tired of portraying what I call 'Smiling Jim, with a toothpick.' I'll go further and say I'm through with that type of role. Comedy, yes; Westerns, yes, but the indeterminate character, the middle-of-the-road guy, definitely no."[10] His wish came true with *The Dark Past* in which he played a violent psychopath killer, a role for which he earned the best reviews of his career to date.

His preparation for that part began a few weeks before the filming. "I believe every principal actor in a scene should be ready to do that scene when the camera starts turning. The only way to accomplish this is for people to rehearse. It also saves money. Lee Cobb, director Rudy Maté and I conferred on *Dark Past* scenes even before we were put on the salary. Finally, Maté put the whole troupe on salary for general rehearsals, and as a result brought the picture in under the budget."[11]

The Dark Past (based on a play by James Warwick) tells the story of an escaped killer convict who hides out with his gang at a psychiatrist's isolated home, taking the family hostage. The psychiatrist (played by Lee J. Cobb) recognizes the mental instability of the convict and tries to understand the roots of his disturbed behavior; the film becomes a compelling battle of the psyches. The value of psychiatric treatment was depicted for the first time in this film at a time when Americans were debating the treatment of criminal rehabilitation and societal re-entry. To look the part, Bill reluctantly got a flat-top haircut. Throughout his career he had kept the same neatly trimmed hairstyle with a weekly visit to the same Paramount barber.

During the making of the picture, Nina Foch, who played the psychopath's girlfriend, noted that Bill had trouble delivering lines with Ts and

Ls. This fact was explained by some as a Midwest peculiarity, while others considered it as a side effect of his heavy drinking.[12] The actress also observed how Bill would easily get depressed when Lee J. Cobb, who had played the role of the father in *Golden Boy* nine years earlier, criticized the quality of the script. Bill's lost confidence was restored only after Foch would offer a few words of comfort.

Holden in *The Dark Past* (1948).

"Extraordinarily fine," "excellent" and "believable" was how critics defined Bill's performance in *The Dark Past*. However, the flattering reviews did not make Bill a star. According to many, Bill's stardom would not be reached until three years later with *Sunset Blvd*.

"A friend in the business once told me that no matter what other types of parts I might play during a year I should take on one Western," Bill said, "It's something to fall back on, and it keeps a man healthy."[13] Following his friend's advice, Bill accepted roles in two Westerns, appearing as a brave captain and town marshal in *The Man from Colorado* and as a violent outlaw in *Streets of Laredo*.

Seven years after *Texas*, Glenn Ford and William Holden were reunited by Harry Cohn in *The Man from Colorado*. Columbia's president assigned the picture to director Charles Vidor, despite their unpleasant legal battle following *Gilda*. At the trial, Glenn Ford was called to testify for Cohn. Since Vidor was still under contract with Columbia, he was forced to direct Cohn's Western. Before shooting began, Ford invited the director to Billingsley's, a Hollywood restaurant popular with Columbia employees, to shake his hand in reconciliation.

"I'd rather shovel garbage," Vidor spat.[14] Cohn made the most of the incident, hoping that Ford would insist on Vidor's ouster as director. But producer Jules Schermer convinced the actor to work with Vidor. When filming began, the atmosphere on the set was very tense. Vidor refused to speak to Ford and used the assistant director or wardrobe workers as intermediaries. Vidor also shot multiple angles and takes for each scene to increase the production cost, enraging Cohn. After only thirteen days, *The Man from Colorado* was already behind schedule and over budget. Vidor was subsequently suspended and eventually replaced by Henry Levin.

The Man from Colorado was a psychological Western set during the Civil War; however, the story was an obvious metaphor for the traumatic experiences suffered by veterans of World War II. Ford played former colonel Owen Devereaux, a war hero who was appointed federal district judge. Bill was Del Stewart, once a captain under Devereaux's command and now town sheriff. Bill's character is forced to turn against his former commanding officer and friend when he deteriorates into a sadistic psychopath. The reviewers were all complimentary about Bill's performance but Ford's interpretation was considered by many to be over-the-top.

Bill took a day off from the filming to sign the contract on a new San Fernando Valley house in Toluca Lake, not far from his current home. Bill and Ardis preferred to live in a suburb far from Bel-Air, Beverly Hills and the social circles of Hollywood. The Georgian-style residence was quite modest by movie star standards. It was designed by architect Paul Williams as a typical American middle-class house and lacked the luxurious comforts of the Beverly Hills mansions. The Holdens worried about the $50,000 loan they had taken to purchase the house and to make improvements like adding a one-story den to make room for their young sons Scott and West. Moving to a bigger residence was long overdue because of their dire straits, which were finally resolved.

Bill tried to spend all his free time with his kids. Scott Holden admits that both he and his brother West had a very special childhood. Bill was a caring and loving father, playing with them like *he* was a child. He would personally try all the toys he would buy them, being the first to ride a new bicycle or a go-kart and entertaining everybody with his funny gags. Even on those nights that he would come home drunk, the children remembered him always in a good mood, joyful and amusing.

Streets of Laredo was the second western Bill shot that year. It was an updated version of two earlier Paramount pictures, *The Texas Rangers* (1936) and *Rangers of Fortune* (1940). Bill was on location the first few weeks, first in New Mexico and then Arizona. The striking Technicolor cinematography by Ray Rennahan was the only thing praised by the reviewers, who did not appreciate "the overdose of sex and brutality" in a very confused plot incorporating a mélange of action and romance. *Streets of Laredo* did not do anything for Bill's career. The same was true for *Miss Grant Takes Richmond,* a light comedy he made for Columbia immediately after *Streets*.

Miss Grant Takes Richmond was originally written for Rita Hayworth. However the actress requested so many script changes that it was decided to use it as vehicle to relaunch Lucille Ball's stalling career. Bill and Lucille had met a couple of years earlier at Columbia while he was working in *The Man from Colorado* and she was the lead in the comedy *Her Husband's Affairs*. Together they proved to have perfect chemistry on and off the set. According to Ball's biographers, Bill and Lucille had a short romance while making *Miss Grant Takes Richmond*.[15]

To promote the picture, Harry Cohn asked close friend Frank Sinatra to watch it and include the movie on the bill at the New York's Capitol Theater where the singer was scheduled to make a four-week engagement. Sinatra found the film a mild comedy but agreed to Cohn's request, over the objections of the Capitol's management. Predictably, the singer's engagement was an enormous success, achieving a first-week gross of $122,000. Thus, Cohn was able to advertise that *Miss Grant Takes Richmond* grossed $122,000 in its first week at the New York Capitol.[16]

Despite the fact that he was often busy working, Bill was dissatisfied with his career (which he defined as "one static blur") to date; it had not taken off like other male leads like Alan Ladd and Glenn Ford, who were now true Hollywood stars. Bill kept his frustrations to himself, alleviating them by drinking hard.

An interesting stage offer came when Henry Fonda temporarily left the hit play *Mister Roberts* due to an injury to his knee. Bill was invited to replace him. "I wanted to do it," he recalled in an interview. "It would have been an exciting Broadway debut for me, but Paramount wouldn't go along with it."[17]

Dear Wife and *Father Is a Bachelor*, Bill's next features, intensified his sense of disinterest and frustration over meaningless roles in meaningless movies. *Dear Wife* was a predictable sequel to *Dear Ruth* in which all the actors repeated their roles; it lacked the freshness and the humor of the original. In *Father Is a Bachelor* Bill was a good-hearted tramp maneuvered into caring for five parentless children. The movie revolved around and contained music, even though it was not a musical. The production used

The cast of *Dear Wife* (1949): Mary Philips, Holden, Joan Caulfield, Edward Arnold, Billy De Wolfe and Mona Freeman.

the real singing voice of the cast members except for Bill. He was dubbed by Buddy Clark, a popular singer who had been killed in a plane crash a few weeks before filming began.[18]

"Almost a complete waste of money and talent," wrote *Variety*. Many critics wondered why Columbia Pictures invested money in a terrible movie that disappeared from screens a few days after its release.

5

Sunset Blvd.

• •

"He photographed like an actor who could possibly have a brain in his head." — Billy Wilder

• •

"I wanted to make things a little harder for myself, I wanted to do that thing which never quite works — a picture about Hollywood."[1]

With those words, Billy Wilder explained how the idea for *Sunset Blvd.* began. The movie that became a Hollywood history milestone also made William Holden a star.

"Originally it was a comedy, possibly for Mae West. The picture become about a silent star and a writer. And we could not find the person to play the great silent star. Mae West did not want to do it. Mary Pickford, no. We were about to sign or not sign Pola Negri for the movie. Then we came upon the idea of Gloria Swanson. It might have been George Cukor who first suggested her. She had already been abandoned; she was a death knell — she had lost a lot of money on the Paramount lot. But I insisted on her. A wonderful idea, that carried with it the great value that she had *been* a silent star, and had made a picture with Erich von Stroheim called *Queen Kelly* [1928], which we could also use on the projector screen in her room. We did a screen test, she did a few lines, where an angry Swanson maintains that she's still the greatest. Now we had a picture. She got a minimal salary, $150,000, less than Holden. And it was a wonderful thing that I also had Stroheim. He had two ideas for the film, one of which I used — the writing of the fan letters himself. The other was, he wished to be seen washing her underwear. Stroheim! Montgomery Clift was to play the writer. Three days before, he pulled out."[2]

Clift, who was at the beginning of his successful career, turned down *Sunset Blvd.* at the last moment probably because he was convinced that the role could harm his image. In those days he was having an intimate friendship with former torch singer Libby Holman, who was fourteen years his senior, and the plot seemed too similar to their real-life story: a relationship between an old, rich actress, Norma Desmond, and Joe Gillis, a young B-movie screenwriter. In addition, Clift had just finished shooting *The Heiress*, in which he played the role of a young man who courted a much older woman.

Wilder began to look for a replacement. The first on his list was Fred MacMurray, who had starred in Wilder's *Double Indemnity*. He did not like the script and turned it down. The director offered the part to Gene Kelly, but MGM did not want to lend their musical star. Finally Wilder thought of William Holden. They had met briefly a few years earlier, when they were supposed to work together on a war film. Wilder sent Bill a copy of the script; he carefully read it and loved it. His only concern was working as a supporting actor opposite the old, forgotten silent actress Gloria Swanson. Paramount executive Larry Ginsberg almost forced Bill to sign the contract (replacing Clift saved Paramount $39,000). It was only after having a drink with Wilder that Bill was convinced to accept the part. Privately he revealed to Ardis his hesitation to risk his image playing a secondary role to a woman who was, after all, a has-been. Swanson remembered in her memoirs that once Bill entered the picture, Wilder shyly asked her to make a second screen test together with the new male lead, because there was concern that she looked too young for him.

"'And who's that?' Swanson asked. 'William Holden,' Mr. Brackett said. [Charles Brackett was the co-screenwriter with Wilder and producer.] 'Joe Gillis, the writer in the script, is supposed to be twenty-five and you are supposed to play fifty. But Bill Holden is thirty-one and nervous that you'll look too young. We may have to age you with makeup. Not too much. Just a little.' 'But women of fifty who take care of themselves today don't look old,' I said. 'That's the point. Can't you use makeup on Mr. Holden instead, to make him look more youthful?' They consented to try, if only out of tact, and after they looked at the test, they decided I was right. They changed Bill Holden's hair and adjusted his makeup and left me a spruced-up fifty, which was exactly my age."[3]

After that screen test, Wilder commented about Bill, "He photographed like an actor who could possibly have a brain in his head."[4] Later,

Gloria Swanson and Holden in Billy Wilder's *Sunset Blvd.* (1950).

the director revised his opinion upward, maintaining that people had always underestimated Bill, who was truly an exceptional artist.

Shooting began on April 11, 1949, in a friendly and relaxed atmosphere. The picture was made, according to Swanson, mostly in continuity. Wilder preferred filming day scenes during the day and the night scenes at night.

"William Holden got just straight base makeup and sometimes not even that — he didn't want to wear any if he could avoid it," recalled makeup artist Karl Silvera.[5] Bill was only thirty-one, but looked much older. Therefore, to emphasize the age difference with Swanson as much as possible, it was suggested he get a very short haircut so that he would look a few years younger. On the set, the costume designers noticed that he wore his suits elegantly, avoiding model-like poses and having his hands in the pockets. He would use the clothes to express his emotions in a simple but sophisticated way compared to Swanson's extreme mannerisms.

Rising actress Nancy Olson was cast in the minor role of Betty Sha-effer, a Paramount screenplay reader. About that amazing experience, Olson remembered Bill as "the perfect person for Joe Gillis at the perfect moment of his life. His career was beginning to slide. He was playing roles like the husband in *Apartment for Peggy* where the picture was about Peggy and not about him. Low-budget, churned-out films. He was already drink-ing too much, he was just a little frayed around the edges."[6]

A few times, Bill showed up drunk and agitated on the set, with shak-ing hands. This element was something that, according to Olson, worked to the film's advantage. A curious thing happened during Olson's first love scene with Bill, in which Betty and Joe had to kiss. On the set that eve-ning was Audrey Wilder, Billy's wife and muse for Betty's character, and Ardis, who had been invited by Bill. Olson was extremely intimidated by the presence of both women, who she had never met before. She was espe-cially terrified by Ardis, but embraced Bill and gave him a long passion-ate kiss in front of her. Olson kept calling Ardis "Mrs. Holden" and later described her as "an icy woman." Before the cameras rolled, Wilder told Bill and Nancy not to come apart after the embrace until he said *cut.* He explained that even if it felt long, his idea was to do a long dissolve so they had to continue to kiss and embrace longer. The two delivered their lines, then embraced and kissed and kissed and kissed ... without any interrup-tion by the director. And all of a sudden there was a female voice screamed: "Cut! Damn it! Cut!" It was Ardis.[7]

Olsen revealed that the reason she was able to work again with Bill in two other films was that he never flirted with her, and therefore their chemistry on the set stayed unspoiled. Bill worked very hard on his role. Early in the shooting he said that he needed to know more about Joe Gillis in order to fill out the character, and that the script was incomplete, unclear, and therefore frustrating for him as an actor.

"How much do you know about Holden?" was Wilder's laconic answer, which troubled him even more.[8] He was afraid to portray a vul-gar, pimp-ish gigolo and continued to express his concerns to Wilder. The director told him simply that he had to visualize a garage mechanic who was living in Des Moines. "And when he goes to see this picture, I want him to say 'There but for the grace of God, go I.'"[9] Ironically it meant that Bill was once again playing the all–American man — the same guy he had already portrayed in almost all his films. Moreover, Bill claimed that he could not relate to the Norma Desmond character until Swanson gave

him keen insight into the industry's pioneering era during a few conver-
sations on the set. Thanks to her, he was able to better understand and
relate to the semi-autobiographical character played by his co-star.[10]

Off the set, Bill had recurrent moments of sadness that he tried to
overcome by drinking. He hid his insecurity and affliction from his friends,
whom he always kept at a distance. He was often moody but his tormented
spirit did not interfere with his craft and professionalism.

Swanson's mother Adelaide had a crush on Bill, as Gloria revealed:
"She came to the set just to watch him." A few years later the old lady,
still infatuated, bought stock in Billy Wilder's *Stalag 17* only because Bill
was the star. It was a profitable investment since the picture was a big hit
and her idol won the Oscar as Best Actor of 1953.[11]

Outside Paramount Studios, a few of the exterior shots were filmed
at a 25-room French-Italian mansion, untenanted for years, located at
4201 Wilshire Boulevard. The property was originally bought by the
tycoon J. Paul Getty in 1936 as a home for a former wife, who kept it after
the divorce. Mrs. Getty did not want a swimming pool built on the property, although a pool was pivotal to the story as a metaphor for Desmond's
success and ruin. Paramount promised to restore the ground when the
shooting was finished. After watching the fancy model being installed, the
owner withdrew her objections before discovering the pool wasn't practi-
cal. Paramount put in a filter and other things and made the pool a gift
to the owner (it was used years later by Warner Bros. in *Rebel Without a
Cause*). In 1957 the house was demolished and a twenty-two-story building — the corporate headquarters for the Getty Oil Company — was
erected.

In the picture, Wilder introduced some minor characters who played
themselves. The great director Cecil B. DeMille, filmed on the set of *Sam-
son and Delilah*, welcomed Norma Desmond in the same studio where he
used to greet Gloria Swanson in the '20s. There was also the "waxworks"
(as Joe Gillis calls Desmond's bridge companions), silent-era stars Buster
Keaton, Anna Q. Nilsson and H.B. Warner. Gossip columnist Louella
Parsons made a cameo, appearing like "a vulture" ready to disclose to the
entire world Desmond's spiraling madness.

After the shooting ended on June 18, the beginning and the end of
the film had to be changed, after two preview screening audiences reacted
with unpredicted laughter. With the reshooting, *Sunset Blvd.* was $180,000
over budget, but Paramount was not terribly concerned since Wilder had

a solid financial track record. By the end of filming, Bill had grown very close to Wilder. The simple guy from Pasadena (as he considered himself) expressed his gratitude to the director not only for the role but also for opening up the world of culture and travel. They later collaborated on three other films and their friendship lasted until Holden's death.

Paramount launched *Sunset Blvd.* with a series of twenty-one private screenings for various leaders of the industry. At one of them, Barbara Stanwyck was so impressed that she reportedly knelt down and kissed Gloria Swanson's silver lamé gown.

Only Louis B. Mayer left the screening in a rage, screaming at Wilder, "You bastard! You have disgraced the industry that made and fed you! You should be tarred and feathered and run out of Hollywood!"

"Fuck you," replied Wilder.

A few days after the official opening, the picture received its first reviews, all positive, even if some found it "disturbing." *Sunset Blvd.*'s world premiere was held on August 10 at Radio City Music Hall. The film was a hit and local papers praised it. The *New York Times* critic wrote, "William Holden is doing the finest acting of his career. His range and control of emotions never falters and he engenders a full measure of compassion for a character who is somewhat less than admirable."[12]

The film performed fairly well at the box office and the following year received 11 Academy Award nominations including Best Picture, Best Director, Best Actor and Best Actress in a Leading Role.

On March 29, 1951, Bill and Ardis nervously sat beside Billy Wilder and his wife Audrey at the RKO Pantages Theater on Hollywood Boulevard at the Academy Award ceremony. The evening was a disappointment. José Ferrer was named Best Actor in *Cyrano de Bergerac, All About Eve* was named Best Picture and its director Joseph L. Mankiewicz won for Best Director. *Sunset Blvd.* won only in three categories: Best Original Story, Best Art Direction–Set Decoration (Black and White) and Best Scoring of a Dramatic or Comedy Picture. After the awards, the Holdens and the Wilders went to the nightclub Mocambo on the Sunset Strip where Paramount had arranged a post–Oscar party. All night Bill managed to keep a sad smile on his face to hide his disappointment in front of photographers. Wilder tried to cheer him up over dinner, saying, "It was a miscarriage of justice. You really should have won tonight."

"Why do you console him?" Ardis asked bitterly. "He was not that good. He did not deserve an Oscar. José Ferrer was much better than Bill."

Holden, Gloria Swanson, Nancy Olson and Erich von Stroheim in a publicity shot for *Sunset Blvd.* (1950).

Although the Wilders were familiar with the Holdens' quarrels, they were stunned by Ardis' insensitive remark.[13] Bill stared at his wife in a state of shock and when that awkward moment ended, he poured himself another drink.[14] Three years later, Bill won his first Oscar for *Stalag 17*, once again directed by Wilder. He thought he had no chance but he was wrong. At a party given by his friends the Clemens, he was comfortably seated in their den, holding a drink, admiring the golden statuette and still expressing his astonishment about his victory. Suddenly Ardis said, "Well, you know, Bill, you really didn't get the award for *Stalag*. They gave it to you for *Sunset Blvd.*"

Bill lowered his eyes and ground his teeth, as he always did when he was nervous. He was still very upset when he returned home that evening, missing the driveway and tearing the fender off his Cadillac. When he woke up the next day, he was sitting in his living room, still in his tuxedo with the Oscar on his lap.[15]

Bill's professional career rapidly took off after *Sunset Blvd.*, in inverse proportion to his marriage that reached moments of great tension and instability. Now that Ardis had withdrawn from the spotlight, she seemed to resent her husband's success and victories. Downgrading Bill became one of her favorite activities. Another embarrassing episode occurred during an interview at home when a reporter asked her what was it like to be married to such a handsome man. Ardis briefly looked at her husband and replied, "Oh, do you think that he's handsome?"[16]

"It was like in *A Star Is Born* just the opposite way," stated Billy Wilder years later. Commenting about the Holdens' difficult marriage: "They were a couple of actors and suddenly he became the main attraction."[17]

At the time, Ronald Reagan and his girlfriend Nancy Davis were two of the few friends Bill and Ardis would see regularly. The couples mostly enjoyed nightclubs or restaurants together and often organized barbeques at the Holdens.' Despite the differences in their backgrounds Bill and Reagan had much in common personally — they liked horses, were wine connoisseurs and shared the same political philosophies. Thanks to Reagan, Bill became an interested, active participant in the Screen Actors Guild; he became its first vice-president. But Bill's influence was greater on Ronald than the other way around. In his next few films, Reagan modeled his performances on those of Bill. He copied a trick Bill had of lighting a cigarette; he wore clothes that had a decidedly William Holden look to them; he even aped Bill's raised-eyebrow, cynical expression.[18]

In the summer of 1950, during a brief visit to New York as vice-president of SAG and to do some publicity for *Sunset Blvd.*, Bill explained to Howard Thompson of the *New York Times* the importance of the Screen Actors Guild to the film industry.

"It may seem like a little thing, and it has nothing to do with wages or unions, but now for the first time we have people of all crafts simply sitting down together and talking over production problems. That never happened before. It's saving time, cutting red tape and production costs, even breaking up typecastings."[19]

On the SAG board, Bill helped chair the Veteran Affairs Committee, which actively sought work for returning actor war veterans, particularly for supporting and bit players.

"It was the least I could do" was his answer to the colleagues who expressed their gratitude. As a member of the Motion Picture Industry Council, Bill also served on the Permanent Charities Committee and, in an honorary post, became the Commissioner of Parks and Recreation for Los Angeles.

Sunset Blvd. was the turning point in Bill's career, but as he later admitted, "That was the big breakthrough that wasn't such an immediate breakthrough. All it led to were a couple of more junk, but more important junk; the junk was getting better."[20]

Alfred Hitchcock wanted Bill to play the role of Guy Haines, the ambitious professional tennis player in *Strangers on a Train*, based on Patricia Highsmith's novel. But hiring him would entail a complicated loan-out from Columbia and would tax the film's budget. The studio countered with Farley Granger, whom Hitchcock had directed in *Rope*.[21]

Instead Bill played in *Union Station*, directed by Rudolph Maté, with whom he had previously worked on *The Dark Past*. The picture was made when *Sunset Blvd.* had not yet been released. Bill was paired once again with Nancy Olson, this time in a suspenseful film noir. He played the chief of security at Chicago's Union Station, who gets involved in the kidnapping of a blind girl. The abductee is the daughter of a wealthy businessman, whose secretary (Olson) falls for him. Paramount released the film two months after *Sunset Blvd.*, hoping to benefit from the publicity of the latter. Despite the presence of the two stars, *Union Station* bombed.

In April 1950, Harry Cohn assigned George Cukor to direct a film adaptation of Garson Kanin's Broadway hit *Born Yesterday*. In 1948 Cohn had paid an incredible $1,000,000 for the rights in one of the biggest deals ever made by Columbia Pictures. However, the project was put on the shelf for months because of casting problems. Cohn assigned it to Rita Hayworth, but she was too preoccupied as Aly Khan's new wife to make up her mind about doing it.

The role of the dumb blonde Billie Dawn had been written by Kanin for Jean Arthur, but the insecure actress had withdrawn during rehearsals. Judy Holliday was asked to learn the role in three days. Holliday scored a huge success in the theater, playing that role for four years in 1,643 performances. Cukor insisted on casting her in the film against the wishes of Cohn, who couldn't envision her as a movie star. After several requests from the director, Cohn agreed to meet with Holliday and as soon as she entered his office he "welcomed" her by saying, just loud enough for her and everybody else in the room to hear, "Well, I've worked with fat asses before."

Nobody had to tell Holliday that she'd had gained a few pounds, just as nobody had to tell her that Cohn was intentionally provoking her. But the actress was a very smart woman and a veteran of 20th Century–Fox president Zanuck's casting couch wars. She did not get offended and, once Cohn was convinced to cast her, she lost fifteen pounds in only three weeks.

In the part of Brock, the junk dealer, the president of Columbia cast Broderick Crawford, who had recently won an Oscar for *All the King's Men*. (Paul Douglas, who played Brock on stage, turned the role down after reading a revised, heavily censored script, completely altering the original play.) Cohn's choice of Crawford was disapproved by Cukor, who believed Crawford was indeed a better actor than Douglas. However, the experience that Douglas had gained playing that role on stage for years and the chemistry he shared with Holliday was far more relevant for the picture.[22]

Bill was offered the role of Paul Verrall, a journalist who becomes the intellectual tutor of Billie Dawn, with whom he falls in love. Bill was reluctant to accept the part, realizing he would be overshadowed by two showy roles. Both Billy Wilder and Garson Kanin (who had just finished a third draft of the screenplay — the first two had been unsuccessfully written by Albert Mannheimer and the brothers Julius and Philip Epstein, successively) advised him to accept, arguing that such a promising project could only advance his career. Holliday became aware of the problem, and confronted Bill about it.

"It's a wonderful script," she said, "and there are a lot of opportunities for everyone."[23] To convince him, she suggested they rehearse the play with Cukor and stage an abbreviated performance for the Columbia employees. After Cohn gave his reluctant approval, a group of carpenters built a 300-seat theater on a Columbia lot. This gave Cukor the opportunity to time the delivery of the lines before they would be filmed.

The cast rehearsed for two weeks, then performed before an audience of studio employees. Later they performed in front of stars and producers (and also Bill's parents). It was an enormous success. On June 15, 1950, the production of *Born Yesterday* shifted to Washington D.C. for location work; Cukor shot exteriors all over town. The itinerary included the Supreme Court building, the Washington Monument, the Treasury Department, the National Gallery, the Jefferson Memorial, the Library of Congress and the National Archives. In this last location, the archives officials feared that the powerful lights used in movie photography might fade

Judy Holliday, Broderick Crawford and Holden in *Born Yesterday* (1950).

or crumble the U.S. Constitution on display under glass. Cukor was forced to have his cameraman reduce his normal lightning by half in a scene where Holliday and Bill were looking at the historic document.[24]

The entire crew of *Born Yesterday* was staying at the Hilton Hotel. Every night Broderick Crawford and Bill would order caviar and champagne, charging it to Columbia Pictures, and having drinking competitions. Two weeks later, the company moved back to Hollywood where principal photography was completed on August 12. There was only one moment of tension during the making of the film, when Crawford asked Cohn permission to leave the set early to retrieve his son from the hospital after an eye operation.

"You leave that set, and I'll sue you for seven million dollars," answered Cohn.

Enraged, Crawford told Bill and Holliday about the exchange, and both advised him to leave the set that afternoon. Shortly before the lunch break, an ambulance entered through a stage door. Crawford's son was on a stretcher in the rear.

Cohn appeared from behind a backdrop, barking, "Now you go home with the boy. And don't you ever tell me you're going to leave the set!"[25]

Born Yesterday was rushed for a year-end release in order to qualify for the 1950 Oscars. The picture had the same financial success as the play, making it an extremely profitable investment for Cohn. The reviews were positive, although the critics agreed the stage version was by far superior to the screen adaptation. Bill received some praises but, as he feared, almost all the attention went to Holliday's performance. She won an Academy Award as Best Actress, beating Gloria Swanson for *Sunset Blvd.*, and Bette Davis and Anne Baxter for *All About Eve*.

6

Hollywood Babylon

· ·

"Every role I ever did for Billy, someone else was supposed to play first." — William Holden

· ·

In 1951, Paramount offered Bill the opportunity to sign a new long-term contract. He refused, explaining that he had been exploited for too long and lent too often to other studios. He decided to be on his own without being tied to a particular studio. It was a brave decision, since at the time only a few superstars had the privilege of choosing who to work with. His choice was disapproved by many in the industry; Harry Cohn expected Bill would be left empty-handed. Others feared that his decision would set an example for other artists to follow and shortly the actors would have taken over the studios, choosing their parts and discussing their salary, shaking the entire Hollywood system. Bill received only one offer, from Jack Warner, who most likely gave him a part just to upset his worst opponent Harry Cohn. Warner Bros., for some reason, pictured Bill and Nancy Olson as a love team of the '50s and paired them yet again in *Force of Arms*, also known as *A Girl for Joe*. This was followed shortly afterward by Paramount's *Submarine Command*. Both films were set during World War II.

Casablanca's Michael Curtiz directed *Force of Arms*. Bill played a service-weary lieutenant traumatized by the death of his comrades during the Italian campaign. His love for a WAC lieutenant (Olson) helps him overcome his sense of guilt. The story was a free modern adaptation of Ernest Hemingway's *A Farewell to Arms* and was almost entirely shot on location in the mountains of Santa Susana in California. When released in the summer of 1951, the picture was panned by the reviewers and ignored by the

Holden on the set of *Force of Arms* (1951) in California's Santa Susana Mountains with his father Bill Beedle.

public. The same fate awaited *Submarine Command*, released at the beginning of 1952 after Bill agreed to sign a short-term Paramount contract. *Submarine Command* director John Farrow called Bill "one of the most competent, sensitive and skillful men in the business." His flattering words did not help the picture at the box office.[1] Many years later, when Ryan

O'Neal (Bill's co-star in Blake Edwards' *Wild Rovers*) told him that *Submarine Command* was one of his favorite films, Bill told him that he did not remember a thing about making it, since he was drunk through the whole picture.

In between the two films, Bill acted along with a dozen Hollywood stars in *You Can Change the World*, a 20-minute "anti–Communist" short conceived by Father James Keller, organizer of the Christopher's Unit of the Roman Catholic Church, and directed by Leo McCarey.

His next two films were *Boots Malone* and *The Turning Point*, both directed by William Dieterle. After *Sunset Blvd.* Bill was being offered roles as the nice all–American guy and also as the "bastard with a heart of gold." The first feature was set in the horse racing world with Bill as an agent for jockeys, temporarily down on his luck, who molded an inexperienced teenager into a first-class jockey. The second Dieterle picture *The Turning Point* was one of the many thrillers based on Senator Kefauver's investigations into organized crime. Bill played a skeptical reporter recruited by a friend to help find incriminating evidence against a syndicate, eventually sacrificing his life.

Bill also found time to work in several radio programs, the most memorable an adaptation of Billy Wilder's film *The Lost Weekend* for *Theatre Guild on the Air*, recorded together with Ardis. The subject of alcoholism seemed terribly autobiographical.

Since they worked together in *Sunset Blvd.*, Bill and Billy Wilder had became close. Bill admired the director's broad culture, his refined taste and his clever mind. At the same time, Wilder was fascinated by Bill's down-to-earth behavior, by his genuine warmth and by his all–American look — something that, as a man from Austria, he could not ever have. The two friends spent so much time together and become so well acquainted with each other's tastes and habits that they became very similar, except for Bill's drinking vice. Once Bill asked Wilder his opinion on an important piece of art he wanted to buy. The director replied, "If I were you — and I am..."[2]

In the summer of 1951, while Bill was in New York to promote *Force of Arms*, Wilder urged him to go see a huge success on Broadway called *Stalag 17*, which he was interested in adapting for the screen. Bill walked out after the first act. He found the play tedious and thought the main character, J.J. Sefton, was obnoxious, lacking any psychological depth. Wilder asked him to read the screenplay he had written together with

Edwin Blum because he wanted Bill to play Sefton. Bill knew that Paramount had already offered the part to Charlton Heston and to Kirk Douglas, who both for different reasons turned it down. He told Wilder, "Second choice again, huh?"

"Well, you didn't do so badly last time, Bill," Wilder replied.

Eventually Bill accepted the role with the stipulation that a couple of lines be added to the script to show that Sefton despised the Nazis. Wilder refused. The director, whose mother, grandmother and stepfather were all dead in Auschwitz, had planned to make a film about a Nazi concentration camp during World War II where a traitor was hidden among the prisoners, so adapting that play *Stalag 17* seemed a very good opportunity for Wilder. He made some changes to the original text, adding several outdoor scenes, but none outside the camp (in order to give to the audience that same feeling of claustrophobia the prisoners felt). In addition, he created a new central character, Oberst Von Scherbach, a sadistic Nazi camp commander. Apart from the central plot and a few character sketches, the director retained very little of the original play. The play's co-author Edmund Trzcinski, who had a small role in the film, did not recognize the character Sefton as portrayed by Bill as the one he wrote as a radiant dramatic hero. He made a terrible scene with Wilder and stopped talking to him after the film became a hit and was praised for its patriotic message.[3]

After a week of rehearsal, *Stalag 17* began shooting on February 4, 1952, at the Calabassas ranch in California (the real Stalag 17 was located near Krems, Austria) where a replica of a prisoner camp exterior was built. Wilder believed in the inviolable sanctity of the screenplay and on the first day of filming he called a meeting of the cast. He had given them an uncompleted script and would not abide the actors rewriting the dialogue.

He asked them if they had read it and after they all answered in the affirmative, he announced, "Gentlemen, if you have something to tell me about your lines or anything else in the script — tell me now. Because once we start shooting not a sentence, not a word, not a syllable, will be changed. Is that clear?"[4] Bill started to open his mouth but then got very red in the face and said nothing.

At Wilder's suggestion, Bill got a flat-top haircut, kept his face unshaved and walked slouch-shouldered with his head cocked sassily to the side to look more the part of a cynical mercenary and less a handsome boy-next-door type. As his confidence grew day by day, Bill became more

Stalag 17's all-male cast: Neville Brand, Don Taylor, Holden, Robert Strauss, Harvey Lembeck, two unidentifieds, Peter Graves, Richard Erdman (1953).

relaxed, even playful. One afternoon he invited a beautiful actress into his dressing room for a tryst. A few hours later, while he was on the set completing a take, he noticed a very pale Ardis looking at him. Bill suddenly felt lost, thinking his wife had heard about his rendezvous.

"Something terrible has happened!" she said.

"What?"

"I smashed up the car."

"Marvelous!" Bill exclaimed, all relieved.[5]

Wilder shot *Stalag 17* in relative chronological order. Until the very end, nobody in the cast knew who the Nazi collaborator character was. German director Otto Preminger was cast as the cruel camp commander. He was paid $45,000 for three weeks' work. Preminger had a reputation as a director-tyrant, but on the set he behaved impeccably, giving a flawless performance as a character he hated as much as Wilder, since like Wilder he had fled Europe before World War II. Robert Strauss' extraordinary interpretation of "Animal" got him an Academy Award nomination as Best Supporting Actor. Dick Beedle, Bill's younger brother, was one of the many extras playing the prisoners of war in the camp.

Vicky Wilder, Billy's daughter, was 15 when her father took her on the set and she met Bill. "I had a crush for William Holden," she confessed many years later. "He looked at me in that special way, and I had the feeling that he seemed to be interested in me, but did not make a play for me as he did not wish to upset Daddy."[6]

The picture was completed in two and a half months, only a

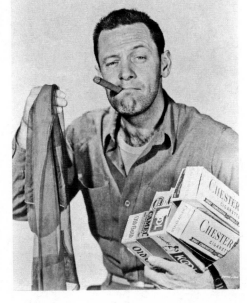

A scene from Billy Wilder's *Stalag 17* (1953).

few days over the scheduled time. Twice Wilder surprised everyone, first inviting his dear friend Marlene Dietrich and later Gloria Swanson, who both agreed to be photographed with each member of the all-male cast.

"All the characters were good in *Stalag 17*," commented Wilder, "because they lived the play. I didn't have the play, but I had the *feeling* of the play."[7]

Stalag 17 became one of his favorite films. "There are five or six minutes, sometimes only thirty seconds that I like in my pictures. Along with *Sunset Blvd.*, *Stalag 17* is one of my favorites, perhaps because there are eight minutes that were any good."[8]

On March 4, 1952, Bill asked permission to leave the set early to be the best man at the Ronald Reagan–Nancy Davis wedding. A couple of weeks earlier, during a meeting of the Motion Picture Industry Council, where Reagan and Bill were Guild representatives, the future president of the United States wrote a note to Bill: "The hell with this, how would you like to be best man when I marry Nancy?"

"It's about time," Bill blurted out. To everyone's surprise they got up without a word and walked out to go celebrate.[9]

The Holdens at the Reagans' wedding in 1952.

The wedding was held at the Little Brown Church in the Valley. It was a very simple ceremony with Ardis and Bill as the matron of honor and best man. Nancy, secretly three months pregnant, was so nervous that she did not know the Holdens had had a fight and weren't speaking to each other. She seemed to go through it in a sort of daze.

When Bill leaned over and said, "Let me be the first to kiss the bride," Nancy panicked and drew back, motioning him to wait — as the ceremony was not over. "You are jumping the gun," she told him.

"I am not!" Bill laughed and kissed her.[10]

After the ceremony, the newlyweds drove back to the Holdens' where Ardis had ordered a four-tier cake and hired a photographer to take wedding pictures. Six months later, Bill and Ardis became Reagan's first daughter Patty's godparents.

Wilder did not release *Stalag 17* for sixteen months until July of 1953. It was an instant hit, making Sefton (according to *Life* magazine) one of *the* most memorable Hollywood characters. Fourteen ex–POWs attended the West Coast premiere at the Warner Bros. Beverly Hills Theater. Despite the discrepancies between real life and their own terrible experiences, they enjoyed the fictional story.[11]

In February 1954, Wilder was nominated for the fourth time for an Academy Award, along with Bill as Best Actor. That year Bill had tough competition: Montgomery Clift and Burt Lancaster in *From Here to Eternity*, Marlon Brando in *Julius Caesar* and Richard Burton in *The Robe*. At the Oscar ceremony, he was caught by surprise when Shirley Booth called his name. The NBC-TV show, sponsored by Oldsmobile, was so filled with commercials that he had no time to give an acceptant speech. His hurried "Thank you, thank you" was the shortest speech in Academy Award history. "I'm very upset. They told me to say 'thank you' and get off. I think they could [have] held off the closing commercial a little longer so that everyone could know how much Billy Wilder was responsible," Bill told the press backstage.[12]

At the post–Oscar party at the ritzy Beverly Hills restaurant Chasen's, Bill met Burt Lancaster and told him that he (Lancaster) deserved to win. Bill shyly did not show off his Oscar, but Ardis sneaked it under her fur coat and put it on the table where they celebrated with close friends. At one point Bill lifted his champagne glass to Wilder exclaiming, "To Billy Wilder ... of course I've always knew it."

In May 1952, after *Stalag 17 was* completed, Bill, Wilder, his old screenwriter friend Charles Lederer and their wives went on a three-month trip to Europe. "Billy was running both of us ragged sight-seeing, restaurant going, shopping," Bill later recalled. "Even mountain climbing. We were at Bad Ischul ... and the previous day we had taken in two churches and one museum and climbed a difficult mountain. I flopped into bed totally wiped out. I told him I was going to sleep all that night and the next day. Well, the next thing I knew the phone is ringing. I pick up. It's him. I looked

Holding his Oscar for Best Actor for *Stalag 17* in 1954.

at my watch. My God, it's six A.M. What does he want at this ungodly hour? He says, 'We're waiting in the lobby, Bill, where are you?' I groaned, 'Hell, Billy, I told you last night I was exhausted. I can't make it.' He got very stern. 'You just have got to come down here and go with us. If you do not come, I will never forgive you.'

"So down I came and Billy had some coffee and brandy waiting for me, and cheese, bread, and ham. I had breakfast and figured I might live another day.

"Well, we started out sight-seeing and we made four important stops that day and that was one of the most wonderful days in my whole life.

"It isn't just his ebullience, his love for life, but that need he has to share his pleasures with you.

"How can you resist the guy?"[13]

About that trip, Wilder's most vivid memory was Bill and Ardis constantly arguing. She did not want to go to Europe: "What the hell is Europe for?" he remembered her saying.

"She was what in Yiddish they called a *Quetsch*—a bore, someone who always complains and is always in a bad mood, spoiling other people's mood too. We arrive in Paris, we check in at the Ritz and we go for lunch in a fantastic Parisian restaurant called L'Espadron. We sit, the waiter arrives and she says, 'I'd like a *peanut butter* sandwich.' The waiter replied, 'I beg your pardon, madam?' In a very upset tone she repeats, 'I'd like a *peanut butter* sandwich. Don't you have one?' When the waiter answers no, she looks at us triumphantly, 'See? I told you! Now you understand why I found Europe such a terrible place'"[14]

Paramount, in agreement with Bill's agent Charles Feldman, rewarded his Oscar victory, offering a new and radically revised contract with a salary of $250,000. It called for two films a year and allowed Bill to make his own outside deals at the rate of one a year.

The Moon Is Blue, Bill's first film shot as an independent artist, turned out to be a very smart move. Otto Preminger (together with screenwriter F. Hugh Herbert) had set up his own production company, Carlyle Productions, to make a film based on the controversial and highly successful Broadway play *The Moon Is Blue*. It was a low-budget project and Preminger offered Bill not only an acting role, but a chance to co-produce it. He accepted the offer, probably responding to a personal sense of rebellion which Preminger had noticed just beneath "the junior-corporate-executive" surface.

"Holden is in constant revolt against authority," Billy Wilder remarked.[15] Making that film meant to Bill not only going against Hollywood censorship, but also getting around the tax authorities, paying less taxes as a co-producer and not as a simple artist. While working on the script, the idea struck Preminger to also make a German version, with a different cast but shooting it simultaneously. As soon as the German cast arrived, rehearsals started and went on for a month. The entire film was completed in two languages in eighteen days. After watching David Niven performing on stage in the play *Nina* starring Gloria Swanson, Preminger decided to cast the British actor against United Artists' will. UA considered Niven "washed up" and advised Preminger to choose someone more commercial. Once *The Moon Is Blue* was completed it did not have an immediate release since its script violated a few of Hollywood's taboos. The picture shocked its first viewers because the dialogue contained words which were acceptable on the stage but seldom heard on the screen. Words like *seduce, virgin* and *lover* were used in an explicit sexual manner and therefore considered immoral. Preminger had faithfully adapted the original play, whose story concerns successful architect Don Gresham, played by Bill, who makes the acquaintance of a young actress Patty (Maggie McNamara) trying to make it in New York. In competition with David (Niven), the father of his ex-fiancée, Greshman tries to seduce Patty, but she fends him off by claiming that she plans to remain a virgin until her wedding night. In vain, both men are determined to find a way around her objections.

The Breen Office, the self-censorship body of the MPAA, promptly refused to pass the film unless the word "virgin" and a reference to seduction were eliminated. Preminger refused to make any cuts. He fought in court and got both New York State and Pennsylvania approval with the support of United Artists (who was not part of the MPAA), despite the disapproval of the Production Code which did not grant the picture a seal. Eventually only Maryland, Ohio and Kansas banned the movie.

"I am not a crusader ... but it gives me a great pleasure to fight for my rights," Preminger said to the press. "[The Code] was written twenty-three years ago and I knew I didn't have a chance when I submitted *The Moon Is Blue*."[16] He explained that the censorship was not updated with the current sexual morality and the right to freedom of speech was threatened.

The mayhem continued after the Catholic Legion of Decency banned it through an intervention of Francis Cardinal Spellman of New York and James Francis Cardinal McIntyre of Los Angeles, who labeled attendance "an occasion of sin." The intervention had a boomerang effect and movie-goers lined up for hours at theaters that were allowed to show it.

"I don't mind the clergy telling their flock not to see it," Preminger commented, "but at the same time I see no reason why they should prevent people of other faiths from seeing it."[17]

The Moon Is Blue was a great success and made a lot of money for everybody connected with it. Bill took home $600,000 as his third of the box office gross. The picture earned Niven a Golden Globe from the Foreign Press Association for best comedy performance of the year, but its biggest achievement was the revision of industry censorship guidelines.

In September 1952, Bill played in *Forever Female* opposite Ginger Rogers and Paul Douglas. It was an unpleasant experience since Bill hated the script, but still owed a film to Paramount under his old contract. *Forever Female* was a sentimental farce inspired by James M. Barrie's one-act play *Rosalind*, repackaged with resemblances to *All About Eve*. Rogers was

Beatrice Page, an aging Broadway star who desperately tries to restore her status. Bill plays a young playwright with the right play but perfect for a younger actress. Page succeeds in getting the part but the show inevitably fails. For the role of Rogers' rival, Paramount cast Pat Crowley, an unknown young actress. Rogers in her memoirs stated that the behavior of her two leading men, Paul Douglas and Bill, suddenly changed when the press reported her romance with young and handsome French actor Jacques Bergerac:

Holden in an early '50s portrait.

The daily response to me from Bill and Paul was one of indif-

ference and downright belliger-
ence. They would go to lunch
and imbibe their share of Man-
hattans or daiquiris. Upon
returning to the set, they sat
beside each other as if glued
together, and behind their
hands they would whisper to
each other, look at me, and
laugh, slapping their thighs. I
felt this was a personal dig.
They never spoke to me unless I
spoke to them.[18]

Bill became friendly with
Douglas. They both stayed
drunk through most of the
filming, causing several problems for director Irving Rapper.
Alcohol seemed to help Bill alle-
viate his sense of guilt mostly
related to the profession he
deeply despised but could not
avoid.

Making *Escape from Fort
Bravo* was, for Bill, a more enjoyable experience than *Forever
Female.* For the first time, he was
in a picture produced by MGM
and with the ravishing Eleanor
Parker. Between shots Bill played
Cupid with her, talking about
his close friend Paul Clemens,
who had just finished painting a
portrait of his family.

Two and a half months
later, while she was making
another film, Parker recalls, "We
ran into each other on the Paramount lot. Paul Clemens was

Top: Holden in *Escape from Fort Bravo*
(1953). *Bottom:* Holden on the set of
Escape from Fort Bravo.

coming over, he told me, and asked if I would like to join them for lunch. The result of that luncheon? On my first day off, I went over to Paul's studio to pose for my portrait. During one of the sittings, the Holdens called to invite Paul to an impromptu barbecue. He told them I was there and they asked him to bring me along. By the time the portrait was finished, we had had several dates."[19] Parker and Clemens were married the following November.

Escape from Fort Bravo, based on a story by Philip Rock and set in 1863 during the Civil War, tells of a woman who helps her Confederate fiancé (John Forsythe) escape from a Yankee prison camp in Arizona. The problem is that she falls in love with the Union officer who had captured her fiancé and delivered him to Fort Bravo.

During the shooting the crew suffered from the heat (most of the film was shot in a desert in New Mexico and in Death Valley, California). The average temperature was 120 degrees. MGM shot it in 3-D; by the time of its general release, however, 3-D's popularity had waned and it was distributed flat. Despite the unoriginal plot, *Escape from Fort Bravo* was quite successful commercially. *Time* magazine called it the best western of the last decade. After watching himself on the big screen, Bill admitted to disliking how his uniform fitted him, emphasizing his slightly out-of-shape figure.

Critics and audiences raved for *Executive Suite*, which Bill made for MGM a few months later with his idol Fredric March. They played executives at a big furniture manufacturing company in competition for the top spot after the president died suddenly. March is an ambitious schemer interested only in profits, while Bill plays a young idealist with new ideas to improve the quality of the products for the advantage of the company and its customers. Director Robert Wise and producer John Houseman assembled a cast of stars: Paul Douglas, Barbara Stanwyck, Walter Pidgeon, June Allyson, Shelley Winters, Nina Foch and Louis Calhern. For the part of McDonald Walling, Wise chose Henry Fonda, who turned it down since he was rehearsing a Broadway musical (which was never produced). Wise's second choice was Bill, who had not read Cameron Hawley's best-selling novel on which the film was based but quickly read and loved Ernest Lehman's brilliant script. He accepted the part after Billy Wilder gave him his blessing. *Executive Suite* was the first major film to deal bluntly with the social phenomenon of corporate power. It intended to provide audiences with a realistic glimpse behind the façade of a typical corporation, allowing the viewers a greater understanding of how the business structure worked.

Wise admitted, "I had a wonderful group of actors. Up until the boardroom [the last scene he shot]. I guess I didn't have them all together in the same room. They were a lot of fun because most of them had worked together over the years. They used to kid each other, joke and tell stories. They'd be sitting around while the lighting was being finished, swapping yarns and needling each other; but the minute the bell rang, playtime was off and they went right back into character."[20]

Bill added, "Everybody was so good — so on his toes — that when you went in there in the morning you had to put on your best. It was a great experience."[21]

Working again with Barbara Stanwyck made him extremely happy. Their scene together had all the fire they showed in *Golden Boy*. Dore Schary, the head of production at MGM, suggested having no musical score to make the film more realistic, and the director agreed. Old MGM set decorations and props from other films were used to reduce the budget. *Executive Suite* cost $1,383,000 and grossed four million. It received four Academy Award nominations and a Special Jury Prize for ensemble acting at the 1954 Venice Film Festival.

On the set, Shelley Winters and Bill met formally for the "first time." They always treated each other like the casual acquaintances they weren't. In 1980, Winters in her memoir revealed a surprising story about how they first met in 1949 at a Christmas party at Paramount where they danced together.

> I didn't know if he knew my name but I knew his. Cornel Wilde in cape and costume did a perfect jump from a second-story window and yelled, "Bill, we're out of ice." Holden took my hand and made for his dressing room across the street to get ice. Bing Crosby was in his dressing room next door — with Joan Caulfield — also looking for ice. I don't remember exactly how it happened, but situations developed in such a way that we forgot about the importance of the ice. So to cut only to:
> Waves pounding on a beach,
> Trees swaying in the storm...
> But Mr. Holden was quite drunk that Christmas Eve and passed out. About 4 A.M. I woke with a terrible headache and wondered what they put in vodka in Moscow. I stumbled around and realized that what looked like Mr. Holden's car was out in front of his dressing room with lots of toys in the back seat. I made some black coffee in the kitchen, but no matter how I tried, I couldn't wake Bill Holden up. There was a sink with a long spray

hose next to his makeup table, so when the coffee was ready I got the water as cold as possible and sprayed him. He woke up, ready to kill me. I shoved the black coffee at him and said, "Mr. Holden, don't you have children at home? It's four A.M. Christmas morning."

He looked around groggily and gulped down the coffee. He took a very hot and very cold shower and insisted I join him. After three more cups of black coffee, when he looked like he could drive, I helped him put his clothes on and he did the same for me. We almost got sidetracked but I wouldn't allow it. I kept thinking of those poor children waiting for their presents. As Holden drove away in the dawn, he shouted back, "By the way, what's your name?" And for some strange reason I answered, "Sonia Epstein."[22]

Their secret meeting happened again every Christmas Eve for the following seven years; Winters kept the secret until the publication of her autobiography. The unexpected news was reported by the media and Bill, who had already divorced his wife, was very amused by it and thanked Winters publicly, stating, "Ardis loved reading the book, because she found out where I had been all those years."[23]

Despite Bill's numerous escapades, the Holden marriage continued to be described in the press as a perfect union. When at the end of 1953 Bob Hope invited Bill to join him at Thule Air Force base in Greenland to do a show for the GIs, Bill accepted under one condition: He had to bring Ardis along. He was not new to entertaining the troops; he had travelled a year earlier to Korea for a two-week show. In addition, Swedish starlet and former Miss Sweden Anita Ekberg and Hollywood columnist Hedda Hopper came along. The company put on a New Year's Eve show in the base gym where two hundred GIs worked night and day to build a stage, lay cables, set up lights and microphones. Bill performed with Ekberg in a few sketches in front of ten thousand men, who gave him a warm and enthusiastic response.[24]

7

Audrey and Grace

"I really was in love with Audrey, but she wouldn't marry me. So I set out around the world with the idea of screwing a woman in every country I visited." — William Holden

Since his impressive performance in *Stalag 17*, Bill was now an international star. The media showed a constant interest in him, and his career was taking off along with a salary proportionate to his popularity. Regardless, he was still afflicted by doubts and insecurity — particularly by fear of waking up one day and realizing that his work was only a big joke. He was uncomfortable being a star, but on the other hand, he could not see himself doing anything else. Being an actor required a strong dose of vanity and narcissism — two qualities he did not have — which put him under a lot of stress. Throughout his life, acting was a challenge, although his lack of confidence was never strong enough to make him quit. Consequently, alcohol became his ally. Drinking would give him the necessary courage to face the cameras each day. Billy Wilder called Bill's shyness the principal cause of his demons and his resulting self-destructive behavior. Bill once confessed to him that he needed at least two glasses of vodka every morning to wake up.

"When we began our collaboration, we were young and didn't care he drank to overcome his shyness — nobody would ever imagine that one day he couldn't live without that stuff," Wilder commented right after Bill's death.[1]

Bill teamed for the third time with Wilder for the comedy *Sabrina*. The picture was not a happy experience for its cast or anyone else. The project started in September 1953 in disarray when Samuel Taylor, author of the play *Sabrina Fair*, abruptly stopped working on the screen adaptation halfway through the rough draft. The culprit was Wilder: Having acquired the rights, he began deleting some parts and, along with screenwriter Ernest Lehman, revised the script. The revision continued through the entire making of the film. Wilder directed by day and rewrote by night. Some changes were made even a few hours before shooting a scene.

But the major source of atmospheric tension on the set was Humphrey Bogart, whose overall animosity along with his difficult personality made shooting extremely difficult. His hostility was directed toward Wilder, Bill and Audrey Hepburn. Cary Grant was Wilder's first choice for the role of the boring, workaholic, tycoon Larry Larrabee, in competition with his playboy brother David for Sabrina Fairchild, the lovely daughter of their chauffeur. Unexpectedly, the British star turned down the part only one week from shooting and Bogart, who had just signed a three-picture deal with Paramount, accepted the role even though he disliked acting in the romantic comedy — a genre unknown to him. Wilder reassured Bogart, who was only five years older than Grant, that he would readapt the role for his more mature look. Despite Wilder's intentions, Bogart felt ostracized by the cast, complaining that the director favored Bill and Audrey Hepburn when shooting close-ups. One day after shooting, Wilder invited Bill, Hepburn, Lehman and others back over for drinks. Bogart was not included. Offended, he became irritable and offensive to Wilder. Nobody was able to escape his rage and any minor issue turned into an excuse to insult the director. "Kraut bastard," "Nazi" and various anti–Semitic epithets were used against Wilder, who was Jewish and had lost members of his family during the Holocaust. Bogart mimicked Wilder's thick German accent, answering "Jawohl!" to all Wilder's instructions. Bogart, extremely insecure, was convinced that Bill and Wilder were scheming against him. When Hepburn commented to someone that Bogie looked very nervous during their romantic scenes together, he got offended and wasted no time getting revenge by ridiculing her, imitating her voice and talking behind her back.

One day on the Paramount lot, Clifton Webb asked Bogart, "How do you like working with that dream girl?"

"She's okay," he replied morosely, "if you like to do thirty-six takes."[2]

Bill's opinion of Hepburn could not be more different. He became her guardian angel since she was rather inexperienced with Hollywood

Humphrey Bogart, Audrey Hepburn and Holden in a publicity shot for
Sabrina **(1954).**

and films, having only made *Roman Holiday* (shot entirely in Rome).
"Before I even met her, I had a crush on her," Bill said later, "and after I
met her, just a day later, I felt as if we were old friends, and I was rather
fiercely protective of her, though not in a possessive way. Most men who
worked with her felt both fatherly or brotherly towards her, while harbor-
ing romantic feelings about her."[3]

On several occasions Bill was very close to physically assaulting Bogart after witnessing his offenses toward Hepburn or Wilder. Only other
people's immediate interventions were able to stop him from hitting his
co-star.

Ernest Lehman was the first to learn of a romance between Bill and
Audrey. After shooting had just finished for the day one late afternoon,
he walked into Bill's dressing room without knocking to drop off some
dialogue changes. To his surprise, he found the two stars standing face to
face, staring into each other eyes with their hands clasped. The embar-

rassed screenwriter apologized but the news of Bill and Audrey's romance leaked the following day.

Falling deeply in love with Hepburn did not make Bill quit drinking. Actress Martha Hyer, who had a minor role in the picture, described Bill as a good actor and a very good person, who nonetheless lacked discipline. Bill reminded her of a cuddly Cheshire cat: "his smile could charm the birds out of trees." Hyer also remembered him drinking so heavily that often he had to rest until he sobered up. "One day," she recalled in her autobiography, "Bill was very shaky, blowing his lines and not really in shape to work. Bogie quietly remarked, 'Methinks the lad hath partaken too much of the grape' — a barb that drove an even-deeper wedge into an already deteriorating relationship."[4]

Bogart's remark was very hypocritical since he was a bottle lover himself. Between takes he would ask for whiskey to be served in his dressing room. Bogie referred to Bill as "Smiling Jim," ridiculing his good looks and implying he was more a matinee idol than a man. He mocked Bill's bleached-blond hair, a look required by his Gatsbyesque role to emphasize the contrast between the Larrabee brothers.

"That William Holden, take a look at him," Bogart sarcastically pointed out to Paramount producer A.C. Lyles. "You know, if I was handsome as Bill Holden, I wouldn't have any doubts why Bacall married me!"[5]

Bogart was resentful of Bill and had not forgotten the run-ins they had thirteen years earlier on the set of *Invisible Stripes*. Bill had his revenge through the press, calling Bogart "an actor of consummate skill, with an ego to match."

Later, when he was asked to comment on the Rat Pack — a group of friends, mostly entertainers in Hollywood informally organized around Bogart — Bill said, "It's terribly important for people to realize that their conduct reflects the way a nation is represented in the eyes of the world. That's why the rat-pack idea makes our job so tough. If you were to go to Japan or India or France and represent an entire industry, which has made an artistic contribution to the entire world, and faced then with the problem of someone asking, 'Do you really have a Rat Pack in Holmby Hills?' what would you say? It makes your job doubly tough. In every barrel there's bound to be a rotten apple. Not all actors are bad. It may sound stuffy and dull, but it is quite possible for people to have social intercourse without resorting to a Rat Pack."[6]

During a scene in which Bogart was the only one to have a close-up,

Bill deliberately smoked to make him cough during his lines. "That fucking Holden over there, waving cigarettes around, crumpling paper, blowing smoke on my face. I want this sabotage ended," he complained to Wilder.[7]

On another occasion, Bogie walked off the set, forcing a shutdown of the production, after a revision of the script was delivered to Bill and Hepburn but not to him. He felt like an outsider among these "Paramount bastards," as he called them. Despite the trouble on the set, the romance between Bill and Audrey evolved into an intense passion. One evening Bill took Hepburn to his home for dinner and introduced her to Ardis, who was resigned to Bill's escapades. She knew of her husband's previous fling with starlets Gail Russell and Diana Lynn; however, this time she realized the affair was more serious. Audrey could not stop feeling guilty all through that awkward evening. Usually at the end of a working day, Bill and Audrey would dine at Lucey's, a fancy restaurant in Hollywood, or at her apartment on Wilshire Boulevard, not far from Paramount studios. Bill was madly in love. He seemed to have found his soulmate: a younger woman, beautiful, classy and sensitive.

"She was the love of my life," he declared many years later. "Sometimes at night, I'd get a portable record player and drive out to the country to a little clearing we'd found. We'd put on ballet music ... Audrey would dance for me in the moonlight. Some of our most magic moments were there."[8]

Audrey adored Bill and she was charmed by the warm, romantic, witty and gentlemanly side of Bill's personality. She couldn't eat or sleep and when she was not working she spent long moments in solitude thinking about him, wondering if he ever would have left Ardis to marry her and have children. She did not know that when the Holdens had their second child, the doctor told Ardis she could not have any more kids, so Bill had an irreversible vasectomy in order not to put her in danger (and probably not to risk an undesired pregnancy from one of his escapades).[9] When Bill, who was ready to leave Ardis, Audrey told the truth (that after marrying him she would never have children), it profoundly shocked her. Heartbroken, she immediately called off the affair. Bill was devastated. Many years later while filming *The Wild Bunch* in Mexico, he confessed to Warren Oates, "I really was in love with Audrey, but she wouldn't marry me. So I set out around the world with the idea of screwing a woman in every country I visited. My plan succeeded, though sometimes with difficulty. When I was in Bangkok, I was screwing a Thai girl in a boat floating in one of the klongs. I guess we got too animated, because the boat tipped over and I fell into filthy water. Back at the hotel I poured alcohol in my ears because I was afraid I'd became infected with the plague. When I got back to Hollywood, I went to Audrey's dressing room at Paramount and I told her what I had done. You know what she said? 'Oh, Bill!' That's all: 'Oh, Bill!' Just as though I were some naughty boy. What a waste!"[10]

It was a typical Hepburn reaction — never critical but always loving with Bill, who was still dependent on alcohol. Despite the intensity of their relationship, in a few months Audrey fell in love and married actor Mel Ferrer while Bill got involved with Grace Kelly, his co-star in his two following pictures.

Sabrina opened ten months from the end of shooting. It was a financial success and received six Oscar nominations, winning only for Edith Head's costumes. (It was an undeserved award since the extraordinary evening gowns were all original creations of French *couturier* Hubert de Givenchy and not even mentioned in the credits.) Bill left the set of *Sabrina* before its completion as he was expected in Tokyo to shoot *The Bridges at Toko-Ri.*

Hollywood had just begun to produce films about the Korean conflict, which was still a confused and complex situation. *The Bridges at Toko-Ri* was the most important studio film to deal with the conflict, but avoided the major issues involved, telling its story in an almost documentary fashion. Based on James Mitchener's bestselling novel, *The Bridges at Toko-Ri* was also a psychological study of its protagonist, a naval lieutenant called back to active duty during the Korean War. The naval officer believed he had already done enough for his country, fearing the consequences of his death on his wife and kids. Producers William Perlberg and George Seaton cast Grace Kelly as Nancy, Bill's devoted wife. Kelly's interest in playing in the movie was low: It was a minor part which covered only 20 percent of a script mostly centered on Bill, Fredric March and Mickey Rooney. Nevertheless she was aware of the producers' prestigious reputation from teaming on such classics as *Miracle on 34th Street* and *The Song of Bernadette*, and accepted the role after MGM agreed to loan her to Paramount. All the scenes between Bill and Kelly were shot on the Paramount lot after the troupe returned from the Far East.

With the full collaboration of the U.S. Navy, cast and crew spent nineteen days off the coast of Japan on an aircraft carrier where they were allowed to use the flight deck as their "sound stage." Admiral Dave Johnson, in charge of the operation, invited the entire troupe to a formal lunch on another aircraft carrier. A helicopter picked up the guests, who had to put on ties and white shirts and were all seated according to protocol. Admiral Johnson was very impressed by Bill and offered his full cooperation in anything the production would need.[11]

Filming *The Bridges at Toko-Ri* was a very moving experience for Bill, remembering his brother Bob had died in the same circumstances as his character Harry Brubaker.

Bill's brief scenes with Grace were shot in three weeks in the fall of 1954. They were enough to create a strong attraction between the two. Grace had just terminated a relationship with her co-star in Hitchcock's *Dial M for Murder*, Ray Milland, who, like Bill, was married with children. Although Bill was still hurt after the break-up with Hepburn, he was also very excited to meet and work with Kelly. He had heard a lot about her and was anxious to find out for himself if she really was as icy as many told him.

In the Paramount publicity hand-out for *Toko-Ri* he stated, "Grace has the faculty of reminding me of my own wife.... Women like Grace Kelly and Audrey Hepburn help us to believe in the innate dignity of man."[12]

According to Lizanne Kelly, Grace's sister, "If a lovely girl and a handsome fellow have to 'play' at being husband and wife all day, they're bound to have problems switching off when the show is over."[13]

Bill and Grace's brief flirt was over once the film was completed and Grace returned to New York. However, fate had them reunited a few months later on the set of *The Country Girl*, where flirting became a torrid, passionate affair.

The Bridges at Toko-Ri was completed in the fall of 1954, but not released until early 1955, after *The Country Girl* appeared in the theaters. The reviews praised Fredric March and Bill's performances along with the intensity derived from the realistic aerial photography. It was considered by many to be one of the best war films ever made.

In 1954 Bill and Ardis traveled to Rome to receive *il Nastro d'Argento*, a prestigious Italian prize awarded to him as Best Foreign Actor for *Sabrina*. Bill was photographed with voluptuous Italian star Gina Lollobrigida. A few weeks later, William Perlberg and George Seaton reteamed

Holden and Kelly. The two producers owned screen rights to the Clifford Odets play *The Country Girl*, for which Uta Hagen had won a Tony for Best Actress. The story concerned Georgie Elgin, a young woman whose promise in life is destroyed by her devotion to her alcoholic, self-destructive actor husband Frank. Finally Bernie Dodd, a Broadway director, tries to help Frank, casting him in a new production, and falls in love with Georgie, who sacrifices her love for him to be once again by Frank's side.

Perlberg and Seaton, who wrote the screenplay, had signed Jennifer Jones to co-star with Bing Crosby as the actor and Bill as the director. But a few weeks before filming, Jones became pregnant. Her husband, producer David Selznick, told the producers that they could use her if they could complete the picture before Jones' condition began to show. The producers realized that the risk was too great and decided to replace her with Grace Kelly, but MGM refused their request to loan her out. Kelly was discreetly approached by the producers, who sent her a copy of the script. After reading it, Grace realized that Georgie Elgin could be her role of a lifetime, finally proving her dramatic acting skills. Finally Kelly's agent, Lew Wasserman, convinced MGM to loan her out by telling them that she would quit if they did not allow her to star in *The Country Girl*.[14]

Holden and Grace Kelly in a publicity shot for *The Country Girl* (1954).

Bill, Bing Crosby and Grace Kelly were summoned to Palm Springs by Seaton, who had rented a space for extensive rehearsals. It was Seaton's idea that in two weeks the stars could learn their lines and the actors would not break the scenes into too many takes when he was ready to shoot.

"Bill Holden is, to me, one of the great technical actors on the screen," Seaton said in an interview in 1974. "He is amazing in his knowledge of the medium. He helped Grace and so did Bing, because when you have the mix of three people like that who admire each other and worked as a team and not to try to shoot off in a different direction and give solo performances, that helps a great deal."[15]

Working together renewed the attraction Crosby and Kelly had for each other (they had met previously socially but quickly drifted apart and did not see each other until then) and they became romantically involved. Bill's feelings for Grace were flaring anew but he discovered that he had a rival when Crosby asked him not to interfere. Bill agreed, and a few days later, after Grace broke Crosby's heart by refusing his marriage proposal, Bill resumed his own romantic pursuit of her. At the beginning, Grace was hesitant to resume an affair with a married man, but Bill was very persuasive and Grace fell madly in love with him.

Mel Dellar, assistant director and good friend of Bill, revealed, "Bill was absolutely crazy about her and they had quite a fling."[16]

According to Bill's therapist Michael Jay Klassman, Grace and Bill were very much in love. Grace was so serious about him that she took him home to Philadelphia. "Cold and hostile" were the words Bill used to describe the unpleasant welcome he received from Jack Kelly, Grace's father. Jack had asked his daughter about the real nature of her relationship with Bill, suspecting she was having an affair with a married man. Grace kept denying it. So he repeated his accusation to Bill, shaking his fist in anger. Equally angry, Bill told Jack to go to hell and left, leaving Grace in tears.[17] Regardless, the affair went on secretly and a small apartment on Sweetzer Avenue in West Hollywood that Grace shared with a girlfriend became their love nest. Bill would go there to pick her up and take her to little restaurants away from prying eyes. They would arrive at and leave the studio separately and be very careful to avoid suspicion by not spending time together on the movie set or in their dressing rooms.

Reporters for the gossip magazine *Confidential* knew about their affair, but they waited for pictures to back up their exposé. Finally they got what they wanted and published a photograph of Bill's white Cadillac Eldorado convertible parked outside Grace's apartment early in the morning. Even though the magazine allegations were true, the evidence was not, since that day Grace's car had broken down and Bill passed by her place on the way to the studio to pick her up.

Their tryst had become public. As he did with Audrey Hepburn, Bill invited Grace for dinner. His marriage with Ardis was on the rocks and their separation seemed inevitable. *Confidential*'s report hurt Kelly's reputation: She was described as a femme fatale, someone who, "behind that frigid exterior, was a smoldering fire," and would go for married men only. The Kellys were so distressed over *Confidential*'s article that Jack Kelly and his son stormed into the magazine's offices and roughed up the editors.

Grace tried to cover up the affair, insisting to a journalist that Bill "drove up to give me a lift in his white convertible. Everyone reported it. He was taking me to dinner with his wife. That was my romance with Bill."[18]

Stories about their affair still appeared in many magazines. Hedda Hopper claimed Kelly was a nymphomaniac. Grace was so distressed that the moment the six weeks of shooting *The Country Girl* was over, she briefly saw a psychologist.

Eventually Bill left Grace. Even though he had told close friends he was deeply in love with her, it seems he came to realize that he would never

Bing Crosby, Grace Kelly and Holden in *The Country Girl* (1954).

win the battle with Jack Kelly; and divorcing Ardis would have been very hard. Years later he confided to Broderick Crawford that Grace had many virtues although he felt her innermost, emotional core was immature. Bill explained that when they had discussed how they might overcome the problem of Grace's Catholicism and his existing marriage in order to get married themselves, she said that her priest told her that if Bill became Roman Catholic, his previous marriage would be considered invalid. Then she felt they could get married in church and be a respectable couple.

"I'd be damned," Bill told his friend, "if I'd let any church dictate what I could do with my life."[19]

Those close to Bill confirmed that, despite his widely known desire to marry Grace, Bill had no intention of divorcing his wife, especially after breaking up with Audrey Hepburn. They quoted him as saying, "If I were to lose Ardis, I would lose everything."[20]

In 1955, Grace received from Bill's hands the Best Actress Oscar for her highly praised dramatic performance in *The Country Girl.*

8

Golden Holden

••

"I'm a limited talent, not a great actor. My forte always has
been playing a kind of contemporary character that the audience can sympathize with." — William Holden

••

In March 1955, Bill flew to Hong Kong for two weeks of location
shooting *Love Is a Many-Splendored Thing*. He was besieged by numerous
reporters who welcomed him warmly at the airport and followed him to
the Peninsula Hotel where he lodged with co-star Jennifer Jones. Bill sometimes required police protection from the hordes of fans, armed with auto-
graph books, camping day and night in front of the hotel.

Directed by Henry King, *Love Is a Many-Splendored Thing* was based
on the life of Eurasian Dr. Han Suyin, played by Jones, who falls in love
with Bill, a married war correspondent, and fights prejudice at the hospital where she works. She loses both her fight and her lover at the film's
end. Production began before screenwriter John Patrick had even finished
the screenplay.

Bill and Jones were striking screen lovers; the chemistry between them
was perfect, but off-screen they disliked each other, barely speaking. Bill
complained that she chewed garlic cloves every time they had love scenes.

Jones' obsession with her performance completely turned Bill off on
making her another of his sexual conquests, as her husband David Selznick
feared. Jones complained to her husband about Bill's lack of warmth; Bill
tried to improve their relationship by presenting her with white roses,
which she threw in his face.[1]

Bill agreed to shave his chest for a few shirtless scenes, while light

Jennifer Jones and Holden in *Love Is a Many-Splendored Thing* (1955).

makeup was applied to Jones' eyes to fit her Eurasian role. Jones' difficult behavior was directed not only at Bill but at many others involved in the production. She was dissatisfied with her makeup and hair which she felt made her look older.

Love Is a Many-Splendored Thing was completed in three months as scheduled. Bill employed his off-camera time, surveying the territory of Hong Kong and developing interests and partnerships in businesses such as exporting and importing, aviation and radio stations. He invested in a Hong Kong radio station that broadcast on three channels in Cantonese, Mandarin and English. He later bought a piece of land in Port Dickson in Malaysia, where he planned to retire one day. Bill was investing in different business areas in case his luck in his profession would change suddenly.

Regarding that intense time of work and travel, Bill said, "When I began making movies around the world, I was being paid to satisfy my deep curiosity about people and geography. In all the four-walled hotel rooms, I would lie awake and think, 'You lucky son of a bitch!'"[2]

In addition, Paramount asked him to take a trip around the world to promote VistaVision, their newly introduced widescreen process. Bill stopped in Rome, one of his favorite cities, where his arrival caused a big fuss. Ardis joined him and together they watched *Sabrina* in a local theater. Bill was very amused to hear himself dubbed by a baritone voice.

Love Is a Many-Splendored Thing was a huge success, making $4 million domestically. The public considered the picture one of the most romantic movies ever produced, but the reviewers were significantly less enthusiastic.

Grace Kelly and Bill both had their eyes firmly set on *Giant* (based on Edna Ferber's bestselling novel), which director George Stevens was preparing. Bill was very anxious to play Bick Benedict, the stubborn Texas rancher who becomes a millionaire after finding oil on his land. Kelly was in competition for the female leading role with Elizabeth Taylor, who eventually got the part. Bill competed with Clark Gable, Gary Cooper and a promising young actor named Rock Hudson. Bill met with Stevens several times and was pretty sure he'd get the part. Later he learned the role was given to Hudson. Very upset, he went to relax at the Universal gym and took a steam bath. Walking into the steam room nude, he found a nude Hudson, who had just learned the news. Bill recognized his rival and, even if a bit embarrassed, wished him luck on the picture.[3]

Harry Cohn offered Joshua Logan the chance to direct a film adaptation of William Inge's Pulitzer Prize–winning play *Picnic* which Logan had directed it on Broadway in 1953. Bill was cast as the lead, since he still had two more pictures on his old Columbia contract. He had already turned down two Columbia films, but this time he could not avoid Cohn's direct request.

"Although he was really too old for the part of Hal," confessed Logan in his autobiography, "he was such a vital, virile, talented man with such a youthful body, that I felt he would be strong in the part."[4]

Picnic told the story of Hal Carter, a young, muscular vagabond who rides a freight train into a small town to see his rich college friend, Alan Benson. Carter stays on to find himself involved with Alan's fiancée Madge Owens. During the annual Labor Day picnic, their growing physical attraction leads to events affecting many lives around them.

In the role of Madge, Cohn wanted Kim Novak, who had just finished shooting *The Man with the Golden Arm* opposite Frank Sinatra. The moment Logan saw her, he was stunned by her beauty. Although he tested Janice Rule (who had created the role on stage) and Carroll Baker, neither convinced the director as Novak did. Kim was very shy and accepted the role even though she was frightened by the idea of working with a superstar like Bill. A few weeks before the start of shooting, Logan and Bill met over lunch to go over the part. The director was anxious to know if Bill knew how to dance, since the climax of the film was an extremely sensual dance sequence between Hal and Madge.

While sipping a martini, Bill said, "Aw, for Chrissake, you're worried about the dancing — look at this." He jumped to his feet in the middle of the restaurant, did a kind of hurried shuffle, and sat down. His movements had nothing to do with dancing, but he seemed to feel they did, so Logan said, "Of course — that was great."[5] Bill laughed cynically because he knew Logan didn't mean it.

Bill then plunged into a physical fitness regime in a frantic attempt to prepare for the role. Rehearsals began ten days later on a Columbia soundstage to be used later for part of the dance sequence. Novak was tense and almost impossible to hear, while Bill did everything but leap on the table and stand on his hands in an effort to show that he was calm, collected and (above all) young enough to play the part. When Logan began working on the love scene between Bill and Kim, she was terrified. Bill had overcome his shyness, and threw an arm around her waist, walking with her to a corner of the set.

"Kim," he said. "We can work together on this if you want. It might help." Kim nodded a weak yes as she broke free of his grasp. Bill took it as a rejection.[6]

Logan had many difficulties in convincing Novak to wear a long blonde wig, since her short hair hardly suited the part of the hyper-feminine Madge. Likewise Bill complained about shaving his chest daily in order to look younger than thirty-seven — and also to comply with the censors who thought hairy chests inappropriate.

Years later he told a British journalist, "Do you think it's fun standing in front of a mirror running a razor all the way down to your navel at six o'clock every morning? I hated it, I hated everything phony about the movie business. I refused to wear corsets or chinlifts or hairpieces in any of my films. I never did costume films because I never felt comfortable being that kind of actor who walks around wearing a beard and a toga. I don't have the legs for togas. I always said they should give those parts to Charlton Heston. I'm a limited talent, not a great actor. My forte always has been playing a kind of contemporary character that the audience can sympathize with."[7] And Hal Carter was indeed the typical, all–American boy that audiences could relate to.

Picnic's cast, which also included Rosalind Russell and young Susan Strasberg as Madge's young sister, flew to Salina, Kansas, where Logan shot the rest of the film. Two days later the crew moved to nearby Hutchinson and lodged at the old, multi-storied Baker Hotel. At the end of each day Bill shouted, "Warm up the ice cubes," an expression that meant he was about to leave the set and was ready to drink.

"He never drank before the end of the shooting day," revealed Logan. "But once we had reached that part of the day, the gin industry began to prosper. Yet somehow it never seemed to affect him. It did not alter his speech, his wit, or his warmth. He was simply a red-blooded American boy who wanted to have a good time and believe me, he did. Quite often he would take a bunch of us to a local restaurant where he had trained the ice cubes to warm up at double speed."[8]

The evening before shooting the game section scenes of the picnic, Bill invited Logan and a few cast members to his suite on the top floor of the Baker Hotel. Suddenly, while the guests were making conversation, Bill went out the open window and hung by his fingers from the ledge outside, screaming at those present to look at him while he was dangerously hanging by just eight fingers. Depending on whom you asked (the stories varied from witness to witness), Bill's reasons for the crazy maneuver ranged from forcing an apology from Logan for something he had said, to demonstrating his virility, to just plain exhibitionism. Rosalind Russell and all the others gasped and pleaded, which only encouraged Bill. Everybody pretended to ignore him and moved to Russell's suite, and a few moments later there was a knock at a window. It was Bill, who climbed to her balcony.

"He was strong as an ox, stubborn as a donkey, and luckier than anything," Russell wrote in her autobiography.[9]

Logan went down to the ground floor to relax after that stressful experience; there he met Novak, who was coming back from midnight mass (she was a fervent Catholic and attended mass daily). "You won't believe what I saw," Kim said. "When I got out of my car, I happened to look up, and halfway up I thought I saw a man hanging out of the window. But of course I probably didn't."

"Oh, really," Logan replied. "I wonder who that could have been — that is, if you saw anyone."

"Well, you know, it's funny — as a matter of fact it's ridiculous that I should even think such a thing — but the way he moved and the way he kind of hung there so calmly, I thought just for a minute, that's Bill Holden."

"Bill Holden?" the director said. "That's ridiculous."

"Of course. Well, good night — see you in the morning."[10]

On the set, Bill appeared very unhappy about his role and tried to ease the tension with drinking. He also proved to be very impatient with Novak, who would ask for frequent retakes, dissatisfied with her acting skills. He complained to Russell that, "This girl has absolutely no sense of humor. She's like ice water." He also criticized Novak's twice-daily visits to the local Catholic church. "You know, Roz, she ought to spend more time studying her lines and less time contemplating her rosary."[11]

When reports of that conversation reached Novak, she was crushed. Someone overheard her saying, "If I'm like ice, Mr. Holden should love me, since he has a thing for whiskey on the rocks!"

The dance sequence between Hal and Madge was the hardest to shoot. Logan knew that was the story's pivotal point. He was very nervous because neither Bill nor Novak was a dancer. Choreographer Miriam Nelson had rehearsed doubles for the two stars for the long shots and had worked very hard with Bill and Kim themselves, hoping Logan could catch a few moments of them really dancing. Only then the audience could feel their closeness and sexual attraction. The results were still very poor. Bill threw up his hands and walked over to Logan.

"I won't do it," he told the director. "You've got to use a double. I can't dance." Shooting a dance scene in *Sabrina* had been for Bill an unnerving experience he did not want to repeat. Logan officially closed the Kansas production and moved back to the Columbia Ranch in Bur-

Kim Novak, Susan Strasberg, Holden and Cliff Robertson in *Picnic* (1955).

bank, where Nelson managed to coax Bill into dance rehearsals with her. To calm his nerves, Bill drank so much that when he shot the scene he was completely drunk.

After consulting with cinematographer James Wong Howe, Logan agreed to use doubles for long shots, and film the two stars from their waists up for close-ups. Howe rigged tiny spotlights with different colored gels, so as Bill and Kim danced (or, rather, walked) across the platform looking into each other's eyes, their faces moved in and out of constantly changing colors. Afterward Logan added in the film's musical score mixed with "Moonglow," making the sequence one of the most sensual dance scenes in film history. (Another major love scene between Bill and Kim had to be completely reshot because back in Hollywood someone noticed they had filmed it in a waist-high field of marijuana.)

Nominated for six Academy Awards, *Picnic* won two Oscars and grossed $6 million. Columbia paid Bill $38,000—somewhat higher than the weekly $25 Cohn shelled out to Paramount when he signed him for *Golden Boy*, but significantly less than his actual salary. Bill swore never again to work for Columbia, which had exploited him for years; however, he did not keep his promise for long. A year later, he accepted work, this time for a different salary, in *The Bridge on the River Kwai*.

Between 1953 and 1956 Bill's name topped the lists of the highest paid actors in America. His popularity was at its peak. Bill was named actor of the year by magazines such as *Photoplay*. The Hollywood Women's Press Club voted him the Golden Apple as the most cooperative male star in 1955 and on February 27, 1956, he appeared on the cover of *Time* magazine. His fame brought him to TV in his best-ever comic role, as a guest star in *I Love Lucy*. Lucille Ball had not seen Bill since *Miss Grant Takes Richmond* but their chemistry on the set was perfect. In the episode "L.A. at Last," Lucy is lunching with Fred and Ethel when she spots Bill, her favorite movie star, at the Brown Derby Restaurant. In the excitement she causes a pie to hit Bill in the face and she flees from embarrassment. Ricky later brings Bill to their hotel to meet her. Still embarrassed, Lucy disguises herself with eyeglasses and a false nose. When Bill lights her cigarette her nose catches fire; she extinguishes it in a cup of coffee. Bill's timing was perfect. The false nose moment was an homage to the scene in *Sunset Blvd.* where Bill waves a cigarette lighter in front of Nancy Olson's face to examine her nose job. The funny episode became Ball's favorite and an instant TV classic.

Bill spent the summer of 1955 in the Virgin Islands shooting *The Proud and Profane*. The heat was unbearable and alleviated only for a few hours by the sudden tropical showers. George Seaton adapted Lucy Herndon Crockett's World War II novel *The Magnificent Bastards* (but couldn't use that title because the censors would not permit the word *Bastards*).

To play the tough and ruthless Colin Black, a half–Indian Marine lieutenant colonel, Bill dyed his hair pitch black and wore a thick black mustache and dark makeup. The result was quite grotesque and Seaton regretted it once the film was completed. He admitted years later, "It was a successful picture, but I learned another lesson on that, and that is, with Bill Holden, don't put a mustache on him.... It's not his good looks. I don't know if the same thing is true today, but the heavies always wore mustaches. Although he was the heavy, there's no doubt about that, but you had to understand him, you had to feel sorry for him."[12]

On the set, Bill and co-star Deborah Kerr, who played a Red Cross worker, had a great professional relationship. However, their on-screen chemistry did not impress the critics, who also criticized Bill's bizarre look.

According to Bill, Kerr was "the most no-problem star I have worked with, and she has a salty sense of humor which surprises everyone. She's an unusual, charming individual."[13]

The Proud and Profane was one of many films Paramount shot in Vista-Vision. When it was released in Europe, many local Paramount executives discussed eliminating Bill's mustache from the film's billboards because it spoiled his beloved clean-cut image. Eventually the posters went untouched.

At the end of the '50s, Hollywood stars like Yul Brynner, Gary Cooper, Kirk Douglas, Alan Ladd, Burt Lancaster and John Wayne were assuming financial and creative control of their own films, founding their own production companies and benefiting personally from tax gains and profit sharing. Bill took advantage of his "golden moment" to embark on his first independent venture, forming Toluca Production. After two years of searching for the right screenplay to produce together with his partner, producer-director Mervyn LeRoy, Bill finally chose *Toward the Unknown*. "What I want in a script," he explained in an interview, "is a combination of spiritual values and optical satisfaction."[14]

Lloyd Nolan, Virginia Leith and Holden in *Toward the Unknown* (1956).

In the film, Bill was an Air Force pilot turned a supersonic jet test pilot whose credibility is doubted by his commanding officer. As executive producer, Bill was able to supervise the entire project in its pre-production. He was an unrelenting worrier and a perfectionist, personally choosing many technical details, from the soundtrack to the film's locations (it was shot in the Mojave Desert and at the Edwards Air Force Base in California). The film's title *Toward the Unknown* was in fact a translation of Edwards' motto, "Ad Inexplorata." To prepare himself for the role, Bill flew in a TF86 Sabrejet piloted by a friend to experience breaking the sound barrier. "It's far less exciting than what I thought it would be," he admitted after landing.[15]

With special aerobatics by the Thunderbirds and military technical advice, *Toward the Unknown* reaped the benefit of authenticity along with slick aerial photography. Warner Bros. bought and distributed the picture, which disappointed the critics and flopped at the box office. It was a temporary setback in Bill's career that led him to dissolve the Toluca Production company.

In an interview he revealed how boring it had been working behind a desk, adding, "I made *Toward the Unknown* as an actor by day and, by night, a caster, a cutter and a producer. I'll never do anything like that again!"[16]

9

The Reluctant Hero

• •

"I've taken quite a few risks in my film career, but *Bridge on the River Kwai* was the ultimate adventure of my life." — William Holden

• •

Bill received dozens of scripts every week. After initial filtering from his agent, he would only read a few, and then only partially. In 1956, *The Bridge on the River Kwai* particularly impressed him. The screenplay had all the right ingredients to become a classic.

Producer Sam Spiegel came up with the idea of making the film after he read French writer Pierre Boulle's novel, to which he later acquired the screen rights. British director David Lean showed his interest in directing the movie and planned on a faithful adaptation. After several Hollywood directors (including John Ford, Howard Hawks and William Wyler) had turned down the script, Spiegel and Lean met at the New York home of their mutual friend Katharine Hepburn. Following their second meeting, Lean and Spiegel signed an agreement and became equal partners. Lean was unhappy with the script written by Carl Foreman, who was ostracized in Hollywood after being blacklisted as Communist and forced to move to London where he wrote pseudonymously. (The screenwriter had optioned the rights to Boulle's novel and wrote a script with the desire to make a picture with Humphrey Bogart, directed by Carol Reed.) Things changed after Foreman sold the rights to Spiegel. Spiegel asked him to write a second draft, but it was not as interesting as the original novel. Lean decided to revise it himself, calling for the help of blacklisted writer Michael Wilson, who had won a 1951 Oscar for *A Place in the Sun*, a superb adaptation of Theodore Dreiser's *An American Tragedy*. In the screen credits Spiegel credited as screenwriter neither Lean nor Wilson but Pierre Boulle, who did not write a single line of the script since he barely spoke a word of English. Prior to the picture's premiere, Spiegel also breached his fifty-fifty agreement with Lean when in a *New York Times* announcement he wrote that the film was presented by "Sam Spiegel Productions," not mentioning his business partner who was credited only as the director.

The film's action takes place at a prison camp in the heart of a Siamese jungle, where a regiment of British soldiers and their officers are the prisoners by a small force of Japanese soldiers who force them to build a railroad bridge on the River Kwai to transport Japanese soldiers and supplies. The plot presented two different stories: the first about the personal conflict between British Colonel Nicholson and Japanese Colonel Saito, the second about American war prisoner Shears, who escapes from the camp and is recruited to blow up the bridge. The role of Shears was not in the novel but was created to enhance the film's potential in the American market. It was for that part that Spiegel hired Bill for $300,000 plus ten percent of the profits, making him one of most expensive actors in the business. "I'm like the chorus girl who was offered an apartment, a diamond necklace and a mink coat," Bill enthused.[1] (Originally Spiegel had offered that role to Cary Grant, but Grant's answer was not received until after Bill had accepted. A broken-hearted Grant approached Bill directly, begging him to withdraw.)

Spiegel said, "All this, as sad as it is, because of Cary's hurt feelings, should be very cheering to us as indicating the effect that this script has on two intelligent actors."[2]

According to Spiegel, the good-looking, all–American Bill had a unique gift and could do no wrong with the audience. "If Holden wanted to kill his mother," the producer once explained, "you'd want him to get away with it. Whereas if Richard Widmark wanted to save his mother, you wouldn't give a damn."[3]

The eight-month shoot began in Ceylon in October 1956, and Bill arrived in late December. The production had settled in Kitulgala, a small village two hours from the Colombo airport through rice paddies, tea plantations, and elephant herds. Barracks were set up for the crew, while the cast lodged in the huge, villa-style Galle Face Hotel, which was once part of a large tea plantation.

Filming on location for such a long time was a tough and sometimes unpleasant experience for all concerned, given the searing heat, terrible humidity and poisonous snakes and insects. The logistical demands of building such a complex set in the middle of the jungle were compounded by strokes of bad luck. A car crash killed one of the assistant directors, broke the back of a makeup artist and seriously injured another assistant. Then half of a two-man crew working the generator fell sick and the second man did the work alone, resulting in a union strike which had to be settled in London. Tempers were short and Lean often found himself working against the actors and the crew, who failed to see his broader view of things. There were major disagreements between Lean and Alec Guinness over how the actor should play Colonel Nicholson. Guinness was not the only candidate for the role; Charles Laughton and Cary Grant were both considered. Later Spiegel and Dean offered it to Laurence Olivier, who declined because he was preparing to direct and star with Marilyn Monroe in *The Prince and the Showgirl.* Noël Coward turned it down along with Spencer Tracy, who had loved the book but was convinced that the role had to be played by an Englishman. Finally Guinness, who was very hesitant to accept it, got the role of the gentleman colonel obsessed with his military rank.

In the final days of filming Guinness, the relationship between Lean and the actor degenerated to a point where they were not on speaking terms. The day before Bill's arrival on the set, Guinness and few crew members had a bitter dispute with the director about how a certain scene was to be shot.

At the end of the day, the director exclaimed, "Now you can all fuck off and go home, you English actors. Thank God that I'm starting work tomorrow with an American actor. It'll be such a pleasure to say good-bye to you guys."[4]

Once on the set, Bill heard of the crew's complaints about their "genius director," who they felt had grossly insulted them and created a standoff. Bill instinctively took matters into his own hands and told those assembled, "Now, just hold it. You've got a great script here, a really good story, and a director who knows what he's doing. So, come on, you sons of bitches, let's get to work."[5] Nevertheless, the quarrels continued until the last day of shooting.

Bill and Lean got on well from the start. "I supposed you could say he was a bit of a college boy," said Lean, "But he was highly professional.

Worked like hell, never late, knew his lines. Had I said, 'We'll start the day with you standing on your head under that tree,' he'd say, 'Oh, I see. Okay.' And he'd do it. If you asked some of the English actors to do much less, they'd start to argue. Trouble was, he was the biggest box-office star in the world when he did *Kwai*. He was so good-looking and so accomplished that people kind of smiled — 'Dear old Bill Holden, yes, very good' — and dismissed his talent. He had a huge talent and because it was apparently effortless, Bill never got the credit he deserved. After all, *Sunset Blvd.* was no easy part."[6]

Bill's presence on the set irritated Guinness, who wrote to his wife Merula, "Our life here has received the influx of Holden (who does love to pontificate)." In another letter he added, "I do wish Bill Holden would stop boasting of the famous actors he has employed in his company, or indeed of the fortunes he has lost. And he talks as much about *Sunset Blvd.* as Martita [Hunt] did of *The Mad Woman of Chaillot*. Isn't that an extraordinary habit that certain actors have."[7]

Bill, who was an animal lover, bought a wild monkey that he tried to tame and chained it to a tree on a long lead. One day the monkey came very close to Sam Spiegel.

"Sam," announced Bill, "there's a monkey on your back."

"Don't anyone move," came the petrified command from Spiegel, while the animal was plucking a hair off the producer's bare chest and nibbling it. Since the monkey had already bitten two people, actor Jack Hawkins suggested that someone get a gun.

"Don't anyone shoot!" ordered Spiegel "You may hit me." They finally coaxed the monkey away with some food and sent it back into the jungle."[8]

Ticks were very common in the jungle of Ceylon. One bore into Bill's knee and he had great pain in his legs for three years. Then one evening at the dinner table in his house in Switzerland, he had enough and jabbed a fork into his knee, finally locating the head of the tick and pulling it out.

In March 1957, a rare set visit from Spiegel coincided with one from Ardis. At a dinner that evening, Spiegel's wife Betty turned to a slightly inebriated Bill and told him how totally exhausted Sam was from his journey. This incensed Bill. "Whaddya mean, Sam's exhausted! There's David up at the bridge, working his ass off in a hundred percent humidity and you're telling me Sam's exhausted!"

Jack Hawkins, Anne Sears, and Holden in a publicity shot for *The Bridge on the River Kwai* (1957).

He ranted on for a while and then said to Betty, "You know what, Betty, you're a c — t." Betty complained to Sam while Doreen Hawkins, Jack Hawkins' wife, tried to calm Bill down. Bill replied, "You know what, Doreen, you're a c — t too!" At this point an enraged Sam stood up, as if he was going to punch Bill. Suddenly he stopped because he knew that if he had knocked Bill out, he would lose the star of the film, which would cost the production thousands of dollars per day! Ardis began to cry, at the same time trying to silence Bill. Turning on his wife, Bill added, "And what's more, Ardis, you're a c — t too!" Bill finally realized that he had gone too far and walked out.

The following day at the bridge location, Bill, usually professional and punctual, failed to make an appearance when he was called for a shot. Lean and the crew got on with another scene that did not involve him. At lunchtime a very apologetic and hung-over Bill appeared and, full of remorse, explained to the director what had happened.

"I behaved badly at dinner last night, I'm afraid, I called all the women at the table c — ts, including my own wife. I've been out searching Colombo high and low all morning for flowers but since I couldn't find any flowers I bought all the c — ts baskets of fruit instead."[9]

During his stay in Ceylon, Bill was voted the No. 1 box office star in the movies by American theater owners. Afterwards he received a cablegram from his friend, John Wayne, whom he supplanted as top film star, reading simply, "You sneak."

In his autobiography, Jack Hawkins described him as a "super actor to work with" and revealed that he discovered, during that long stay in Asia, Bill's obsession about fireworks. "I suspect this is because in America one is not allowed to let off fireworks in a garden, and displays are always big public affairs. One evening after shooting he and I walked down to the little village a short way from the camp to buy a few things from the store, which was like a jungle supermarket. I had just paid for some shaving soap when Bill pointed to a box of cardboard tubes on a shelf above the storekeeper's head.

"'What are those?' he asked the Singhalese proprietor.

"'Those,' he replied, 'are very fine, very great Roman candles.'

"Bill's eyes lit up like fireworks at this intelligence, and before I realized what was happening he had bought the lot.

"'You like fire-balloons?' the storekeeper inquired.

"'Sure.'

"The man then went into the back of the shop and came out with a huge bamboo globe covered with tissue paper. This was about ten feet high, and had a little burner which fitted underneath it. This was added to the collection and we carted the lot back to the camp."

That night Bill organized the first of a series of fireworks displays, which he repeated the following night after he bought all the fireworks the store had in stock. When Sam Spiegel returned to the location, Bill decided to have a pyrotechnic show in his honor, culminating in the launching of a big fire-balloon. When the balloon started to drift towards the bridge on the river Kwai, Spiegel nearly went mad.

The producer saw there was a good chance that his precious bridge could burn down before he had the chance to blow it up. With a cry of despair he jumped into his Jeep and sped to the bridge to make sure nothing would happen, leaving Bill literally dancing with delight.[10] The bridge was 425 feet long and 90 feet high, consumed 1500 trees, cost a quarter of a million dollars, and took five months to build. It had to be blown up as a train (a real one, a gift from a local maharaja) was travelling across it. Seven cameras were hidden, with slit trenches next to them in which crew members would be protected from the explosion. A signal was given to the train driver to jump off just before the train reached the bridge. Lean had planned the entire shooting according to that scene which was the last to be filmed. Nevertheless, the blowing-up of the bridge was a significant change from the novel, as the author Pierre Boulle revealed: "For three years I fought them over this change. In the end I gave up."[11]

Bill refused a stunt man for the difficult scenes. He had to argue with Spiegel and Lean, who knew that if something happened to him, the production could lose its star.

"I'll never forget *Bridge on the River Kwai* because it was the most dangerous film I've ever made," Bill revealed in an interview in 1973:

> During the six torturous months it took to complete, my co-stars and I risked our lives in just about every imaginable way. The likelihood of injury was so high that a special medical unit was on location at all times.... The plot called for a lot of acting in the water, and we were constantly peeling huge leeches from our bodies. Also the river was full of sharp, jagged rocks that would cut you open if you brushed against them.... I was nearly killed the day we blew up the bridge. The script called for me to swim through the river's rock-strewn rapids and place dynamite charges at the base of the bridge. The scene required split-second timing and had to be filmed in one continuous shot. I love taking risks, so I refused a stunt man. Director David Lean tried to talk to me out of this decision, but I insisted. The cameras rolled and I drifted downriver and into the rapids. I was halfway through when I hit a hidden rock headfirst. The blow dazed me and I was pulled under by the churning current. Somehow I managed to fight my way to the surface. I finally made it to the bridge and completed the scene. I've taken quite a few risks in my film career, but *Bridge on the River Kwai* was the ultimate adventure of my life.[12]

After the shooting was completed, no one from the crew was allowed to leave the country until the film safely reached London for processing and editing. For two long, anxious weeks the footage of the final sequence was lost, and then it was found undamaged, sitting in the sun on a runway of Cairo Airport in Egypt.

To work in the film, Bill had agreed to lower his salary considerably to $300,000, but he had insisted on ten percent of the film's gross. However, Bill's lawyer put a special clause in his contract that whatever the profits, he was to receive no more than $50,000 a year in order to avoid excessive taxes in the same tax year. Spiegel agreed, not imagining that *Kwai* would earn more than $30 million at the box office between 1957 to 1980.

The Bridge on the River Kwai premiered in London on October 2, 1957, and in New York on December 18 and was praised by critics on both sides of the Atlantic. The "Colonel Bogey" theme music topped the charts throughout the world and the film received eight Academy Award nominations. It won seven, including Best Film and Best Director. Alec Guinness won an Oscar as Best Actor. He later admitted to feeling guilty since he thought Bill was the real star of the picture.

Bill congratulated him on his well-deserved victory, exclaiming, "You keep the Oscar, I will keep my ten percent!"

In the early '70s Guinness declared, "Mr.

Top and bottom: Snorkeling on holiday.

Holden and I have exchanged vows to work again. I've been called what I consider a huge compliment — the quintessential Englishman — and doubt I am, but if I am, then Mr. Holden is the quintessential American. He represents the positive aspects of what has pushed your country from humble origins to a respected, likable and capable position."[13]

After the success of *Kwai*, Bill was offered a series of roles in mediocre action movies, all of which he turned down. Rather than making Paramount's *The Jayhawkers!* or *The Trap*, he preferred to temporarily retire from the screen. He also refused to appear in John Huston's *The Roots of Heaven*; when David Selznick suggested casting him in *Tender Is the Night* he suddenly became "unavailable."

The right proposal finally came from Carl Foreman, with whom Bill became friends while on location in Ceylon. The screenwriter convinced him to work for the independent company Open Road Productions that he (Foreman) had just started. Although he lived in London after being blacklisted in Hollywood, Foreman was writing anonymously and was able to convince Columbia to partially finance a project for a film directed by Carol Reed, who was considered one of Britain's greatest directors with three hits in a row (*Odd Man Out*, *The Fallen Idol*, and *The Third Man*). David Lean had been Foreman's first choice but the director refused because he was busy with the pre-production of *Lawrence of Arabia*. Anxious to continue his filming experiences abroad, Bill accepted Foreman's proposal to work in England.

The picture, *The Key*, was based on *Stella*, a war novel by Dutch author Jan de Hartog. The film title referred to the apartment key of Stella, a Swiss girl living in World War II Plymouth. When her fiancé, a tugboat captain, dies the night before the wedding, the young woman tries to forget him. She sleeps with other seamen who all eventually became war casualties.

As Stella, Carol Reed cast 23-year-old Italian star Sophia Loren. Bill played David Ross, one of the tugboat captains smitten with Stella. The fifteen-week shooting schedule began in mid–July 1957. Taking advantage of the summer weather, Reed filmed first all the scenes at sea, not requiring Loren's presence on the set until the beginning of October. When the actress finally arrived in England, Foreman and Reed seemed to have changed their mind about her, and tried amiably and gently to persuade her to withdraw.

"They had come to realize that I was really too young for that part, that I just wouldn't be believable with Holden, who was much too old for me," Loren stated years later. "They needed someone much more mature for the part, Foreman said, and Ingrid Bergman, was ready to take over."[14]

Loren, who desperately wanted to play the role she found challenging and intriguing, overcame her impulse to withdraw. "I'm sorry," she said, "but I don't agree with you. This is a part that I feel committed to. I don't think there will be any discrepancy with Mr. Holden. I have signed a contract and I want to do the film."[15]

Reed had no choice and went forward with the Italian actress. Before *The Key* was finished, Foreman told Loren how pleased he was that she had not withdrawn. Sophia's beauty, charm, and class mesmerized her fellow co-stars and the entire crew. Bill met her for the first time at a dinner at Carol Reed's, and still remembered the details of the evening fifteen years later.

> She didn't walk in, she swept in. Never saw so much woman coming at me in my entire life. I have always made it a rule as far as actresses are concerned, to play it absolutely cool, almost cold on the outside ... I just don't want anything in a relationship with an actress to be misunderstood at the time. You have to work with them terribly intimately, particularly in love scenes, and unless you play it neutral you may well have a situation on your hands. I've had that difficulty with Jennifer Jones, Grave Kelly, Audrey Hepburn and Kim Novak ... in all the relationships I've had with leading ladies, and I consider the one with Sophia a very important one, I found that the less involved I was with them the better.[16]

About that first meeting, Foreman's opinion was slightly different. "Both Bill and Carol were, of course, happily married men. But the impact Sophia had on them was so devastating, without realizing it they began to compete with each other. They were clearly both excited by this stunning Italian creature, each determined to achieve, platonically of course, the relationship with her. What was happening was that they were fighting for the possession of her psyche."[17]

At the beginning, Bill's false indifference on the set puzzled Sophia and though they worked capably together, neither was completely at ease. Sophia quickly became aware of how Bill, Howard and Reed felt about her and used it to her advantage, although never becoming personally involved with any of them.

Bill's outward indifference toward Sophia persisted until one day on the set when someone handed him a photograph from an Italian tabloid dated 1951 with a topless Sophia on the set of *It's Him ... Yes! Yes!* Bill reacted with bitter scorn and Sophia said, "What is it?"

"This," said Bill, handing her the magazine. "Isn't it dreadful?!"

"I don't think they're dreadful," Sophia said. "They look pretty good to me."[18]

Bill smiled. Later he admitted, "I got to think about it, and I thought: Goddamnit, they *were* beautiful. What the hell was I doing knocking it?! It was just my moral concept of the time. I realized how chic Sophia had been about it. From then on we began to get through to each other. But it was a long time before we showed any affection. It was always there as far as I was concerned but I never wanted to express it because of her bloody beauty and everything else, I don't go out of my way to place myself in jeopardy."[19]

According to Sophia, Bill was perfectly cast. She remembers him as full of self-doubts: "When viewing rushes, he leaves the projection room before the lights go on, because he can't stand the critical reaction of others. For me he made a gallant exception. He stayed and said: 'Sophia, you've really got it!'"[20]

During the filming, Bill was invited to the annual Royal Film Performance, which that year featured *The Bridge on the River Kwai*. Dressed in a gorgeous white evening gown, Sophia was his official escort. Bill wore for the occasion tails and a white tie. The stunning couple impressed everybody and they were the first to meet Queen Elizabeth II.

During the day, on the set of *The Key*, it was hard work with all concentration focused on making what everybody hoped would be a superior film. But in the evening, while Sophia would lock herself in her hotel room to assiduously work on the script, Bill would go to the studio bar to get drunk with Trevor Howard and other crew members. Bill was one of the few American actors Howard liked. (The Hollywood star system forbade the British star from travelling in the same car as Bill, who since the phenomenal success of *Kwai* received five-star treatment.[21])

For his newspaper, journalist Donald Zec organized a newspaper competition in which he invited readers to write in a few sentences why they would like to have dinner with William Holden and Sophia Loren and what they would say. According to Zec,

I arranged the winners to be brought to the hotel. Mr. Holden had won a Mrs. Patricia Dyer of Frinton in Essex ... I sensed over the oyster, the turtle soup, the chicken and the Niersteiner wine, that Bill Holden had had a hard day. Mrs. Dyer was nervous and stared into his face from her position on his left. Bill stared back without speaking. It was going to be quite an evening.

With Sophia Loren in Carol Reed's *The Key* (1958).

Finally, Mrs. Dyer, drawing on the inspiration of all the sages, leapt in with, "What's your favorite film?"

Holden twisted his lips into a dangerous smile. "It hasn't been made yet," he said.

"If you quit show business altogether," faltered the lady, "what would you do?"

"Die," Bill Holden said, pouring himself another drink.

Mrs. Dyer's voice was now a whisper. She geared herself for the final question which had won her scintillating, forthcoming, informative superstar of the evening.

"With what five people have you most enjoyed working?"

"None."

Mrs. Dyer took refuge in her chicken. The evening was taking on third degree burns.[22]

When the studio work was complete, the film was scheduled for a royal premiere on May 29, 1958, before Princess Margaret. On July 2 it opened in the United States. Reed was forced by Columbia to shoot two endings, one for the Americans in which the final, surviving captain married Stella, another for the British in which they drifted apart. On both sides of the ocean, *The Key* was as tepidly greeted. Reviewers generally did not praise Bill's work as much as Howard's and Loren's. In an interview with an Italian magazine, Loren admitted to being surprised to learn that the American newspapers described her relationship with Bill on the set of *The Key* as "stormy."

"We had a lot in common," the Italian star said. "However, after the film was complete, we shook hands and we went separate ways back to our privacy."[23]

10

World Citizen

....
"I really couldn't care less about what they say about me in
Hollywood. I'm going to live the way I want to live, and
nobody's going to tell me how." — William Holden
....

Bill's friendship with John Wayne began during his early years in
Hollywood. Sharing agent Charlie Feldman, they also partied together
often. Both felt great personal and professional respect for each other and
every time they met they promised each other to work together one day.
The occasion came at the end of summer 1958 when producer Walter
Mirisch budgeted $3,600,000 to make *The Horse Soldiers*, based on Harold
Sinclair's novel. For the first time, the legendary Western director John
Ford agreed to make a picture set during the Civil War — a historical period
he knew well. Although James Stewart and Clark Gable were the initial
choice for the main roles, the producers eventually decided that the pair-
ing of Wayne and Bill, the two biggest stars in Hollywood, was a better
bet.

Paramount tried to keep Bill off the film, claiming that he was exclu-
sively committed to them under a 1956 oral agreement. On October 13,
after exhausting and fruitless negotiations, a Federal judge ended the legal
battle, refusing to grant an injunction sought by Paramount against Bill,
allowing him to be in the film. Pre-production was a long and complicated process since Wayne, Ford and Bill had their own production companies (Batjac, Argosy and William Holden Productions, respectively).
Along with co-producer Martin Rackin's Mirisch Company and United
Artists, there were six corporations involved in the contractual negotia-

tions. Six sets of agents, lawyers and accountants spent six months drawing up one of the most complex contracts ever written. In September 1958 all parties signed a 250-page agreement stating that the film would cost about $5 million, $175,000 going to Ford and $750,000 each to Wayne and Bill. Each star was also given 20 percent of the profits and Ford was allotted 10 percent of the producers' share.

The Horse Soldiers was filmed from the end of October 1958 to January 1959, including 28 days on location 80 miles from New Orleans in Natchitoches, Louisiana, and in Mississippi south of Natchez. Nineteen days of interiors were shot at MGM and Columbia Studios. The shooting was logistically complicated and physically strenuous for the 64-year-old Ford. He was unhappy with the final script and uncomfortable associating with co-producer Martin Rackin, who was constantly supervising the director's work on the set.

From the first day of work, Bill was shocked by the brutal manner that Ford used with Wayne: "Ford treated Duke [Wayne's nickname] badly because Ford was on the wagon and took it out on Duke and wouldn't let him have a drink." Bill said in an interview years later,

> He also told me I couldn't drink. So I found myself lodging in Shreveport where Ford couldn't stop me having a drink after work. I liked Duke a lot. I wasn't sure how we'd get on, but he was a really nice guy. But I was pretty disgusted with the way Ford treated him. Ford would yell at him and treat him like he was a newcomer. I said to Duke, "Why do you let that old bastard treat you like that?" He said, "Aw, Bill, that's just his way of making sure I give him a good performance." I said, "Duke, you've been at this longer than me. You got nominated for an Oscar, didn't you?" He said, "Yeah!" I said, "And what film was that for?" Of course I knew the answer. *Sands of Iwo Jima.* I said to Duke, "Did Ford get a good performance out of you for *that*?" He said, "Ford didn't direct *Iwo Jima*." I said, "That's what I mean." ... Duke would just do anything for Ford, and I admired his loyalty. But I wasn't having Ford talk to *me* that way. I told him. I said, "Jack, I'll sweat blood to give you a good performance, but if you ever talk to me that way you talk to Duke, I'll walk off and I won't come back." Ford said, "Oh Bill, I don't need to force a good performance out of you. I saw *Sunset Blvd.* You're twice the actor Duke is. He *needs* me to bully him."[1]

A few days later, Wayne paid Bill the highest compliment after observing him in a scene: "Someday I'll kill that guy. He makes acting look so easy."[2]

Two days after Wayne's sleeping pill–addicted wife Pilar arrived, she was sent back to Hollywood where she attempted suicide. John was in desperate need of a drink. Bill and Rackin felt sorry for Wayne being under Ford's no-drinking edict and devised a plan to get him away from Ford for a whole day. Rackin told the director that Wayne's teeth looked off-color in the early rushes and they needed to be cleaned. They made an appointment with a dentist in Shreveport, drove him there for his cleaning, and spent the remainder of the day drinking. When Ford found out, he stormed furiously into Wayne's room, prepared to confiscate bottles.

One day, Bill had a touch of the flu and his remedy was a flask of brandy. Observing Bill's strange behavior, Ford asked actor Denver Pyle if he had noticed it too. Knowing Bill had a hangover, Pyle replied that he heard Bill was not feeling well, avoiding the topic of alcohol. Amidst 100 men on horses, Ford called for a ladder and began framing with his hands.

"Get me Bill Holden," he barked. "I want him on a horse."

Bill gamely mounted up and came over for his instructions.

"Bill, start over there across the stream and ride towards me here into a big close-up."

Bill dutifully followed the instructions, moving across the river into the frame. Then Ford struck.

"Your lower lip is shaking, Mr. Holden."

"Well, I've had the flu, and..."

"Are you a little hung over, Mr. Holden?"

"No, but I've been having a little brandy for this cold, trying to break it up..."

"Well, I can't have you in a close-up with that lower lip. All right, that's a wrap! We'll start here tomorrow, if Mr. Holden feels better."

The company was dismissed and Bill was chastised for unprofessional behavior.[3]

Despite the on-set arguments, Bill explained in an interview, "I thought we were getting some good stuff on film. I liked the edge Duke and I had to play. I was a doctor who hated war and blamed people like the character Wayne played for all the miseries war caused. And he was a soldier who hated doctors because they'd botched an operation on his wife and killed her ... I hated war, so it wasn't difficult for me to believe what I was saying."[4]

The shooting was blighted by the death of stuntman Fred Kennedy. Overweight and out of shape, Kennedy pleaded with Ford to allow him to take one more fall. At first the director was adamant in his refusal, but he reconsidered when the stuntman insisted he needed extra money to help his family.

To play a trick on actress Constance Towers, Ford told her to rush in after the fall and plant a big kiss on Kennedy's lips. They set up for the scene, Ford called for action, and Kennedy galloped the horse toward him, taking the fall on cue. But Kennedy landed the wrong way and broke his neck. Towers ran out to him, took his head and shoulders into her arms, and leaned down for the kiss. He was desperately sucking air through his broken neck. Abruptly she looked back to Ford and screamed, "This man is dying!"[5]

Kennedy passed away before reaching the hospital. Ford blamed himself for the accident, fell into depression, started drinking again and lost interest in the project.

The Horse Soldiers received a tepid response from critics when it opened in June 1959. It died at the box office, grossing only $10 million, barely covering its cost.

On the set of *The Horse Soldiers*, Bill was interviewed by *New York Journal American* columnist Phyllis Battelle, about the persistent rumors of trouble in his seventeen-year marriage.

Lying shamelessly, Bill said, "I have no intention of ever considering marriage with anyone else but my wife.... We were fortunate enough to have a family. And we've been able to work out any difference of opinion, which everybody has, especially in a business where you're constantly away from home, with a reasonable and intelligent approach."[6]

Despite his assertions, Holden's marriage was indeed on the rocks. Bill remained away from home much as he could, accepting work in productions made abroad.

"My blueprint is to make one very important picture a year," he said, "that is not only artistically satisfying to me but successful at the box office. Ideally I'd like to spend six or seven months on my vocation and five or six months on my avocational activities."[7]

In the middle of 1959, Bill announced he was selling his home in Toluca and moving to Switzerland with his family. That decision was largely motivated by financial reasons; many actors had moved to Switzerland to avoid paying taxes which amounted to three-quarters of their earnings. The only exception made by the American government was if someone resided abroad for at least five years. Bill explained his choice to the media, stating that the main reason was his sons' education; the move would give them the advantages of learning other languages. In addition he remarked that living in Central Europe helped cut costs since he scheduled two pictures to be made there. However, the American press condemned him for taking jobs away from American craftsmen. They claimed he forced producers to make their films abroad when hiring him. For more than three years the media harshly attacked him, depicting him as a greedy traitor and someone interested more in money than in his homeland, turning his back on his country to avoid paying taxes.

Bill responded calmly to the accusations: "It seems to me that Americans have always been noted for moving around, for being unafraid of new challenges and new frontiers. Now certain people are trying to tell us to stay home and not to work abroad. It's a form of isolationism."[8]

When a few even suggested that his U.S. citizenship should have been revoked, he reacted more aggressively: "For many years I regularly paid taxes, sometimes even eighty percent of my earnings. Now I am tired of Hollywood and of many other things ... like paying hefty sums to the Internal Revenue Service! On the other hand, I plan on working only overseas from now on and I don't see any reason why I should bankroll the Federal treasury. I will only pay my taxes on the income received in that country."[9]

On August 20, 1959, Bill moved his family into a beautiful home he bought in St-Prex, near Lausanne.

At the end of 1958, before settling permanently in Switzerland, Bill took a two-month trip to Kenya together with Indiana oil tycoon Ray Ryan and Swiss banker Carl Hirshmann. Bill had met Ryan in Palm Springs where they become friends and later travelled together in Ryan's private jet in search of new oil investments. When the magnate took a trip to Africa he invited Bill to go along together with Hirshmann, an old business partner. Bill was captivated by the wild country of Kenya, so different from the golden and fake Hollywood world he detested.

"Originally I planned to be the great white hunter with a Nikon camera," he told reporter Joe Hyams, "but when I got to Africa I found the boys depended on the hunters for meat. Before I knew it I was out shooting meat for camp, rugs for my children and zebra skins for Billy Wilder's office. I don't believe in shooting anything you can't eat, walk on, or hang up."[10]

Among his hunting trophies Bill listed a magnificent gemsbok which he described as "the Audrey Hepburn" of the gazelles because of its delicate long neck. However, he confessed that about half the animals he had taken the licenses for, he did not have the heart to shoot. He also once feared for his life when a female rhinoceros charged his Land Rover to protect a cub, hidden from view of his fellow hunters. The wild animal hooked the end of the car and knocked the group about ten feet. "That was the first time in my life I've really smelled fear. It was in the car like a fog."[11]

The highlight of Bill's trip was the purchase of the fifty-room Mawingo Hotel with 93 acres of fruit and vegetables, and flower gardens at 6,900 feet on the slope of Mt. Kenya (about 126 miles from Nairobi). Bill and Ryan were shareholders with 45 percent each; Hirshmann had 10 percent. The trio planned to form the Mount Kenya Safari Club which had to support established societies for the preservation of game. The hotel was originally part of a British chain; the three partners decided to refurbish it, adding tennis courts, a nine-hole golf course, two swimming pools and rows of modern, luxurious white bungalows. To promote the resort, special honorary membership cards were sent to celebrities from the entertainment, financial and political worlds. Bill took charge of the renovations, designing the bungalows and finding and hiring qualified personnel. He imported a chef from Vienna and organized native dancers to entertain guests. Slowly Africa got under his skin and became his spiritual home. Four years later Bill renounced his past as hunter and, with the help of game catchers and conservationists Don Hunt and Julian McKeand, established a 1,260-acre wildlife preserve surrounding the club, to safeguard the native flora and fauna.

"In our club we do not kill animals," Bill explained in an interview. "We have created it to give an example how to save nature from mankind." He added on a different occasion, "Ecologically, there is a point of no return. At the rate we were decimating wild animal herds until a few years ago, whole species — cheetahs, rhinos, lions, zebras — would have become no more than names in the encyclopedia. To see a tiger, you'd have to visit a zoo. There is a beautiful balance in nature. Each animal has its own defenses, its own predators. When man — the supreme predator — steps in, he upsets that balance. And it's all so selfish. At least, when you shoot game for food, or survival, there's an excuse. To kill a living creature to decorate your living room is unthinkable."

Thanks to Bill, the Mount Kenya Safari Club acquired an international reputation, but it had little commercial success. To Bill, Kenya and in particular his property always remained a special place, a hideaway where he could return to restore himself spiritually and physically.

Bill returned to work aiming to earn as much as possible to keep financing his investment in Kenya. The first film he made after moving to Switzerland was *The World of Suzie Wong*. Shot in London and Hong Kong, it was a love story between an American painter and a young Chinese prostitute. It was Bill's eightieth time visiting Hong Kong, one of his favorite cities, where he had bought an apartment and made some profitable investments. It was no coincidence that he was offered the job of narrating the CBS-TV documentary *Report on Hong Kong* which aired the following year.

The World of Suzie Wong was based on a drama by Paul Osborn, inspired by Richard Mason's book; its production was long and difficult. When location filming was over and the crew flew to London, trouble began. Co-star France Nuyen, who had played Suzie Wong on stage, was distressed by her rocky relationship with her lover Marlon Brando; she was fired for her odd behavior after a nervous breakdown. She was replaced by dancer Nancy Kwan, daughter of an Englishwoman and a Chinese architect; producer Ray Stark had noticed her in Hong Kong. Eventually Stark fired director Jean Negulesco and asked Hollywood director Richard Quine to immediately come to complete the film. On a second trip to China, Ardis accompanied Bill despite the rumors of an imminent separation. Only a few weeks earlier, Hedda Hopper had reported in her gossip column, "When Brenda Marshall married, she was a happy, fun-loving woman. The last time I saw her at a party ... at Lausanne, Switzerland, her old contentment had gone bye-bye."[12]

Bill told the press he did not mind making the same film twice because he firmly believed that with Nancy Kwan, it would be a better picture. But *The World of Suzie Wong* bombed at the box office, panned by the critics as too unbelievable and sentimental.

Two weeks after *The World of Suzie Wong*'s premiere at New York City's Radio City Music Hall, Bill announced a donation he made (along with his partners of the Mount Kenya Safari Club) to build a school that would provide a free education up to the fifth grade for the children of the club staff and employees of neighboring farms.

"I guess the idea came to the three of us simultaneously. We aren't charging any fees and we felt it was the least we could do for the Africans who live around the club."[13]

A year had gone by since the Holdens had moved to Switzerland, yet Bill was still receiving insulting mail from Americans regarding his alleged tax evasion. He seemed not to worry that much, expressing to the press his immense satisfaction regarding that choice. His children were attending an international school and planned to go to college in the States.

"Living in Switzerland has been the most rewarding experience of my life," he told to a reporter, adding that his family liked it there and so there they would stay. It was easy for Bill to make those statements since he had actually only spent a few weeks at home, otherwise travelling extensively for business and work all over the world. Some of his trips were an excuse to be far from Ardis and their frequent arguments. She was always moody from being bored at home, alone and nervous in a country that she disliked. When Bill was offered the chance to star in *The Counterfeit Traitor*, scheduled to be made in Germany, Denmark and Sweden, he did not think twice and accepted George Seaton's offer. The director had written a screenplay based on a book by Alexander Klein, who told of the real adventures of Eric Erickson, an American son of Swedish immigrants who returned to live to Sweden. Erickson was an oilman who was pressed into service as a spy during World War II. Allied intelligence agents were hoping to tap his contacts within Germany by having him pretend to be a Nazi sympathizer.

Seaton was able to convince the real Erickson to fully cooperate with the project to make it more realistic. Erickson showed the crew the exact places where the events had happened and the prison where he was incarcerated.

Lilli Palmer was cast as a spy in love with Erickson, played by Bill, who is captured and sentenced to death by the Germans. Palmer recalled in her autobiography the day when the crew started the location shooting in Hamburg; Seaton intended to use the Herberstraße in the heart of the red light district for a night. He tried to bargain with the madams of the whorehouses, where the girls were displayed in the windows, but the $100,000 asked was too high and he had to shoot across the real crowd of sailors, tourists and prostitutes. As the crew was slowly moving in that street, a fat lady in green corsets leaned out a window, pointed a finger at Palmer and started to sing a popular song the actress performed in one of her earlier films. Palmer was recognized by other bystanders, and they joined in the song.

Lilli Palmer and Holden on the set of *The Counterfeit Traitor* (1962).

"They seemed to know you," Bill said, looking at her with new respect. "How come? Have you ... er ... worked here before?"[14]

Seaton said in an interview that Bill and Palmer worked very well together and the only problem the production encountered was created by actor Hugh Griffith, who had a drinking problem and was not easy to handle.

During the making of *The Counterfeit Traitor*, Bill found a way to be closer to his sons. In the production, sixteen-year-old West worked with the still cameraman and fourteen-year-old Scott helped with men's wardrobe. The production had several delays due to weather and the short daylight hours of the winter season, and so the rest of the shooting was postponed to the following summer. On June 1961 when production resumed, the crew noticed a dramatic change in Bill's look. He appeared tired and aged, with puffy eyes from his alcohol abuse in the months during the break. The director decided to give him extra time to rest.

The Counterfeit Traitor was Bill's last hit for nine years. It was greatly acclaimed by the reviewers, who praised his superlative performance.

For economical reasons Bill made the big mistake of refusing the hero's role in of the biggest hits of 1961, *The Guns of Navarone*. "My price is now $750,000 plus 10 percent of the gross," he told Carl Foreman, producer and screenwriter of the picture, who replaced him with Gregory Peck. Peck's salary, together with David Niven's and Anthony Quinn's, did not amount to Bill's asking price.[15]

Instead he starred in *Satan Never Sleeps*, based upon *The China Story*, a novel by Nobel Prize–winning author Pearl Buck. Set in 1949, it was the story of Father O'Banion, played by Bill, on his way to relieve the older Father Bovard (Clifton Webb) at his mission in Southwest China. O'Banion is delayed by a flood, from which he saves a beautiful native girl, Sui Lan (France Nuyen). She falls madly in love with him and becomes his shadow, following him to his new post.

Director Leo McCarey together with Claude Binyon adapted the book into a script using Communism as a metaphor for personal and social rigidity. Being a film critical of the Chinese communism government, it could not be shot on the real locations; it was made in England and Wales and later completed in a London studio using the set of *The Inn of the Sixth Happiness* (another picture set in China).

Satan Never Sleeps was not an easy film to make as Bill was distracted and uninterested in his job. He admitted to some friends that he had lost interest in being an actor, a job he was doing only for economical reasons, and diluting his dissatisfaction with the help of alcohol. McCarey often was involved in Bill's binge drinking. The director was so frustrated by the interference of 20th Century–Fox and their modifications to his script that he eventually walked off the production, and the final five days of shooting were left to an assistant. McCarey would never direct another picture. The released version of *Satan Never Sleeps* was edited without McCarey's input which may explain the film's bizarre happy ending. The picture was a critical and commercial disaster. *The New York Post* described it as "embarrassingly predictable until it becomes so bad that you couldn't even imagine it."[16]

Meanwhile in America, the Hollywood press still could not comprehend why William Holden, a model citizen and a former soldier, suddenly had lost any positive feeling toward life in the States. Many of his fans, colleagues, and friends disapproved of his decision to leave his country, which they associated with the motives of a "dollar-slave." For the umpteenth time Bill replied to those allegations: "After forty-five motion pictures I have no illusions about myself. I'm not an actor. I've never been one. What I am is a contemporary reporter. Films set in a sound stage no longer hold any glamour for me. They're just a place to work. To be an actor, you have to be one of two things: calloused or talented, and I'm neither."[17]

In May 1962 when *The Counterfeit Traitor* opened nationwide, members of three key movie unions picketed theaters in New York, Los Angeles and San Francisco protesting the rising trend by American moviemakers to shoot films abroad to take advantage of tax loopholes, foreign subsidies and cheap labor. Bill was their first target. Picket signs read "DO NOT SEE WILLIAM HOLDEN IN ANY PICTURE"; "WHY DOES WILLIAM HOLDEN DECLINE TO BE A RESIDENT OF THE UNITED STATES?" AND "WE PROTEST ACTORS WHO LIVE OUT OF THE UNITED STATES WHO DO NOT PAY THEIR SHARE OF THE TAXES."

The three unions were hoping that the picketing could dramatize their campaign for Congress to eliminate tax advantages for American stars who established foreign residence. They explained that every time Bill refused to make a movie in the United States, it meant that about $7,000,000 was taken away from movie workers each year.[18] This time Bill was extremely irritated by the allegations and replied with a less diplomatic and more eloquent tone.

"I really couldn't care less about what they say about me in Hollywood. I'm going to live the way I want to live, and nobody's going to tell me how."[19]

11

Booze and Tragedy

••
"Why the years of desperate drinking?"—"Let's just say inner
turmoil."—William Holden to Bernard Drew
••

Since falling in love with Kenya, Bill looked for a chance to make a
film that reflected his beloved Africa and his interest in the big-game preservation farm, using the facilities of the Mount Kenya Safari Club. After
a project with producer Darryl Zanuck fell through in early 1962, Bill
convinced 20th Century–Fox to finance the construction of a soundstage
and other permanent facilities on his African property to make *The Lion*.
Based on a novel by Joseph Kessel, author of the controversial *Belle de jour*,
The Lion was the story of a lawyer who goes to Africa to visit his ex-wife
and discovers that his daughter has befriended a wild lion. The thin plot
was an excuse to show the world Kenya's natural scenery and the wild flora
and fauna that Bill was trying to preserve.

On the set, Bill was reunited with Trevor Howard, with whom he
had enjoyed working in *The Key*. Howard had a great admiration for Bill
and his wily dealings with major film studios.

"You've got to hand it to Bill Holden," the British actor said in an
interview. "He was the one actor in *The Bridge on the River Kwai* who
seemed to figure it was going to be such an enormous hit and, while Jack
Hawkins and Alec Guinness accepted a flat fee to do it, Bill insisted on
ten percent of the profits to be paid yearly, and that, he told me, worked
out to about $50,000 a year. After that he was in such big demand he was
getting like 20 percent of the profits from his films as well as a huge fee
up front. When we made *The Lion* he must have been one of the highest

paid actors around. But he never let it go to his head. But I do think he drinks too much. Not a good thing for his liver. Happily, I've got low blood pressure so I can drink as much as I like."[1]

His low blood pressure was a nice excuse for Howard to justify his after-work drink binges. Drinking had become a serious problem and Bill showed the characteristic puffy eyes and deep creases along his forehead and around his mouth.

Gorgeous French actress Capucine was the picture's leading lady. The moment he met her, Bill was infatuated. "My friend call me Cap," she said when she was introduced to Bill.

He replied to everybody to hear, "She is the most beautiful woman in the world."

Capucine, whose real name was Germaine Lefebvre, was born in Toulon, France. She changed her name after she moved to Paris to become a fashion model for legendary French designers including Dior and Givenchy. In 1950 she was married to French actor Pierre Trabaud for a brief eight months. In the late '50s she left Europe for New York to improve her English and seek higher modeling fees. She was scouted in a restaurant by agent-producer Charles Feldman, who offered her a role opposite British star Dirk Bogarde in the film *Song Without End*, about composer Franz Liszt. It was followed by *North to Alaska* with John Wayne and *A Walk on the Wild Side* with Barbara Stanwyck and Jane Fonda. She became Feldman's girlfriend and he recommended her to Fox for the role in *The Lion*.

Shortly after Capucine's arrival on the set, Ardis showed up at the Mount Kenya Safari Club on holiday. On the set a few days later, Bill and Ardis began to argue violently in front of the entire crew. Everybody knew that Ardis was jealous of Capucine even though neither Bill nor Cap had visibly displayed any sexual interest in each other. Once Ardis left Kenya, the situation returned to normality and Bill's attraction to his beautiful co-star became incontrollable. However, he felt a strong sense of guilt not only because of Ardis but also Charles Feldman, who was a dear friend. Disloyalty toward his friend gave him another excuse for more drinking. His health quickly deteriorated and once shooting was over, he found he had contracted hepatitis. Suddenly the situation precipitated. Shortly after being admitted to a local hospital, he had to be carried out by stretcher and flown to Italy for treatment at the Tuscan Montecatini Terme spa resort. In just one month, doctors were able to restore his health through

Holden, Zamba the Lion and Capucine in a publicity shot for *The Lion* (1962).

a strict detox diet. He briefly returned home to Switzerland, where he spent his days racing his motorboat (in Lake Geneva) or his Bentley.

After that episode, in early July 1962 he left for Paris where he was expected on the set of *Paris When It Sizzles*. "I remember the day I arrived at Orly Airport for *Paris When It Sizzles*," Bill confessed to Ryan O'Neal on the set of *Wild Rovers* in 1970. "I could hear my footsteps echoing against the walls of the transit corridor, just like a condemned man walking the last mile. I realized that I had to face Audrey [Hepburn, his co-star] and I had to deal with my drinking. And I didn't think I could handle either situation."[2]

Fear made him drink, this time with devastating effects not only on himself but on the picture.

Hepburn was delighted to work with Bill again, and the fact he was in the cast convinced her to accept the part. "I hadn't seen him for about ten years. In fact, I think the last time we even said anything to one another was when I introduced him to Mel [Ferrer], who was my fiancé at the time, at some nightclub in New York."[3]

Although he was sentimentally involved with Capucine, Bill still had strong feelings for Audrey and the idea she would discover he was an alcoholic troubled him. Years later when a journalist asked him what made him an alcoholic, Bill answered, "Let's just say inner turmoil."[4]

Audrey was not fully aware how bad Bill's drinking had become. With her marriage with Ferrer on the rocks, she encouraged Bill's attentions, hoping to make Ferrer jealous. Gossip columnists played up the rumors of an affair between the stars.

"Everybody in the know had his finger crossed that the romance between two big married stars is just a passing fancy that will be forgotten when the picture they're doing together is finished," wrote Hedda Hopper. "Meanwhile it's proven to be such a juicy bit of gossip that the names Liz and Burton have almost been forgotten."[5]

Some tabloids even reported the false news that Hepburn was seeing a European psychiatrist to help her decide what to do about this romantic tangle. Yet when Ferrer heard reports of his wife being seen too close to Bill, he responded by stating that they were just "old friends."

Paris When It Sizzles, the story of a broken-down screenwriter who encourages his secretary to help him act out his stories, was a remake of the 1952 French movie *La Fête Henriette*, directed by Julien Duvivier. Paramount wanted Blake Edwards to direct, but he had prior commitments and recommended his close friend Richard Quine, director of *The World of Suzie Wong*. Edwards thought Quine knew how to handle Bill's heavy drinking.

At the Studios de Boulogne, where the film was made, the mood was very tense. Bill would often show up very late and very drunk, insisting on rehearsing and shooting his daily scenes despite his awful state. Once he arrived on the set with a little monkey on his shoulder. Knowing that Bill would be useless that day, Quine decided to suspend the filming. Audrey Hepburn tried to stay calm but working with Bill was tormenting her. The actress was going through difficult times and felt very insecure. She began to believe she was unattractive and insisted that cinematographer Claude Renoir (nephew of the great director Jean) be fired because he was not able to photograph her well. Quine replaced him with Charles Lang, upsetting the local union that threatened to go on strike.

Screenwriter George Axelrod, author of the script *Breakfast at Tiffany's*, remembered a night Bill climbed a tree by a wall leading to Hepburn's room. She finally came to her window and leaned out; Bill kissed her and then slipped and fell from the tree, landing atop a parked car below. Quine was so distressed when he saw Bill limping on the set the following day that he had Paramount fly in Ardis to try to control her husband. "Bill was like a punch-drunk fighter, walking on his heels, listening slightly, talking punchy. He didn't know he was drunk," the director recalled.[6]

Ardis' presence made things worse. Finally the director persuaded him to enter the Château de Garche, an alcoholic rehabilitation center, to dry out for a week. Quine used those seven days to shoot Hepburn's close-ups and a few cameo scenes with Tony Curtis.

Upon his release, Bill returned to work looking sober and younger. He behaved as if nothing had happened and no one dared remind him. Immediately director and screenwriter tried to make up for the lost time, shooting as much as possible (and removing any physical strain that Bill could not handle).

Noël Coward, who had a little part in the film, wrote in his diary on October 1, 1962, "Bill Holden, off the bottle and looking 15 years younger, absolutely charming to work with. We exchange confidences and bottles of eau de cologne in the interminable waits."[7]

Bob Willoughby, the set photographer, was one of the very few to have nice memories of that film, particularly of Bill, with whom he spent hours talking. "He told me about his love of Africa, and the plans for his safari club, but never discussed work. I could see he was lonely and needed someone to talk to. Often on the way home from the studio, he would ask me to come in for a quick drink at his hotel.... Everyone was in love with Audrey, but no one more than Bill."[8]

Production (originally scheduled for three months) took four because of Bill's behavior. With only one last scene to be shot, Bill announced he would go back to Switzerland for the weekend to ride in his new Ferrari. Quine begged him to wait just a few days, film that last sequence and then go back home. Bill stubbornly did not listen and showed up on the set the following Monday walking on crutches and with an arm in a splint. He explained he had crashed the new car into a wall. Quine shortened that last scene because of Bill's injuries. Hepburn tried to console him being closer to him, but her friendly behavior was once again misunderstood with tabloids reporting a romance between the two stars. Audrey said in a later interview that after that car accident, "All I did was 'mother' him a little. Anyway, I'm glad that Capucine is now getting all the publicity."[9]

It did not take long for Bill to start drinking again and a few weeks later he was admitted for the second time to Château de Garche. This time Capucine came to Paris to assist him during his entire stay in the clinic. Her presence was a great help. She was able to put him in a good mood and to facilitate his speedy recovery. Bill was impatient to leave the clinic and work with her in *The 7th Dawn*, a film scheduled to be filmed in Malaysia. After a brief stop in Kenya, Bill flew off to Kuala Lumpur where he was expected on the set. This time his relationship with Capucine was not a secret to anyone, since he had been separated from Ardis for some time. Bill was once again drunk during the entire making of the film. At the end of the production, he had seizures, collapsed and lost consciousness. He was hospitalized in Switzerland where the seizures continued for several days. Doctors feared he could be left with brain damage.

At the hospital, Capucine met with Ardis. The French actress was living in Lausanne and visited Bill at the hospital every day. She was at his bedside when he woke up. Ardis had known of Bill's affair from a letter written by her friend Nancy Reagan. (Nancy had travelled to Kenya with her husband and noticed that what Bill and Capucine were sharing was more serious than just a fling.) When the worst was over and his doctor confirmed that there was no brain damage, Bill was discharged from the hospital. He immediately asked for a legal separation from Ardis and moved into his own apartment in Lausanne. The press began to speculate on an imminent marriage with Capucine, but neither of them wanted to get married.

Many years later, writer Boze Hadleigh probed Capucine: "At one point, it seemed as if William Holden was going to divorce his wife for you."

"That would not have happened," was Capucine's firm answer without commenting any further.[10]

In the summer of 1963, Bill returned to the States to visit his adopted daughter Virginia, who had just had a baby. In that period, Blake Edwards recalled seeing Bill and Capucine at a screening of *Days of Wine and Roses* (a movie whose subject was alcoholism) after which Bill turned to her and said, "Was I that bad?"

"Worse," she said.

"Did I put you through that?" he asked.

"More," she replied.

Bill's gratitude to her was proved by the substantial financial help he provided for her after the flop of her later European films.[11]

Special sneak previews of *Paris When It Sizzles* revealed that the comedy was a failure. The offbeat humor and cuts back and forth between the real story of the two main characters and their fantasies did not amuse audiences. Paramount delayed its release until April of 1964, when their fears confirmed by unfavorable reviews and disastrous box office results. Five months later, *The 7th Dawn* suffered the same fate.

In December, Bill and Capucine accepted Sam Spiegel's invitation to cruise the Caribbean on his yacht, which was anchored in the South of France where they boarded. The couple was alone with the crew on the boat, since the other guests and Spiegel joined the cruise in Barbados. Those ten long days crossing the Atlantic were crucial to their relationship, which suddenly changed after that holiday. Capucine left for Hollywood to make a film and her romance with Bill was over. Nonetheless they stayed friends and Bill left her $50,000 in his will.

For over two years, Bill was away from movie sets. His last five films were all colossal flops and he seemed to have lost his allure as a Hollywood star. His reputation as an alcoholic made things worse. Many directors considered him for parts but were overruled by producers who feared his irresponsible behavior. Despite the great publicity, the Mount Kenya Safari Club was still incurring serious losses, not attracting enough visitors to cover the expenses. In April of 1965, in agreement with his partners, Bill closed the club to concentrate his efforts on looking after the animal reserve he had created around the property.

While on a trip in Thailand, Bill learned the tragic news of his younger brother Dick Beedle's death. During a business trip in Peru, the former Air Force pilot chartered a small plane to move faster around the country. During a flight off the coast he suddenly sent out an SOS that the plane was out of fuel; then the aircraft disappeared off the radar. Neither the wreckage nor Dick's body was ever found. Bill and Ardis flew to Lima where he met with his sister-in-law. Local authorities insisted that they had made every effort to find Dick.[12]

After Dick's tragic death, Bill felt a sense of guilt like the one he experienced when his brother Bob was killed in the Second World War. He also felt a great sense of guilt over his treatment of Ardis whom he had constantly betrayed and his children whom he loved immensely but spent very little time with. Once again, the only consolation — alcohol.

To his great surprise, an offer of work arrived at the end of 1965 from Columbia. He was offered the lead in *Alvarez Kelly*, a Western based on an actual Civil War incident. Bill played the title role, an unscrupulous cattleman who runs afoul of the Confederacy in his effort to deliver beef to the Union Army. He is captured by a Confederate colonel (Richard Widmark), who persuades him — by shooting off a finger — to deliver the cattle to the starving Confederates in Richmond.

After travelling across the States searching for the perfect location, director Edward Dmytryk (who had directed Bill's very first picture *Million Dollar Legs*, in which he was an extra) chose a large plantation not far from Baton Rouge, Louisiana, where the shooting began in December. A few days earlier, Dmytryk had summoned screenwriter Daniel Taradash to revise the final script, which he found unoriginal and clichéd. Taradash arrived to Louisiana, where he worked night and day. However he suddenly realized that his lines were changed in front of the cameras.

He complained to Dmytryk, saying, "What is the sense of my sweating out this dialogue if you're gonna let Bill Holden ad lib whatever he wants to say?" The director replied, "Dan, you take the script too seriously." Taradash revealed in an interview that every day he and Dmytryk would meet in Bill's room after the shooting and go to dinner. Bill would drive so erratically that Taradash would shut his eyes.[13] The director in his autobiography recalled the troubles Bill caused on the set.

> Bill Holden, like many of his colleagues, had a "drinking problem" (it was no problem for him — he liked to drink). When the film took shape in Hollywood, Bill was a little concerned one evening when he told me he had taken "the cure" in France, and the French were not as stuffy as the Americans —

they did allow him the drinking of the wine after the cure. And for a man accustomed to Paris, Rome, and Hong Kong, Baton Rouge can be a boring community — and boredom is the enemy of good sense. One morning, as I was about to call the actors for the first shot, Widmark approached me, took my elbow and pulled me aside.

"We are in trouble," he said.

"How?"

"Come on back to the trailer," he said, nudging me along the way.

"Holden is out," he explained. "I don't think you'll get anything out of him today. He's gone!"...

What surprised me most about the situation was Widmark's attitude. Knowing his temper and his feelings about nonprofessional behavior, I expected him to blow sky-high. Instead, he behaved like a solicitous mother. He drenched Holden with black coffee, walked him around a bit, and in about 45 minutes Bill was sitting his horse and ready to get on with the scene — a bit surly, but serviceable."[14]

Dmytryk also wrote that in spite of all the troubles, "Bill is a professional, and he did his best with a role I was never quite sure he believed in."[15] The shooting of *Alvarez Kelly* was completed in Hollywood, where reporters (who had not seen him there in seven years) were eager to interview him. But Bill was not the same available star he had been in the past; he had become extremely wary of the media that had written too many stories on his drinking problem, his extramarital affairs and his "anti-patriotic" behavior.

"You gotta approach Holden carefully," a press agent told the *New York Times* Peter Bart, who was about to interview him. "Holden doesn't like to talk about his business interests, why he lives abroad, his family, his politics, his love life, his movie plans." The long list of don'ts left very little for the poor journalist to discuss. After a firm but icy handshake, Bart realized he was not welcome. He asked Bill how he was feeling after a recent month-long bout with a form of typhoid. "I don't talk about my illness with the press," he replied coldly. He was then asked why he hadn't made a picture in two years. The reply came quickly: "There have been other things I've been more interested in doing." When Bart asked him to explain the failure of his last films, Bill exploded: "I've been going wrong because I've taken the advice of so-called Hollywood producers. From here on I follow my own instincts, I'm through with advice." Bill got angry when he was asked to talk about Africa: "Why should I tell anyone, what I think about anything?" he said. "Just because I am a star and supposedly have an image to uphold, why does that mean I should pat orphans on the head or play benefits every night or give my opinions to reporters? I don't give a damn about my image. My only obligation to the public is performance — what they see on that screen. That's all the public should ask of me. Anyway, that's all I'm giving."

Afterwards he complained bitterly about agents, lawyers, fans, reporters, interviews and invitation to cocktail parties. "I didn't ask for any of this. None of it at all."[16]

The reason for his grumpy and hostile behavior was probably the fact that, a few weeks earlier, he had received divorce papers from Ardis' attorney.

Alvarez Kelly opened in November 1966 with poor reviews and, like Bill's past five films, it was a box office failure.

The Hotel La Pace in Montecatini Terme, Tuscany, had become one of Bill's favorite destinations when he felt the need to detox. In the summer of 1966 he drove in his Ferrari from Lausanne to Montecatini to spend a few weeks relaxing at the spa. He checked into the same suite he always occupied and, under medical supervision, began a personalized diet along with a fitness program, took hot therapeutic baths and drank mineral water. At the spa Bill met Sarah and Susan West, girls from New York in their early twenties, on holiday with their family (he later found out they were granddaughters of writer Anita Loos). On the evening of July 26, the two sisters wanted to go to Viareggio, a village not too far from the spa, to visit some friends, and Bill offered the girls a ride in his Ferrari. They left at a fast speed along the highway called Firenze-Mare. At 10:15 P.M., Bill began to pass a slow-moving car, but before he could return to his lane, he collided with a small Fiat 500 coming from the opposite direction. The driver 42-year-old Giorgio Valerio Novelli, who was on his way to join his family on holiday, died in an ambulance before reaching a hospital. Bill and the West sisters escaped unhurt.

The accident was in the news all over the world. Bill was so shaken that he stayed in his hotel suite and refused to see anyone except the police, his two Italian lawyers and the American consul from Florence. He claimed that he had had two glasses of wine. On August 13, Bill was informed by his attorneys that he was formally accused of manslaughter and that he could face from six months to five years in jail. He was allowed to collect his car and leave Italy while waiting for the sentencing. Fourteen months later, on October 26, 1967, the Italian court in Lucca sentenced him to eight months in jail but suspended the sentence, citing extenuating circumstances (the slow-moving Italian driver had failed to make enough room on the highway after Bill signaled that he wanted to pass). The court also banned him from driving in Italy for eight months. Bill was not present for the verdict; he called from Switzerland to get the news. The feelings of guilt were overwhelming and his drinking went from bad to worse. Less than a month after the trial, Bill's father died of a respiratory ailment in Palm Springs.

At the end of that difficult year, producer Charles Feldman offered Bill $40,000 to play a cameo in *Casino Royale*. It was a plotless spoof of spy films, based very loosely on Ian Fleming's first James Bond's novel. Made by seven directors and an extraordinary all-star cast, the picture was shot in England; Bill, who looked prematurely aged and heavier, appeared only in its first ten minutes as one of a group of international agents together with John Huston (who was also one of the directors), Charles Boyer, Kurt Kasznar and David Niven, who played an elderly, retired Sir James Bond. *Casino Royale* was a $12 million disaster.

Bill was excited when he was offered the top role in *The Devil's Brigade*: Robert Frederick, of whom Winston Churchill said during World War II, "If we have a dozen men like him we would have smashed Hitler in 1942. He's the greatest fighting general of all time!"[17] The picture was similar in story and execution to *The Dirty Dozen*, which had opened a few months prior to great acclaim. Bill played Frederick when he was still a colonel in charge of training a group of misfit G.I.s and Canadian troops for a dangerous mission in the mountains of Italy during World War II. *The Devil's Brigade* was filmed on a Utah mountaintop; on location, Bill drank only wine, explaining that his body could no longer tolerate hard liquor. However, when the crew moved to Italy, things suddenly changed and he started drinking vodka.

Cliff Robertson, who was in the cast and had already worked with Bill in *Picnic*, became a close friend. He had a different explanation for Bill's alcohol problem: "He knew I understood him and he felt that not a lot of people understood him. He wasn't so complex; he was just a fellow all round, a good guy not that complicated. People tried to fix his tendency to drink as an indication of a great complicated personality. I think it was just the opposite. Because he wasn't a complicated personality, he probably felt a little out of sync with the complicated environment."[18]

A dangerous accident occurred because of Bill's drinking. Bill and other actors were crossing a creek holding their machine guns on their heads. Bill, who had been drinking since he woke up, noticed on a bridge a group of local people observing the scene. Suddenly he was taken by an uncontrollable rage and opened fire with his machine gun. People screamed and ran while the crew remained speechless, shocked by his violent action. After realizing his extreme behavior he was so embarrassed that left the set and went to have a drink in a little bar in the local village. The following day, with the help of a doctor called from Paris and a pretty Italian girl who "entertained" him between takes, he was able to complete his work.

At Charles Feldman's 1964 New Year's party in Hollywood, Bill had met Patricia Stauffer, a pretty blonde everybody called Peep (Bill called her "Winker"). Stauffer was from a wealthy family, she attended schools abroad and worked as a model for a few years before marrying Ted Stauffer, owner of several Hollywood restaurants and cafes. They had a daughter but divorced five years later. Patricia had all the qualities Bill liked in a woman: independent, educated and good-looking. But above all she was not an actress and therefore she was out the Hollywood circles he detested. It was not another flirtation, as many thought. The couple dated for a while and began a relationship-friendship that continued with ups and downs until Bill's death. Patricia played a key role in Bill's life: She went along on his trips around the world, visited him on the set of his last movies and most of all tried to make him overcome his personal demons, supporting him in the battle against alcohol.

One of their first trips together was to Kenya. Bill wanted to share with Pat his love for Africa, something that Ardis never really felt. Upon their return home, he announced to the press his partnership with David L. Wolper, the producer of *The Devil's Brigade*, in a series of documentaries on East Africa. He hoped they would break the myth that Africa was nothing but a continent of thick jungles, pulsating drums and strange tribal rituals, as was usually portrayed on the screen.

"There has been a lot of nonsense shown about East Africa," he explained to a journalist. "I want to show what it is really like." He hoped that when the films were completed, they would provide a useful history of Kenya.[19]

Bill planned to travel to all the chosen locations as the narrator of the nine-part TV series. The documentaries would stress conservation efforts and deal with the conquerors and invaders of East Africa, the effect on hunters on the area, and the importance of tribal superstition and magic. On December 26, 1967, Bill traveled with a group of researchers to find the most appropriate locations. Each of the nine hour-long episodes was budgeted at $500,000. Bill did not like TV, but understood that was one of the best media to get messages across and he accepted immediately a CBS bid on the series, which was called *William Holden: Unconquered Worlds*. Twenty-five-year-old David Seltzer was chosen to write the scripts and to direct. Seltzer hired a crew of Dutch technicians and 21 locals. The first episode, "Adventures at the Jade Sea," dealt with the land around Lake Rudolf (now Lake Turkana) in northwest Kenya and southwest Ethiopia, a remote area with a Moon-like landscape. Once on location, Bill started drinking beer and Campari and soda. He behaved in a difficult way, making everything hard for Seltzer, who was shocked by Bill's sudden transformation and bizarre conduct and almost quit. For a few days, Seltzer and Bill did not talk to each other. Bill continued drinking but the director was able to complete the first episode. Seltzer admitted years later that despite everything Bill put him through, he respected him professionally. However, he described him as an afflicted human.

"Adventures at the Jade Sea" aired at the end of March 1969. The other eight episodes were never produced.

12

The Wild Bunch

"You listen to people like Holden. That guy's a gas. He's lived
nine or ten lives." — Ryan O'Neal

In 1967, Warner Bros. approached director Sam Peckinpah with a
project called *The Wild Bunch*. (The storyline resembled that of a television production he had previously directed.) Peckinpah also collaborated
on the screenplay with Walom Green. *The Wild Bunch* depicts the final
days of an aging bandit gang, headed by Pike Bishop. The gang attempts
to rob the railway office of the small Texas town of San Rafael, but are
stopped by a band of mercenaries dressed like U.S. cavalrymen led by Zeke
Thornton, Bishop's former friend. Then the action moves to Mexico, where
Bishop's group gets involved in the local war against Pancho Villa and a
final challenge from Thornton.

Peckinpah wanted to cast Lee Marvin in the role of Pike Bishop,
but the actor (who had initially expressed great enthusiasm) backed away
in favor of another film. Charlton Heston, Burt Lancaster, Gregory Peck
and Robert Mitchum all received scripts from producer Phil Feldman,
but it was Bill who was finally cast in the role of Bishop. Despite Bill's
career missteps and his difficult reputation, Feldman thought that the name
William Holden was still solid, especially abroad, and he was able to hire
him for the bargain salary of $250,000 plus a percentage of the picture's
box office gross. Peckinpah agreed with Feldman's choice, believing Bill
was perfect for the part. Years of heavy drinking had thickened Bill's perfect body and curved his shoulders. But he still had charisma, with the self-
possessed cynicism of his early films giving way to a tired melancholy.

"[Pike Bishop was] what Bill Holden is today," Peckinpah said. "Fifty, middle-aged, wrinkled, no longer the glamour boy."[1]

On March 25, 1968, the complete cast, which included Robert Ryan and Ernest Borgnine, gathered around the Mexican villages of Parras and Torreon, where Peckinpah began filming. On the first day there were tense moments. Bill left the set after he watched how brutally Peckinpah treated everyone in a scene in which he (Bill) was not involved. The director asked him where he was going and Bill replied, "If that's the way things are going to be on this picture, I want no part of it."

Three days later, when Bill had his first scene, Peckinpah screamed at everyone but Bill. However, the two had another confrontation when the director asked him to wear a false mustache in the entire movie. "Like hell I will!" was Bill's immediate response, explaining that the only time he had worn a mustache, the movie had been a flop. But Peckinpah persuaded him and by the time the cameras were rolling, Bill was wearing a mustache almost identical to the real one the director had.[2]

As the shooting progressed, Bill began to resemble Peckinpah. It was not only the mustache; he also began to take on the vocal qualities and the mannerisms of his director. Editor Lou Lombardo recalled, "I told Holden one day after the dailies, 'I got you figured, you're doing Sam.' He was running that Wild Bunch just like Sam was running the movie. His gestures, his tone of voice, it was all Sam. He picked up on that. I told Sam that. He said, 'Ah, you're full of shit!' I said, 'No, I'm telling you, the guy's got you!'"[3]

Sharon Peckinpah got the same impression. "Holden was wonderful. He was a great reflector of something in my father. There are so many things that he did in *The Wild Bunch* that reminded me of Dad. In the scene were they're in Angel's village, the way Holden was sitting, his physicality reminded me very much of my father. He kind of rests his elbow on his knee and says to Jamie Sanchez, 'Either you learn to live with it or we'll leave you there' and I thought, 'Oh, Dad, I must have heard things like that a million times from you.'"[4]

"As I recall, all six of us this day had a low," said Bill about his first group scene. "The first rehearsal was just absolute chaos. It was an eight-minute scene on film, which made it long and involved. Well, Sam sat there and looked at us. And nobody knew his lines because we had somehow all felt that there would be plenty of time to get sharp on the thing. Anyway, Sam said, in this very calm but menacing voice, 'Gentlemen, you

Ben Johnson, Warren Oates, Holden and Ernest Borgnine in *The Wild Bunch* (1969).

were hired to work on this film as actors and I expect actors to know their lines when they come to work. Now I'm willing to give you twenty minutes and anyone can go wherever he wants to learn his lines. But when you come back, if you can't be an actor you will be replaced.' Well, you've never seen so many frantic people wondering off behind sagebrush and everything else leaning against adobe walls ... but getting those lines down."[5]

Peckinpah's difficult but extremely creative way of directing did not make things easy on the set. He kept replacing all the minor actors, extras and technicians who did not follow his instructions precisely. The situation became unbearable after the unit publicist was fired. Former Warner Bros. publicity head Max Bercutt had to fly down to Mexico to hear an explanation. Before meeting with Peckinpah, Bercutt talked with Bill, his old friend, who told him that the director was crazy.

When Bercutt confronted Peckinpah, Peckinpah refused to allow the publicist back on the set. "He doesn't pay attention and he annoys me."

Bercutt insisted, and Peckinpah threatened to close the set in response. Bill stepped in and said, "You better listen to Max. Let this guy stay or I walk."[6] Finally the director accepted and Bill winked at Bercutt.

The production provided Bill with a private house with servants, where he often invited people from the crew and the cast for dinner or to play poker. Pat Stauffer's visit lasted for a few days. To avoid confrontation, Bill had to move Stauffer when Ardis made a surprise appearance. Bill behaved professionally throughout the filming, drinking only Heineken beer.

He also became very close to Ernest Borgnine. Years later he told his Palm Springs neighbor Edd Byrnes that on the *Wild Bunch* set he unsuccessfully tried to find ways to steal scenes from Borgnine.[7] Borgnine also remembers Bill's great sense of humor: "William Holden ... kept the boozing to a bare minimum, at least during the shoot. And he never came to the set inebriated. Part of that, he told me, was because he wanted to marry his girl but she refused unless he gave up the bottle. He would stop for a while, but he couldn't control it. It was just too much for him, I guess."[8]

By the time *The Wild Bunch* wrapped, the budget had nearly doubled to $6 million, and the schedule had stretched to 81 days. Peckinpah had shot over 330,000 feet of film with 1,228 camera set-ups. His final cut would contain over 3,600 shot-to-shot edits — more than any other color film made up to that time.

Thanks to the director's skill, Bill was able to show Pike Bishop's vulnerability and authority. Once again, Bill proved to be a great actor, something many had already forgotten.

On May 1, 1969, over 1,000 people showed up at the Royal Theater in Kansas City to watch a sneak preview of what the Warner Bros. publicity department had called "one of the year's biggest movies!" The response to the ad in the local paper was so overwhelming that all the available seats sold out in minutes, leaving 500 people outside the theater. During the first half of the screening, several middle-aged members of the audience were so repulsed by the violence that they left the theater, some to vomit in the alley. However, for over two and a half hours, most of the audience stayed glued to their seats, horrified but also excited by the images appearing on the screen. The spectacular opening and closing shootout scenes were impressed in everyone's memory. The spectators were shocked by the extreme, graphic violence explicitly shown for the first time on film. After listening to comments from the audience, Peckinpah was convinced to cut 20 minutes, creating a version 143 minutes long with an intermission. But there were still complaints about the length and it was further cut to 115 minutes, this time against Peckinpah's will.

Rarely had a film stirred such controversy and dissension among critics. Some proclaimed *The Wild Bunch* to be one of "the best westerns ever made," a true masterpiece; others found its violence to be revolting and sickening, calling it "the bloodiest movie ever made." Most viewers either hated or loved it. Meanwhile, Bill was in the Bahamas with Borgnine and Peckinpah at the Warner Bros.–Seven Arts Film Festival, where *The Wild Bunch* was part of the program. He justified the violence in the film, explaining that what was shown was exactly what death and violence are in real life.

"When you get shot, you bleed," said Bill. "For the first time, we show it…. As far as the violence is concerned, you can see much worse on the television news reports any night of the week. We weren't trying to glorify killing; we just wanted to show what it's like getting shot."[9]

The Wild Bunch was Oscar-nominated for Best Original Story and Screenplay and Best Original Music Score and many of the film's scenes became legendary. There was a modest box office response in the States but the picture was extremely popular in Europe, where it was received with great acclaim and later became a cult movie.

In September 1969, Bill appeared in *The Christmas Tree*, produced, directed and written by Terence Young. (Young was in great demand after the success of his three James Bond films.) The British director cast Italian actress Virna Lisi as the female lead and arranged to shoot in Paris, Nice and on the island of Corsica. Bill played a widower whose eleven-year-old boy contracts leukemia through atomic radiation during a holiday in Corsica. The father and his girlfriend try their best to make the child's last six months of life memorable. The making of the picture went smoothly until the day Bill had to play a love scene with topless Lisi. Never before in his career had he shot a sex or nude scene and he refused to do it, insisting that it was vulgar and unnecessary. Young considered it realistic and a perfect touch to balance the affection between the two lovers. Nothing or nobody was able to persuade Bill to change his mind; he disappeared into his dressing room and stayed there, drinking alone. Someone from the production called Pat Stauffer in California for help and explained the situation. Pat took the first flight to Paris and convinced Bill to do the scene after the director promised more sophisticated, less vulgar nudity in it.[10]

A few months earlier, in an interview with the *Sunday Express*, Bill had clearly stated his opinion about sex scenes in films and plays, revealing the Puritanism typical of his upbringing. His views on the subject of sexual images were antithetical to his tolerant attitude toward the disturbing violence displayed in some of his previous films. "I was brought up very strictly," he said, "and what's going on now in novels and in the theater has nothing to do with my life. I understand it, but I don't have to like it. I don't want to be shown on stage how to conduct my sexual life. If a bunch of people want to sprawl around naked on the stage, that's their affair. It's got nothing to do with me."[11]

The Christmas Tree had only moderate success in Italy where Virna Lisi was a popular star, but was dismissed elsewhere by critics as a cheesy tearjerker. Its release in the States was brief and limited.

The following year Bill returned to work in *Wild Rovers*, a Western written, produced and directed by comedy master Blake Edwards, director of the hits *The Pink Panther* and *The Party*. Bill's co-star Ryan O'Neal was at the height of his popularity after the remarkable success of *Love Story* (he received the news of his Academy Award nomination on the set of *Wild Rovers*). Bill and O'Neal played two tired, bored and disenchanted cowboys who decide to brighten their dull existence by robbing a bank and fleeing to Mexico, tailed by the sons of the ranch boss. Filmed in Utah and Arizona, *Wild Rovers'* production encountered several problems, this time not caused by Bill. First, veteran actress Kim Stanley, who had a brief role, had a nervous breakdown, and Edwards had to quickly replace her. Then the new actress had a conflict of schedule and a replacement for the replacement had to be found. There were also a few electrical problems which nobody realized it until Edwards saw the dailies; several retakes were required.

A deep friendship developed between Bill and Ryan O'Neal. Bill told him his personal experiences during Hollywood's golden era, his trips around the world and his sexual adventures, as O'Neal listened with great fascination. "You listen to people like Holden. That guy's a gas. He's lived nine or ten lives," O'Neal said in a *New York Times* interview.[12]

Karl Malden, who was also in the cast, remembered that Bill "constantly sought dinner companions," enjoying being among people. Blake Edwards remembered him quite differently: "Bill was strictly a loner, who would often just take off in his car without anyone knowing where he was going and without anyone knowing how long he'd be away. He liked his privacy."[13]

Wild Rovers got a cold reception from test screening audiences, and major cuts were ordered by MGM. Edwards was reluctant but agreed after he was promised that MGM would not interfere in his next project. Forty minutes were cut and the result was disastrous. Of his arguments with MGM honchos James Aubrey and Douglas Netter, Edwards said, "There was no discussion; an integral part was simply removed. If I take a chair and remove one leg, you still have a chair, but it won't stand up, will it?"[14] He added, "[Aubrey] cut the heart right out of it. I wrote and conceived it as a classic Greek tragedy. Aubrey and Netter just said, 'The audience wants to see Ryan O'Neal.'"

In the friendship between a young and an old cowboy, many critics found homoerotic undertones. The drastic cuts made the story too confusing and its symbolism too obscure for the audiences that agreed with those reviewers who found *Wild Rovers* long, unfocused, pretentious and mostly pointless.

In the fall of 1971, Bill accepted another Western, *The Revengers*. Producer Martin Rackin had high hopes for this picture because it was reteaming Bill and Ernest Borgnine in the same Mexican location as *The Wild Bunch*.

Director Daniel Mann cast Susan Hayward in a small part because she was one of his favorites (she had previously worked with him in *I'll Cry Tomorrow* and *Ada*). Twenty-nine years earlier, Bill and Hayward had appeared in *Young and Willing* and since then they had been very good friends. Bill invited her to visit his Mount Kenya Game Ranch; she accepted but Bill later became furious when she shot a big cat during a safari and had a photograph taken of herself with her kill. The whole point of Bill's sanctuary was to preserve the lives of animals and make his celebrity guests aware of the problem of the endangered species — something Hayward seemed not to have understood. Bill forgave her eventually.[15]

Bill's 26-year-old son Scott, who had just graduated with a degree in business administration, made his screen debut in a bit part as a cavalry lieutenant. Scott nursed acting ambitions against his father's wishes;

however, Bill helped coach him. Scott received an honorable mention in *Variety*.

Although Bill drank a lot of beer on the Mexican set, he was able to do his work smoothly. Hayward was very satisfied by the experience of working with him; she told an interviewer, "As an actor, he's generous. He has enough ego that you respect him and he does his level best, and enough so he has room left over to care about the actor standing next to him."[16]

The picture was completed at the end of November, and when it opened the following June it did not meet the expectations of the reviewers. They found it too contrived, trite and disappointing; none of the glory of *The Wild Bunch* was recaptured by Wendell Mayes' script and the attractive cast.

In 1971, Bill and Ardis' divorce became final. Gossip columns said Bill's next wife would be Pat Stauffer, but Bill said that he had no wish to marry again.

Of his divorce he remarked, "Cost me a small fortune ... I had my independence, but the divorce was necessary to my way of thinking." He added that his relationship with Ardis was now "marvelous."[17]

Bill was going throughout a period of sobriety. He was very excited to star in *Breezy*, Clint Eastwood's third film as director and his first without starring in it. The picture told of the brief but intense love between a middle-aged real estate salesman and Breezy, a hippie teenager. The script was written by Jo Heims, who had previously collaborated with Eastwood on *Play Misty for Me*. The screenwriter wrote the role of Frank Harmon with Clint in mind, but he was 43 and not right for the part. Bill, twelve years Clint's senior, was perfect for it. Producer Bob Daley remembered that Eastwood said the film would not "make a dime" but he wanted to take the challenge, partly out of affection for Heims, partly because he wanted to test himself as a director with different material. Some speculated that Eastwood was attracted to the script because he was involved in a relationship with a much younger woman. Casting the title role was difficult. The actress had to be young (seventeen, according to the script) and capable of managing a few nude scenes. Eastwood selected fifteen candidates who shot screen tests, playing one scene with Bill. When the director noticed the perfect chemistry between Bill and Kay Lenz, he knew she was Breezy.

Breezy began shooting in November of 1972 and was completed in only a few weeks. It was filmed entirely in L.A., a convenient location for Bill, who had bought a beautiful Palm Springs villa seven years earlier as his primary residence when he was in California.

Breezy was a low-budget production (under $1 million) and Bill agreed to work for Eastwood for no salary, receiving instead a percentage of the profits. The movie was not a great hit and, six months after its release, the Screen Actors Guild contacted Eastwood and told him that, to comply with union rules, he had to pay Bill $4000, the minimum wage.[18]

Eastwood said of Bill, "He was just a prince to work with; he was always the first guy there ready to work." Bill returned the favor and praised his director: "I'd forgotten what it is like to make pictures this agreeably. I'll work with Clint any time he asks."[19]

On the set, Kay Lenz was full of energy. Her limited background included only a few television appearances, so working with Eastwood and Bill was an invaluable, formative experience for her. Eastwood granted her veto power over the nude scenes; unless she approved them, he would not include them in the final cut. Lenz also remembered Bill's kindness, especially during their love scenes. When she was about to undress, he would keep looking only at her eyes to make her feel comfortable; he would quickly drape his shirt around her as soon as a take was over. The actress later admitted that she could not have done those scenes without Bill's help.

In a *New York Post* interview, Bill said he found something in *Breezy* that was reminiscent of *The Moon Is Blue*; he specified, though, that his new film would not provoke a scandal like the Preminger picture did. He also asserted proudly that he had never seen a porn movie and the only X-rated film he had watched was *Midnight Cowboy*, about which he refused to comment.[20]

In *Breezy*, Scott Holden played a small part as a veterinarian; it was his last attempt to pursue an acting career. The picture had a limited release in November 1973 and hardly recovered the money invested. Universal gave *Breezy* a second chance with a nationwide release the following summer. Despite many critics' praise for Bill's performance, the audience attendance was still disappointing.

To a reporter who asked if he was ready to retire, Bill replied that he couldn't because he needed the money to finance his other interests. He also admitted that he was less well-off than the press was reporting due to bad investments and the divorce. However, he still hoped to realize a project at Wuvulu, near New Guinea in the South Pacific; there with some associates he planned to study and research endangered bird species and primates.

In 1973 Bill was persuaded by NBC to appear in one of the first TV miniseries ever produced, *The Blue Knight*. He was offered a contract and a basic salary but with a very high percentage from the theatrical release overseas. Opposite Lee Remick, Bill played Bumper Morgan, a veteran Los Angeles Police Department street cop who is near retirement age and is obsessed with solving a prostitute's murder.

The Blue Knight was entirely shot on Los Angeles locations with a high budget due to the use of a big cast and numerous extras. Between takes, Bill was often mistaken for a real cop by bystanders. Each morning he would arrive on the set on his new Black Honda motorbike, which he usually rode at high speed around the Palm Springs desert; his passion for fast vehicles was ongoing despite the tragic accident that occurred in Italy.

The four-hour miniseries was very well received when it aired in November 1973, receiving high ratings. All the critics raved about Bill's impeccable and compelling dramatic performance, which gave him a new popularity. A shorter but more explicit version was prepared for the foreign market, where it was shown in movie theaters. A few months later, Bill was nominated and deservedly won an Emmy. NBC offered him the opportunity to play Bumper Morgan in a series of 26 weekly TV episodes inspired by the miniseries but he turned them down, disliking the idea of temporarily moving back to Hollywood. The series character was played by George Kennedy.

After the amazing success of *The Blue Knight*, many wondered why Bill bothered to appear in a cameo in *Open Season*. The film was a combination of gratuitous scenes of violence and sex shot in Spain and Michigan. *New York Times* critic Nora Sayre wrote, "William Holden appears briefly in an early scene; you then spend the rest of the movie waiting for him to come back. Perhaps he was just visiting the set or taking a short cut on his way to an appointment on the lot."[21] Bill accepted the role for purely venal reasons: He made a sizable amount of money for appearing in two scenes as a *deus ex machina* to resolve the plot.

The Towering Inferno was the first picture co-produced by Warner Bros. and 20th Century–Fox. Both studios had planned to make a film with the same premise: a new glass skyscraper full of offices, apartments and restaurants suddenly goes up in flames. Producer Irwin Allen, eager to repeat the success of his *The Poseidon Adventure* (made two years earlier), convinced the two studios to join forces and produce one film instead of two similar. A $15 million budget was set, and Warner and Fox agreed to split the domestic and international gross. The direction was split between British John Guillermin, who handled the actors, and Allen, who directed the action sequences. The cast was filled with big names: Paul Newman, Steve McQueen, Fred Astaire, Robert Wagner, Jennifer Jones, Richard Chamberlain, Robert Vaughn, O.J. Simpson, Fay Dunaway and Holden.

Bill was very hesitant about making the film; he found the Stirling Silliphant script "lousy" and considered his role one-dimensional. However, the William Morris Agency, which represented him, and Pat Stauffer persuaded him to accept it. What *really* convinced him may have been the $750,000 salary, the best offered to him in years. "Guess I can't refuse good money or a good role," Bill said, justifying his choice in an interview just before the film's release.[22]

Towering Inferno shooting began on May 13, 1974, and it was scheduled to be completed within 72 days. The production needed four different filming crews and the construction of 57 sets, most of them to be burned. Among the stuntmen used in the most dangerous and spectacular sequences were future film director John Landis and Paul Newman's son Scott. According to Guillermin, there was no rivalry among the stars, who behaved like a big family on the set. The only moment of tension happened two months into the filming when Bill, distressed by the occasional tardiness of Faye Dunaway, reportedly shoved the actress against a wall and physically threatened her if she was ever later again. Dunaway suddenly became extremely punctual.

Bill's dressing room was located in front of Robert Vaughn's and the two stars got to know each other very well. Between takes they would sneak off the main set to go watch the stuntmen doing the dangerous scenes on the action set. Joseph Musso, a production illustrator, remembers Bill's kindness and friendliness with set visitors, especially members of the crew's families, who were curious to meet the stars and would ask to take pictures together with them.

As Jennifer Jones confirmed in an interview, "Bill is a gentleman of taste, manners, and kindness. He's one of the genuinely popular people in Hollywood, and in the world. Everyone has a few favorite Holden films."[23] During breaks, Bill loved to reminisce with the old crew members about films and colleagues from the past.

Postproduction of *The Towering Inferno* was rushed so the film could open for the Christmas holidays and qualify for Academy Awards. On December 10, 1974, the picture had a spectacular New York premiere and received very good reviews. It earned $55 million in the United States and almost double abroad, becoming the top grossing film of all time. In addition, the picture had an impact on changing fire laws in hotels and office buildings. "We were all very proud of that," recalled the movie's costume designer Paul Zastupnevich.[24] However, Bill was not too proud of his work, defining his character as "a cardboard cut-out."

"Everyone knows the star of that movie was a burning building," he said to the *New York Times*.[25]

13

A New Kind of Love

"Bill and I were soulmates.... He helped make me back into a human being." — Stefanie Powers

In 1974 Bill checked in at the La Costa resort and spa center in Carlsbad near San Diego to undergo a series of health treatments. There he met actress Stefanie Powers, who was participating in a celebrity tennis match and to whom he had been previously introduced at a party. By chance they met again a few weeks later in the anthropology section of a Los Angeles bookstore. Bill asked her out and slowly their friendship evolved into a romantic relationship.

Stefania Zofia Federkiewicz was born in Los Angeles on November 2, 1942. Her father, a Polish immigrant, split with her Polish-American mother when she was still a child. As a teenager, Stefanie wanted to be an archaeologist, but her mother, who had been a professional dancer, encouraged her to audition for movies.

Her first efforts were not in vain: A screen test for *West Side Story* led to a role in a film. After playing little parts in several films, Powers signed a contract with Columbia, which loaned her to other studios. In a few years she starred in fifteen films, one directed by Blake Edwards. Then in 1966 she took the lead as a sexy spy in TV's *The Girl from U.N.C.L.E.* While working on the series, Powers married actor Gary Lockwood, who later starred in Stanley Kubrick's *2001: A Space Odyssey.* The couple divorced in 1974.

Powers became a familiar TV face, appearing on several popular programs. When Bill met her, she was 32 years old and still struggling with the failure of her marriage. "Bill and I were soulmates. He came along at the lowest emotional point in my life.... He helped make me back into a human being," remembered Powers.[1]

The couple traveled extensively. Bill took her to Hong Kong, where he still owned an apartment and shares in a local radio and TV network. In less then a year they visited Malaysia, Singapore, Iran, New Guinea, Europe and finally Africa.

Stefanie immediately fell madly in love with Kenya as she explained in an interview: "I'll never forget that first trip to Africa, the primordial landscape around Lake Turkana, inhospitable as hell, a barren place, but I never felt more serene in my life."[2]

She joined forces with Bill, working for the preservation of the animal species and in the fight against big game hunting. Bill finally looked at his future with a renewed enthusiasm. At 57 he refused to think that his most significant accomplishments were behind him. He told *People* magazine about this new kind of love and Powers' positive influence on him. He even replaced alcohol with strong black coffee and cigarettes. When they were not travelling, they saw each other usually only on weekends. They also loved to ride on Bill's Honda Windjammer III. Despite 24 years difference in age, their relationship worked perfectly based on respect and fidelity.

After the media reported the couple's imminent wedding, Bill explained to *People* magazine, "Marriage isn't a consideration at all. Why ruin it? Our visits are properly spaced so that each of us can go off on our own tangents."[3] He said in a different interview, "When we got to know each other, we realized we had this great opportunity to use movie locations to study the cultures of people in remote places instead of just the amount of celluloid that has to be accomplished. Some people spend their time on location looking for good restaurants; we spend our time studying the heritage, the art, the rituals, ceremonies and mores. I've never had a relationship with any woman so fulfilling."[4]

"We were both insatiably curious about the world, about traveling to unconventional places.... It was very interesting and uncanny how much we shared," Powers revealed in a documentary about Bill.[5]

Stefanie visited Bill in Germany on the set of *21 Hours in Munich*. It was an ABC-TV film about the 1972 crisis where the Israeli Olympic Games team was taken hostage by Arab commandos during the games. Bill played the chief of the German police, Manfred Schreiber, who negotiated with terrorist leader Issa, played by Italian actor Franco Nero (one of Bill's biggest fans). ABC budgeted $2 million for production, offering $150,000 to Bill along with a percentage of film sales abroad. Bill liked the script and, since he had no other offers, accepted it and, moved for a month to Munich, where they filmed on the location where the events took place.

One day Bill invited his old friend Edd Byrnes, who was in Munich on business, to the set. Byrnes wrote in his autobiography, "I spent the afternoon with him. He was always joking about and remaining so courteous to everyone around him. He teased the director, 'I know you originally wanted Bob Mitchum for this role, but he asked too much money, so you settled on me.' He had a great self-deprecating kind of humor."

Byrnes maintained that Bill had been sober for three years and appeared to be in fantastic shape for a man in his late fifties. "As he was getting fitted for his wardrobe, I jokingly told him that he had the same body he did when he played Hal Carter in *Picnic*. He looked fit and tan and seemed to be very content with himself."[6]

21 Hours in Munich aired in prime time on November 7, 1976. The ratings were so low that ABC never broadcast it again. Although the German government cooperated on the film's production, it was never broadcast in Germany; it did air in several Arab countries.

In September 1975 Bill travelled to China on an art-buying and business trip with Stefanie and Richard Talmadge, a Manhattan lawyer friend. One evening in Beijing, Talmadge was returning to his hotel with his wife and friends after watching the New York Cosmos play a Chinese soccer team when he was stabbed by a Chinese man. Bleeding from his chest and arm wounds, the lawyer was immediately admitted to a hospital. The assailant was seized by the local police and faced the death penalty. Asked by reporters to comment about the episode, Bill described the assailant as "a mentally disturbed man." He also added, "This could have happened in any city."[7]

Upon his return to New York, Bill helped to promote photographer Peter Beard's book about vanishing Africa entitled *Longing for Darkness*, for which he wrote the introduction. Beard, now an acclaimed photographer, shared with Bill a mad love for the Dark Continent; the two had previously collaborated when Bill planned his series of documentaries on Africa.

At the end of that year, director Sidney Lumet read a script about the television industry written by Paddy Chayefsky, who had worked on it for over two years. Lumet and Chayefsky had a long history together: Now major figures in the movie industry, they first worked together in the early days of television. Lumet became very excited about being part of the new project, *Network*. Lumet agreed to direct it without changing a word of Chayefsky's script. Lumet's last three hits (*Serpico*, *Dog Day Afternoon* and *Murder on the Orient Express*) were very different films but all of them had deep psychological significance, as *Network*'s screenplay did.

The first to be cast in *Network* was Faye Dunaway. In the lead role of Howard Beale, Lumet insisted on casting an American; he was not convinced that an Australian actor like Peter Finch was a right choice, as Chayefsky had suggested. However, after Finch sent an audiotape in which he read *The New York Times* with a perfect American accent, Lumet changed his mind and cast him. The second major male role was Max Schumacher, for which several names were mentioned: Charlton Heston, Marlon Brando and Robert Mitchum (strongly pushed by Dunaway), but Lumet was hesitant.

Suddenly Bill's name crossed his mind. As he recalled in an interview, "I heard various rumors about him. I heard he was very taciturn, very private, unresponsive, did his work, went home, etc., etc. I heard that in the past there been a drinking problem and I didn't really know what to expect, except I just knew that there was something so perfect about him for that part."[8]

Holden, Robert Duvall and Peter Finch in *Network* (1976).

Lumet also spoke about noticing a real look of sadness on Bill's face in his most recent movies. The expression gave him a sense of human dignity that resembled the one Schumacher's character had.

Bill read the script, realized what a great opportunity it was, and accepted immediately. "I thought that Paddy Chayefsky had written something that contained an awful amount of truth in it, and if it wasn't completely true at this particular time it was going to be in the near future. I felt that Paddy had drawn a true-to-life character with considerable honesty and integrity and I wanted to do it. I thought it would be fun to work with people who were terribly professional and it was exactly that. It was more than fun."[9]

In March 1976, *Network*'s cast and crew rehearsed for two weeks in the ballroom of the Diplomat Hotel on Sixth Avenue and 43rd Street in New York. Production assistant Susan Landau remembered that it was during the rehearsals that the two male stars first met. "Bill and Peter took to each other instantly. I have never seen such love and recognition like that between two people; such mutual respect. Both men had been there and back in their lives, you might say, and both had been away from films for a long time. They shared so much together. Anger and respect for acting, and pride in acting. And they loved swapping stories about the old days."[10]

Bill had never rehearsed a movie for that long, but Finch and Dunaway showed him how to make use of Lumet's method. After the two-week rehearsal, the production moved to Toronto to shoot the television studio sequences. Chayefsky remembered that in Canada, "Bill and Peter and I had lunch every day and dinner every evening together and we looked so forward to these meals we almost couldn't wait for the day's shooting to be over."[11]

"Bill Holden was wonderful to work with," Faye Dunaway said in her autobiography. "He played Max with a crusty elegance and just the right mix of street smarts and schooled intellect. He and I had brushed up against each other briefly in *Towering Inferno*, a movie that has left a bad taste in his mouth. He felt the film had so exploited our names that he wanted to talk to me before we began *Network* so that we could provide a united front in making sure that didn't happen again."[12]

When the day of shooting a long love scene with Dunaway's brief nudity arrived, Bill again was terrified to do it. He expressed his point of view to Lumet, which he also repeated in an interview with the *New York Times*. "In general, I don't care for scenes of copulation. Certain functions of the human body are bloody private."[13]

The director explained to him the importance of that particular scene, which confirmed the awkwardness of Diana's character (played by Dunaway) in a funny-sad sequence. Lumet's argument convinced Bill, who trained himself internally to reach the right emotional and physical balance the scene required. Even though it was a closed set on that day, the scene was still not easy. Dunaway said it was the most difficult love scene she had ever done. Lumet shot that sequence in a series of cuts, all carefully orchestrated. It was filmed a piece at a time, from every angle, and then in the editing phase he was able to make it look continuous and fluid.

"The only way we all got through it was with a huge measure of good humor," recalled Dunaway. "It all worked to relieve the tension both Bill and I felt, and there was tension on that day to spare."[14]

Lumet completed *Network* eight days under schedule and $700,000 under budget. Film distributor United Artists was very nervous about this crude, fierce satire on TV — a new and delicate subject never showed on the big screen. *Network* told the story of a TV network that cynically exploits an ex–TV anchor's ravings and revelations about the media for their own profit. When he announces that he will commit suicide on live television in two weeks, what follows, along with skyrocketing ratings, is the anchorman's descent into insanity, during which he fervently rages against the medium that made him a celebrity.

Network made a great deal of money and received ten Academy Award nominations; Bill and Peter Finch were both nominated in the same category (Best Performance by an Actor in a Leading Role). In January 1977, the Australian actor suddenly died of a heart attack and two months later became the first actor to win the award posthumously. Bill knew that *Network* was the best film he had made in fifteen years and wanted to win; however, when Finch's widow accepted the Oscar on behalf of her husband, his teary eyes proved his genuine happiness for his departed friend.

After *Network*, Bill was once again in great demand. He accepted $750,000 to star in *Damien: Omen II*, a sequel to the 1976 horror hit *The Omen* in which Gregory Peck had played the lead. (Bill had previously turned down the role in *The Omen*.) In this sequel, Bill was Richard Thorn, Damien's uncle, brother of the character played by Peck.

Because Richard Donner, director of *The Omen*, was busy filming *Superman* in England, the film's producer and screenwriter Harvey Bernhard offered it to Michael Hodges. The Chicago production of *Damien* was plagued by a series of problems. First a crew member was involved in a fatal traffic accident, and then the whole crew came down with a rare form of influenza, despite no reported outbreak in Chicago. Ten days into shooting, 20th Century–Fox replaced Hodges because his perfectionism was pushing the production over budget. Don Taylor finally completed the film, only a day over schedule. Taylor had a personal relationship with Bill, having acted together with him in *Submarine Command* and *Stalag 17* in the 1950s.

Bill said to the press regarding *Damien*, "That first picture did very well with audiences. They found it enjoyable, and I found it interesting to work in a picture of this genre. But it's not *my* genre."[15]

By the time *Damien: Omen II* hit theaters in the

Holden in *Damien — Omen II* (1978).

summer of 1978, its paperback was already a bestseller in bookstores. It grossed nearly $30 million but received mixed reviews. Many found the plot predictable with "no scares" and "few surprises," lacking the depth of the original. Bill's performance was considered "a waste." However, Fox was so satisfied with the results that it immediately financed a third installment, followed by a fourth many years later. Both later sequels were unsuccessful.

That summer Bill announced to the press that his next film would be *Cormorant* with French actress Anouk Aimée and E.G. Marshall under Costa-Gavras' direction. "*Damien* might not reach an audience that'll appreciate what Costa-Gavras has to say," he declared. "So, in a sense, I'm broadening the spectrum of audience reaction to my work."[16] The international project was ultimately aborted and Bill ended up working with his favorite director, Billy Wilder, for the fourth time.

Bill arrived on the Greek island of Corfu in the end of May, where the shooting of *Fedora* was about to begin. Wilder had chosen to make another Hollywood Gothic, a *Sunset Blvd.* variation. It was a melodrama about eternal youth and fame linked to the cynical movie industry.

Fedora was based on Thomas Tryon's novel *Crowned Heads*, in which

American independent producer Barry Detweller arrives on Corfu to offer Fedora, a film star who had inexplicably gone into seclusion at her peak, the chance to star in an *Anna Karenina* remake. Detweller finds out that Fedora's daughter has assumed the appearance of her mother, the latter having been disfigured by an overdose of special pharmaceuticals in an effort to keep her young.

For the role of Fedora, Wilder wanted Greta Garbo, but no one could convince the legendary actress to return to the screen in what could have been the most sensational comeback in Hollywood. Wilder sent the script to Marlene Dietrich, offering her the part of the old Fedora, and Faye Dunaway the young one. Offended by the proposal, Dietrich sent it back immediately and included a five-word note written in huge capital letters, "HOW COULD YOU POSSIBLY THINK!"

At Sydney Pollack's suggestion, Bill gave both roles to Swiss actress Marthe Keller (star of *Bobby Deerfield* and *Marathon Man*), a bad choice which he quickly regretted. To play old Fedora, Keller was supposed to wear a special silicon mask, but Wilder found out that the actress had been involved in a traffic accident and undergone surgery that made her facial tissues too sensitive to tolerate the mask. He was then forced to split the role as originally conceived and cast veteran German actress Hildegard Knef.

Bill played "difficult" before accepting the Barry Detweller role, which required his presence for the entire shooting in Greece, Paris and Munich. He demanded a hefty sum through his agent, but Wilder knew that he would lower his asking price eventually. Wilder's only concern about casting Bill was that it would reinforce the parallel with *Sunset Blvd.*

"He has a seriousness, a presence, a maturity, a solidity which makes him indispensable.... He's maybe the only actor in Hollywood his age who hasn't had facelifts. It's remarkable in a city where, with pieces of skin that have been cut from the face of one star you could make five or six new ones."[17]

From the beginning, Keller and Wilder were a mismatch. The actress complained that the director treated her like a puppet, not giving her a chance to act a scene the way she felt. Wilder told her that he would print only those scenes she performed the way he ordered her. Keller was in tears on the plane from Greece to Munich. She told Bill she could not work any longer with a director like that. Bill consoled her, but also observed that every time he had made a film with Wilder he got an Oscar nomination.

She later confessed to have found Bill a bore and avoided socializing with him. She complained privately that all he did was tell stories about the Hollywood "golden era" she had already heard. Wilder made things harder when he started ridiculing Al Pacino, Keller's current boyfriend, who was visiting her on the set (he only wanted to eat hamburgers, despite being in Europe). Keller was so distressed that she nearly quit. When the film was completed, Wilder said that Keller lacked charm and class, but above all she lacked passion (probably, he maintained, because of her Swiss origin). "If I had it to do over again, I would rewrite 60 percent of it, and I would test and test and test [for the female lead role]."[18] After he realized that Keller's voice didn't sound similar to Knef's, Wilder had both parts dubbed by actress Inga Bunsch.

Fedora completed its sixty-day shooting schedule on August 31, 1977, with a $7 million budget. In Santa Barbara, a preview audience's reaction was disappointing. In May 1978, the picture had its official premiere at the Cannes Film Festival during a special Billy Wilder retrospective. French and Italian critics loved *Fedora*, but not the American press. A year later the film opened in New York quite successfully thanks to the local critics who trumpeted it. Nevertheless, the picture had a limited nationwide release. It performed very well in Germany and France.

Aware of all the criticisms the film received, Bill commented diplomatically, "I find it hard to be objective any more. The movie works if you're a Billy Wilder buff. It's highly stylized, and, to me, highly reminiscent of *Sunset Blvd.* Yet it's not in the storytelling, though it does concern itself with the film business and an aging actress." He also remarked once again how rewarding it was working with Wilder "and hearing his constant barrage of witticisms. On top of it, he's very understanding of actors."[19]

In 1979, Bill returned to Kenya with Stefanie Powers, this time to play a cameo in an unmemorable adventure called *Ashanti*. The location and the financial reward were good reasons to accept that job. Bill played a helicopter pilot who loses his life helping a World Health Organization doctor save his kidnapped wife from a sex slave trader. He shot all his scenes in two weeks. He became a good friend of Michael Caine, the film's lead, and stayed in touch with him after he returned to the States.

Despite the exotic scenery and an international all-star cast including Peter Ustinov, Rex Harrison, Omar Sharif and Kabir Bedi, *Ashanti* scored below-average at the box office. Caine admitted that the picture was the worst he ever starred in and the reviews confirmed it.

On April 3, 1978, looking elegant in a black tuxedo, Bill appeared with Barbara Stanwyck at Hollywood's Dorothy Chandler Pavilion for the fiftieth Oscar ceremony, presenting the Best Achievement in Sound. Master of ceremonies Bob Hope introduced the couple saying, "There's a lot of gold being given out tonight, but Hollywood will never run out of it as long as we have treasures like the next two stars. He made his sensational screen debut in *Golden Boy*, and we'll never forget his leading lady whose performances were never less than twenty-four karat. The Golden Boy and the Golden Girl are together again tonight. William Holden and Barbara Stanwyck!"

After a roar of applause Bill launched into an impromptu speech: "Before Barbara and I present this next award, I'd like to say something. Thirty-nine years ago this month, we were working in a film together called *Golden Boy*. It wasn't going well because I was going to be replaced. But due to this lovely human being and her interest and understanding and her professional integrity and her encouragement and above all, her generosity, I'm here tonight."

Stanwyck was so moved, she was only able to whisper, "Oh, Bill." After they alternated reading the nominees, she gave the envelope to him and said, "And here, my golden boy, you read it."

At the end of the year, while visiting Stefanie on the set of her film *Escape to Athena*, Bill decided to appear as an unpaid and unbilled extra playing an American prisoner of war. It was a brief sequence in another bad movie, shot on the Greek island of Rhodes and featuring international stars. A real role was offered him in 1979 when *The Towering Inferno*'s Irwin Allen began casting *The Day the World Ended*. Bill accepted it, hoping to be part of another blockbuster, but unfortunately was a big mistake.

Based on the 1969 Gordon Thomas–Max Morgan-Witts novel, it was about the 1902 volcano eruption near the tropical island resort village of St. Pierre in Martinique, where 30,000 people lost their lives. Some scenes played like a remake of Mervyn LeRoy's 1961 *Devil at Four O'Clock* with Frank Sinatra and Spencer Tracy.

The Day the World Ended was shot on location on the Kona Coast in Hawaii, where Bill was reunited with Paul Newman and Ernest Borgnine and met new co-stars Jacqueline Bisset and Burgess Meredith. Director James Goldstone was aware of the weaknesses of the script and insisted on rehearsals in a local hotel before filming began, with the purpose of receiving input and suggestions from all cast members to give more depth to its characters and more suspense to the story. Working in humid conditions in tropical heat and sudden rains put the production behind schedule and made the shoot physically demanding. When Goldstone filmed some scenes in natural caves on the islands, Allen wanted the special effects men to add some fake geysers to make things more visually interesting. A few days later the island was hit by a strong earthquake and steam naturally burst from underground.

Part of the problem the production encountered was that Allen didn't have enough financial backing. As Ernest Borgnine admitted, "Shooting in Hawaii was extremely costly and meant cutting corners on the sets and all the important special effects, which were downright cheesy."[20]

On the set Bill behaved bizarrely as a consequence of an alcohol relapse. He was often nervous and restless and controlled himself only when Stefanie visited him for a few days. The director and other cast members feared that in that condition, it would be impossible for him to perform the most difficult scenes, which he did eventually. However, Goldstone became so preoccupied that Bill asked for medical help. His health did not improve.

Afterward, the set moved to the Burbank Studios and MGM's Stage 30 to film all the interiors. One day when all the principal actors were required to shoot close-ups for a difficult scene, Bill showed up hours late and completely drunk. He almost passed out and the set had to be closed. The next day, deeply embarrassed by this behavior, Bill agreed, on Stefanie's suggestion, to enter St. John's Hospital in Santa Monica, returning to the set one week later to complete his work. The delay was costly for the film's producers, but no one told him out of respect for his professional reputation.

The picture was in trouble long before its opening. Advance word on it was bad, insiders predicting a major flop. Warner Bros. decided to change the title to *When Time Ran Out* but the $20 million movie was indeed a flop when it opened on March 28, 1980, grossing a pitiful $1.7 million and bringing the era's disaster cycle to an end.

14

Lousy Fadeout

....
"People look at me and say, 'My God, you've aged.' And I say,
I'm glad you found the formula not to."—William Holden
....

Bill's relationship with Stefanie Powers deteriorated. Bill was unable to cope with his drinking problem any more; Powers was enjoying great popularity thanks to the success of the television series *Hart to Hart*, written by Sidney Sheldon and co-starring Robert Wagner. Tabloids reported on their failing romance, telling how violent Bill became when drunk, how remorseful when sober. There was a rumor of an incident in which Bill held a loaded gun to his head for 90 minutes because Stefanie had refused to marry him.[1] Unsuccessfully, the actress tried different ways to help him. In the end she had to break off the relationship because she could not take it any more.

In June 1979, Bill was asked to star in a film to be shot in the wild Australian bush. After reading the script, he felt it was a particularly good role as well as an opportunity to get his relationship with Powers back on track. Before leaving the country, he attended group therapy in an alcoholic rehabilitation center for a few weeks in Orange, California. *The Earthling* was the story of Patrick Foley, a man dying of cancer who finds a lost seven-year-old orphan in the forest where the man plans to die. Unable to accompany the boy back to the civilized world, he reluctantly brings him on his trip and teaches the boy rugged survival.

British director Peter Collinson was also dying of an inoperable prostate cancer (he passed away two months before the picture opened in the States) and knew it. His approach to the film (which was supposed to be about a joyful celebration of a boy's coming of age) became something very pessimistic, departing from the story's real meaning. Once again, Collinson confirmed his reputation as a difficult director, his attacks aimed mostly at the Australian crew and at nine-year-old Ricky Schroder, who would become extremely popular after starring in Franco Zeffirelli's worldwide hit *The Champ* a few months later. On the Australian set, Collinson tormented Schroder heartlessly until Bill intervened. He warned the director to stop his despicable behavior or pay the consequences. Despite their gap in age, Bill established a wonderful friendship with Schroder, whom he told stories of his trips around the world. Bill showed him a collection of several old maps which later became Schroder's passion. Years later Ricky named his first son Holden in honor of Bill.

The Earthling cost $4 million; the production company, Filmways, disliked the final product and feared a loss. They ordered drastic re-editing while also adding a different musical score. When the picture was first shown in Australia in July 1980, many complained how little action was present in the plot. Bill and Schroder were profoundly disappointed watching the new cut; both had hoped that the changes would improve the film.[2] American theaters showed the film for a very limited time in February 1981.

During the entire shooting of *The Earthling*, Bill stayed away from alcohol. On his way back home he stopped in Hong Kong, where he had sold his pied-à-terre but maintained his investments in communications broadcasting. At his hotel he celebrated the end of the film by drinking until boarding his flight to California the following morning. He landed without remembering anything he had done in the past few days. Back in Palm Springs, his drinking binges went on and Pat Stouffer, with whom he had resumed his friendship before leaving for Australia, tried to rescue him. Bill was sober when he completed the dubbing of some *When Time Ran Out* scenes and when he delivered the eulogy for Stouffer's father. Suddenly, in December 1979, the situation worsened again when he showed up very late and completely wasted outside Stefanie Powers' house during her Christmas party, embarrassing Powers and her guests.

During the Hawaiian shooting of *When Time Ran Out*, when Bill's behavior was out of control, actress Ava Readdy suggested calling Michael Klassman, a close friend and psychotherapist specializing in the treatment of alcoholics and drug addicts. Klassman flew from Los Angeles to Hawaii and found Bill in a severe stage of alcoholism with signs of intense depression. The doctor-patient relationship was very stormy. Bill denied having a drinking problem and refused to discuss it. When events escalated, Klassman was able to persuade Bill to enter St. John's Hospital in Santa Monica. Klassman then visited Bill's Palm Springs home every day for four months, spending long hours talking to him. In the earliest sessions Bill was very taciturn. The doctor worked hard to gain his patient's trust and have Bill talk freely. Klassman realized that Bill was in denial on some serious issues related to his status as a movie star. Being famous only for his acting ability was unacceptable for him; it was not as satisfactory as any other job in any other field that could help humankind. He was also very lonely; felt guilty about the fact that his brothers had died without knowing how much he loved them; and regretted that he had not been close enough to his children West and Scott. He compared himself to his own father who never hugged him and never verbalized his pride in Bill. Bill thought he had sacrificed his relationship with his children for devotion to a profession he despised. He also felt guilt over Stefanie Powers, with whom he often had talked of marriage but never at the right moment. He had promised her he would quit drinking and never did. Eventually, his horrible behavior drove her away.

Klassman was able to see that the origins of Bill's problems were his parents, who raised him strictly and were detached from him, never showing him any physical affection. Although he had become a Hollywood star, his father never forgave him for abandoning his career in chemistry. The result was that Bill was unable to commit to love, be intimate with anyone, or have a real friendship or lasting relationship. Except at the very beginning, even his long marriage with Ardis had never been a happy one. He considered himself and his life a complete failure. Now alcohol had made him an insomniac and impotent. His health and his body were in terrible shape. His heavy drinking reflected all the typical alcoholic symptoms: a face with deep lines, red nose, puffy eyes and grayish, prematurely aged skin. His liver and kidney were also in very poor condition. Often his hands would shake and his lapses of memory became more frequent. He was profoundly disturbed by the situation but not enough to quit. Klassman persuaded Bill to attend AA meetings, but once there he was too embarrassed to rise from his chair and admit his problem. Getting drunk was easier; it meant running away to escape into another world and to anesthetize himself into a long, slow suicide.

Getting older, Bill had become more aloof; however, thanks to Klassman's therapy he was able to reconnect with his children, especially his long-estranged son Scott. As Scott remembered in an interview, "In the last two years we seemed to run into each other more often than usual.... He did stop by to see us [in Geneva] and he did see his grandchild.... He was thrilled to death about that and there was a different look in his eyes.... I think he tried to reassure me that the love had always been there for us even though he didn't have the time to necessarily express it all the time. And he always did care and his concerns were genuine and he was genuine and consequently we had a much warmer relationship. It was sort like finding each other after so much time."[3]

Earlier that month, the *National Enquirer* ran the story "William Holden's Agonizing Battle to Save His Longtime Love." The tabloid alleged that Bill was getting cured by a German doctor in order to keep Stefanie Powers from abandoning him. After visiting Scott in Switzerland, Bill did meet cancer specialist Hans Napier in Germany to ask advice about his alcoholism; his visit created a pandemonium among the European tabloids that reported him ill with terminal lung cancer. Bill tried to call a few friends in the Hollywood press to set the record straight but the rumors would not go away and he fell into a mild depression.

At the end of 1980, Bill finally snapped out of his gloominess, got back in shape and looked forward to starring in Blake Edwards' new film *S.O.B.* The director was now at the top of his career after the success of *10* and the *Pink Panther* films. He had originally planned and announced *S.O.B.* in the early '70s but was not able to realize until a decade later.

S.O.B. (which stands for standard operational bullshit, referring to the fake but normative way people behave in the show business) was a fierce satire on success in Hollywood, based on by Edwards' own experiences, written with his typical sharp irony and packed with references to Hollywood's past both on and off the screen. It was an original example of life imitating art. Upon its release, the media tried to guess who the real-life models for the fictional characters were. The film told of the last days of Felix Farmer, a Hollywood producer who suffers a nervous breakdown after his big-budget, wholesome family film starring his actress-singer wife (played by Julie Andrews, Edwards' wife) bombs. In the story a series of characters represented the worst Hollywood stereotypes, from the ruthless agent to the opportunist producer.

Working again with Edwards was a pleasant experience for Bill. The director defined him as a "gentleman from a different era with solid values" and remembered him as a "dashing" man, still handsome even in his sixties and arriving on the set on his motorcycle. The role of a lesbian agent went to Shelley Winters. Bill had not seen her in years. Winters had just published her autobiography in which she revealed their Christmas trysts in the 1950s. He treated her kindly but avoided her off the set.

His relationship with Julie Andrews was friendlier as she revealed in an interview: "William is a trouper. When we worked together, I thought to myself, it's true, all I've heard about what fun it is working with William Holden. The whole set, everybody in S.O.B., was like a large family; Blake and William had worked together before and they had real affection for each other, which rubbed off on the rest of us."[4]

S.O.B., Bill's last film, got mixed reviews, with the naysayers calling it vulgar and unfunny. The best reviews came from Europe where the picture was considered a little gem of satire, becoming a cult movie years later.

In January 1981 Bill did not attend the inauguration party for President Ronald Reagan because he feared he might drink too much and make a spectacle of himself. He spent the following summer promoting S.O.B. and resting in his Palm Springs home, often in Pat Stauffer's company. He frequently went to L.A. to discuss the upcoming That Championship Season, in which he was to play the role of a basketball team coach. Bill owned an apartment in the Shorecliff Towers, a luxury condo in Santa Monica overlooking the beach; he used it when he had business in Hollywood instead of commuting back to Palm Springs.

"Even when he was in town he was a loner," remembered his S.O.B. castmate Robert Webber. "Bill did not need a lot of people around him. He could be very self-contained." This remark was echoed by many of his friends, who complained that he had became too solitary, avoiding all social occasions.

Bill's last public appearance was in the spring of 1981, when he attended a tribute to Barbara Stanwyck at Lincoln Center in New York. Bill had some very moving words for his beloved old friend, to whom he was eternally grateful for the support she gave him at the beginning of his career.

In August 1981, Bill was depressed about the death of dear friend Paddy Chayefsky. The offer of That Championship Season and a second film, Dime Novel Sunset, made him eager to return to work.

On November 3, Bill informed Elaine Keating, his housekeeper in

Palm Springs, that he was going to spend a couple of weeks to Santa Monica, and to tell anyone who called that he was out of town. Brian Keating, Bill's butler and Elaine's husband, prepared a suitcase and put it in the trunk of Bill's Mercedes. Thirteen days later, the Keatings had not heard a word from him. For more than a week Bill had not called Pat Stauffer, with whom he was going out again, nor Stefanie Powers. He had fired his housekeeper in Santa Monica and spent all his time locked in his condo after Jason Miller, author of *That Championship Season*, informed him that making of the film had been postponed to January. Bill was depressed and was drinking a lot. He would open his door only to Bill Martin, the manager of the building, who fixed small problems inside the apartment. Bill would lock himself in his bedroom and come out only when the work was done. In the following days Martin did not worry. He would stand outside the door of the apartment and, because he could hear the television or other noises, he assumed that Bill was all right. In his last telephone conversation with Stauffer, Bill told her he wished to take a trip abroad with her. After Bill's death, Stauffer revealed to the press that she and Bill were planning to wed in Kenya on New Year's Eve, the 17th anniversary of their meeting. Many, though, thought that that news was only Stauffer's fantasy since she had said that the only other person aware of their weeding plans was Mary Beedle, Bill's mother, now 86, who was living in the senior community of Leisure World in Orange County.

"He would not have bothered his mother about this," Bill's butler told the *New York Post*.[5] Stauffer replied, "Bill and I were very close and it had been all over between him and Stefanie [Powers] for over a year when we reached this decision. The last time we were together, about two weeks before he died, he talked about how lucky we were to have had a love so few people ever experience, and that it was now time for 'Ma and Pa Kettle' to settle down.... Bill was a very private person and we kept our relationship very, very private from the world. I was in the center of a very guarded world of Bill's that consisted of just a few close people. He kept in touch with Glenn Ford, his old friend from their days at Columbia together, Brian Keating, his butler, with whom he always kept in contact, Stefanie Powers, and myself!"[6]

Billy and Audrey Wilder had planned to spend the weekend of November 14 with Bill at his home in Palm Springs. (Wilder was eager to go, not only to see Bill but also to take a break from *Buddy, Buddy*, the film he was directing.) When Wilder called Bill's home to reconfirm, Elaine

Keating told him that Bill wasn't there. Nobody knew where he was. The Wilders were disappointed and spent the weekend at home.

In his last days, Bill was reading the script of *Dime Novel Sunset*, a western in which he hoped to co-star with Glenn Ford (who might have been the last person to have seen him alive). The actor confirmed that he had met with Bill about four days before his body was discovered.

"I've lost my best friend," said Ford in tears. "He was my best man when I was married.... We were friends since 1938."[7]

Bob Hope, Bill's neighbor in Palm Springs and his friend for thirty years, said, "I don't know what it was that caused those depressive moments when he would drink. His career was a success, he had friends and money. Who knows what causes those things?"[8]

Stefanie Powers heard the news of Bill's death on the radio. She immediately called his apartment to ask the police to wait for her arrival before they removed the body; she wanted to see him one last time. The police did not grant her request. Powers later suffered a nervous collapse. Production of *Hart to Hart* was shut down while she recuperated.

Deane Johnson, Bill's lawyer for thirty-five years, told the press that there would be no funeral or memorial service, per his client's instructions. Bill had given instructions to the Neptune Society, a Burbank corporation, to cremate his body and to disperse the ashes in the Pacific Ocean. On November 22, the first Sunday after Bill's death became known, Stefanie Powers had a small "farewell gathering" at her house for some of Bill's closest friends including Natalie Wood, Robert Wagner, James Stewart, Richard Widmark, Billy and Audrey Wilder, Lee Remick, Capucine, Blake Edwards, Julie Andrews and Bill's goddaughter Patti Davis. Billy Wilder with his subtle irony later commented, "I really loved Bill, but it turned out I just didn't know him. If somebody had said to me, 'Holden's dead,' I would assumed that he had been gored by a water buffalo in Kenya, that he had died in a plane crash approaching Hong Kong, that a crazed jealous woman had shot him and he drowned in a swimming pool. But to be killed by a bottle of vodka and a night table — what a lousy fadeout for a great guy."[9]

A few days later, attorney Melvin Mason made public Bill's will, dated April 6, 1979. Bill made Ardis a beneficiary of a trust holding his residuary estate, which provided that income was to be paid to her, to his children and to his mother. In a codicil to the will, Bill added his niece, the child of Bill's deceased brother, as a beneficiary of his estate. In addition, he made a $250,000 bequest to Stefanie Powers, $50,000 to Capucine and $50,000 to Pat Stauffer. Bill bequeathed his extensive gun collection in equal shares to his sons. Peter and Scott also received $75,000 bequests and were nominated beneficiaries of the residuary trust. Bill's valuable collection of antiques and Oriental primitive art was donated to the Palm Springs Desert Museum. All Bill's property and business interests in Kenya were to be given to a charity interested in the preservation of wildlife and the environment.

Powers took up all of Bill's causes after his death. One of them was the establishment of the William Holden Wildlife Foundation, which she organized with the help and approval of Bill's partners in the Kenya game ranch, Don Hunt, Iris Breidenbend and Warner Communications president Dean Johnson.

In an interview she explained, "We decided to do this purely because we loved him and we wanted to see some of these things not fall by the wayside.... All the projects planned by the group, which would carry Bill's wishes, included a wildlife education center to instruct native Africans in wildlife preservation, repopulating Kenya with ostriches (a species killed by natives for food and plumes) and compensating game wardens injured on duty."[10]

In March 1983, Powers won a legal battle to partially consign that fraction of Bill's estate destined to a charity interested in the preservation of African wildlife to the William Holden Wildlife Foundation instead of the African Fund for Endangered Wildlife selected by the will's executor. She considered the fund unsuitable and obtained an order from a judge that before any money was given, Title Insurance and Trust Company had to monitor the organization's progress in their activities.

Nowadays thanks to its foundation president Powers, the William Holden Wildlife Foundation still carries out Bill's unfinished work and carries on with his dream.

At the Oscar ceremony in March 1982, Barbara Stanwyck received an honorary award. Holding the statuette in her hands, the actress touchingly paid tribute to Bill: "A few years ago, I stood on this stage with William Holden as a presenter. I loved him very much and I miss him. He always wished I would get an Oscar. And tonight, my Golden Boy, you got your wish!"

Billy Wilder wrote an epitaph, which in just a few words described William Holden's true spirit:

Here lies a very successful man, who spontaneously gave up his profession to devote himself to preserve endangered species. He did not take much care of himself so he killed himself. However, what he neglected to consider was that he himself was an endangered species as well: The Handsome American.[11]

Filmography

Prison Farm

1938. Paramount. *Director:* Louis King; *Producers:* William LeBaron, Stuart Walker; *Screenplay:* Stuart Anthony, Eddie Welch, Robert Yost.

    Cast: Shirley Ross (Jean Forest), Lloyd Nolan (Larry Harrison), John Howard (Dr. Roi Conrad), Esther Dale (Cora Waxley), William Holden (Prisoner).

Million Dollar Legs

1939. Paramount. *Directors:* Nick Grinde, Edward Dmytryk; *Producer:* William C. Thomas; *Screenplay:* Richard English, Lewis R. Foster.

    Cast: Betty Grable (Carol Parker), John Hartley (Greg Melton Jr.), Donald O'Connor (Sticky Boone), Jackie Coogan (Russ Simpson), Dorothea Kent (Susie Quinn), Joyce Mathews (Bunny Maxwell), William Holden (Student).

Golden Boy

1939. Columbia. *Director:* Rouben Mamoulian; *Producer:* William Perlberg; *Screenplay:* Lewis Meltzer, Daniel Taradash, Sarah Y. Manson, Victor Heerman, based on a play by Clifford Odets.

    Cast: Barbara Stanwyck (Lorna Moon), William Holden (Joe Bonaparte), Adolphe Menjou (Tom Moody), Lee J. Cobb (Mr. Bonaparte), Joseph Calleia (Eddie Fuseli), Beatrice Blinn (Anna Bonaparte).

Each Dawn I Die

1940. Warner Bros. *Director:* William Keighley; *Producers:* David Lewis, Louis F. Edelman; *Screenplay:* Norman Reilly Raine, Warren Duff and Charles Perry, based on a novel by Jerome Odlum.

    Cast: George Raft ("Hood" Stacey), James Cagney (Frank Ross), George Bancroft (Warden John Armstrong), Jane Bryan (Joyce Conover). Maxie Rosenbloom (Fargo Red), Stanley Ridges (Muller), William Holden (Bit).

Invisible Stripes

1940. Warner Bros. *Director:* Lloyd Bacon; *Producer:* Hal Wallis, Louis F. Edelman; *Screenplay:* Jonathan Finn, based on a novel by Lewis E. Lawes.

Cast: George Raft (Cliff Taylor), Jane Bryan (Peggy), William Holden (Tim Taylor), Humphrey Bogart (Chuck Martin), Flora Robson (Mrs. Taylor), Paul Kelly (Ed Kruger), Lee Patrick (Molly), Margot Stevenson (Sue).

Our Town

1940. United Artists. *Director:* Sam Wood; *Producer:* Sol Lesser; *Screenplay:* Thornton Wilder, Frank Craven and Harry Chandlee, based on a play by Thornton Wilder.

Cast: Frank Craven (Mr. Morgan, the Narrator), William Holden (George Gibbs), Martha Scott (Emily Webb), Fay Bainter (Mrs. Gibbs), Beulah Bondi (Mrs. Webb), Thomas Mitchell (Dr. Gibbs), Guy Kibbee (Charles Webb), Stuart Erwin (Howie Newsome).

Those Were the Days!

1940. Paramount. *Director and Producer:* J. Theodore Reed; *Screenplay:* Don Hartman, based on *Siwash Stories* by George Fitch.

Cast: William Holden (P. J. "Petey" Simmons), Bonita Granville (Martha Scroggs), Judith Barrett (Mirabel Allstairs), Ezra Stone (Alexander "Allie" Bangs), Vaughan Glaser (Judge Malachi Scroggs), Douglas Kennedy (Allen).

Arizona

1941. Columbia. *Director and Producer:* Wesley Ruggles; *Screenplay:* Claude Binyon, based on a story by Clarence Budington Kelland.

Cast: Jean Arthur (Phoebe Titus), William Holden (Peter Muncie), Warren William (Jefferson Carteret), Porter Hall (Lazarus Ward), Paul Harvey (Solomon Warner), George Chandler (Haley), Edgar Buchanan (Judge Bogardus).

I Wanted Wings

1941. Paramount. *Director:* Mitchell Leisen; *Producer:* Arthur Hornblow Jr.; *Screenplay:* Richard Maibaum, Beirne Lay Jr., Sig Herzig, based on a story by Eleanore Griffin and Frank Wead.

Cast: Ray Milland (Jeff Young), William Holden (Al Ludlow), Wayne Morris (Tom Cassidy), Constance Moore (Carolyn Bartlett), Veronica Lake (Sally Vaughn), Brian Donlevy (Captain Mercer).

Texas

1941. Columbia. *Director:* George Marshall; *Producer:* Sam Bischoff; *Screenplay:* Horace McCoy, Lewis Meltzer, Michael Blankfort, based on a story by Lewis Meltzer and Michael Blankfort.

Cast: William Holden (Dan Thomas), Glenn Ford (Tod Ramsey), Claire Trevor

("Mike" King), George Bancroft (Windy Miller), Edgar Buchanan (Doc Thorpe), Andrew Tombes (Tennessee).

The Remarkable Andrew

1942. Paramount. *Director:* Stuart Heisler; *Producer:* Richard Blumenthal; *Screenplay:* Dalton Trumbo, from his own novel.

Cast: William Holden (Andrew Long), Ellen Drew (Peggy Tobin), Brian Donlevy (General Andrew Jackson), Rod Cameron (Jesse James), Richard Webb (Randall Stevens), Porter Hall (Art Slocumb), Montagu Love (George Washington), George Watts (Benjamin Franklin), Gilbert Emery (Thomas Jefferson).

The Fleet's In

1942. Paramount. *Director:* Victor Schertzinger; *Producer:* Paul Jones; *Screenplay:* Walter de Leon, Sid Silvers, Ralph Spence, based on a story by Monte Brice and J. Walter Ruben and on a play by Kenyon Nicholson, Charles Robinson and Paul Jones.

Cast: William Holden (Casey Kirby), Dorothy Lamour (The Countess), Eddie Bracken (Barney Waters), Betty Hutton (Bessie Day), Barbara Britton (Eileen Wright), Cass Daley (Cissie), Gill Lamb (Spike), Jimmy Dorsey and his Orchestra.

Meet the Stewarts

1942. Columbia. *Director:* Alfred E. Green; *Producers:* Robert Sparks, Henry Freulich, *Screenplay:* Karen DeWolf, based on Elizabeth Dunn's *Candy and Mike Stewart* magazine stories.

Cast: William Holden (Michael Stewart), Frances Dee (Candance Goodwin), Grant Mitchell (Mr. Goodwin), Marjorie Gateson (Mrs. Goodwin), Anna Revere (Geraldine Stewart), Margaret Hamilton (Willametta).

Young and Willing

1943. United Artists. *Director and Producer:* Edward H. Griffith; *Screenplay:* Virginia Van Upp, based on the play *Out of the Frying Pan* by Francis Swann.

Cast: William Holden (Norman Reese), Eddie Bracken (George Bodell), Martha O'Driscoll (Dottie Coburn), Barbara Britton (Marge Benson), James Brown (Tony Dennison), Susan Hayward (Katie Benson), Robert Benchley (Arthur Kenny), Mabel Paige (Ms. Garnet), Florence MacMichael (Muriel Foster).

Blaze of Noon

1947. Paramount. *Director:* John Farrow; *Producer:* Robert Fellows; *Screenplay:* Frank Wead, Arthur Sheekman, based on a novel by Ernest K. Gann

Cast: Anne Baxter (Lucille Stewart), William Holden (Colin McDonald), Sterling Hayden (Tad McDonald), William Bendix (Porkie), Howard Da Silva (Gafferty), Sonny Tufts (Ronald McDonald), Johnny Sands (Keith McDonald).

Dear Ruth

1947. Paramount. *Director:* William D. Russell; *Producer:* Paul Jones; *Screenplay:* Arthur Sheekman, based on a play by Norman Krasna.

Cast: William Holden (William Seacroft), Joan Caulfield (Ruth Wilkins), Mona Freeman (Miriam Wilkins), Edward Arnold (Harry Wilkins), Billy De Wolfe (Albert Kummer), Virginia Welles (Martha Seacroft), Mary Philips (Edith Wilkins).

Variety Girl

1947. Paramount. *Director:* George Marshall; *Producer:* Daniel Dare: *Screenplay;* Edmund Hartman, Frank Tashlin, Robert Welch, Monte Brice.

Cast: Mary Hatcher (Catherine Brown), Olga San Juan (Amber La Vonne), DeForest Kelley (Bob Kirby), William Demarest (Barker), Bob Hope, Gary Cooper, Bing Crosby, Ray Milland, Barbara Stanwyck, Dorothy Lamour, Alan Ladd, William Holden, Burt Lancaster, Paulette Goddard, Veronica Lake, Joan Caulfield, Cecil B. DeMille.

Rachel and the Stranger

1948. RKO. *Director:* Norman Foster; *Producer:* Richard H. Berger; *Screenplay:* Waldo Salt, based on the story *Rachel* by Howard Fast.

Cast: William Holden (Big Davey), Loretta Young (Rachel), Robert Mitchum (Jim Fairways), Gary Gray (Davey), Tom Tully (Parson Jackson), Sara Haden (Mrs. Jackson), Frank Ferguson (Mr. Green), Walter Baldwin (Gallus), Regina Wallace (Mrs. Green).

Apartment for Peggy

1948. 20th Century–Fox. *Director:* George Seaton; *Producer:* William Perlberg; *Screenplay:* George Seaton, based on a short story by Faith Baldwin.

Cast: William Holden (Jason), Jeanne Crain (Peggy), Edmund Gwenn (Prof. Henry Barnes), Gene Lockhart (Prof. Edward Bell), Griff Barnett (Dr. Conway), Marion Marshall (Ruth), Randy Stuart (Dorothy), Helen Ford (Della).

The Dark Past

1948. Columbia. *Director:* Rudolph Maté; *Producer:* Buddy Adler; *Screenplay:* Philip MacDonald, Michael Blankfort, Albert Duffy, based on the play *Blind Alley* by James Warwick.

Cast: William Holden (Al Walker), Nina Foch (Betty), Lee J. Cobb (Dr. Andrew Collins), Adele Jergens (Laura Stevens), Stephen Dunne (Owen Talbot), Lois Maxwell (Ruth Collins), Berry Kroeger (Mike), Robert Hyatt (Bobby Collins).

The Man from Colorado

1949. Columbia. *Director:* Henry Levin; *Producer:* Jules Schermer; *Screenplay:* Robert D. Andrews, Ben Maddow, based on a story by Borden Chase.

Cast: Glenn Ford (Colonel Owen Devereaux), William Holden (Captain Del Stewart), Ellen Drew (Caroline Emmett), Ray Collins (Big Ed Carter), Edgar Buchanan (Doc Merriam), Jerome Courtland (Johnny Howard).

Streets of Laredo

1949. Paramount. *Director:* Leslie Fenton; *Producer:* Robert Fellows; *Screenplay:* Charles Marquis Warren, based on a story by Louis Stevens and Elizabeth Hill.

    Cast: William Holden (Jim Dawkins), William Bendix (Wahoo Jones), Macdonald Carey (Lorn Reming), Mona Freeman (Ronnie Carter), James Bell (Ike), Stanley Ridges (Major Bailey), Alfonso Bedoya (Charley Calico), Ray Teal (Cantrel).

Miss Grant Takes Richmond

1949. Columbia. *Director:* Lloyd Bacon; *Producer:* S. Sylvan Simon; *Screenplay:* Nat Perrin, Frank Tashman, Devery Freeman, based on a story by Devery Freeman.

    Cast: Lucille Ball (Ellen Grant), William Holden (Dick Richmond), James Gleason (J. Hobart Gleason), Janis Carter (Peggy Donato), Gloria Henry (Helen White), Frank McHugh (Kilcoyne), George Cleveland (Judge Ben Grant).

Dear Wife

1949. Paramount. *Director:* Richard Haydn; *Producer:* Richard Maibaum; *Screenplay:* Arthur Sheekman, N. Richard Nash.

    Cast: William Holden (Bill Seacroft), Joan Caulfield (Ruth Seacroft), Mona Freeman (Miriam Wilkins), Edward Arnold (Harry Wilkins), Billy De Wolfe (Albert Kummer), Mary Philips (Edith Wilkins), Arleen Whelan (Tommy Murphy).

Father Is a Bachelor

1949. Columbia. *Directors:* Norman Foster, Abby Berlin; *Producer:* S. Sylvan Simon: *Screenplay:* Aleen Leslie, James Edward Grant, based on a story by James Edward Grant.

    Cast: William Holden (Johnny Rutledge), Coleen Gray (Prudence Millett), Mary Jane Saunders (May Chalotte), Charles Winniger (Professor Morderai Ford), Gary Gray (January Chalotte), Billy Gray (February Chalotte), Warren Farlow (March Chalotte), Wayne Farlow (April Chalotte), Peggy Converse (Genevieve Cassin).

Sunset Blvd.

1950. Paramount. *Director:* Billy Wilder; *Producer:* Charles Brackett; *Screenplay:* Charles Brackett, Billy Wilder and D. M. Marshman Jr., based on the story *A Can of Beans* by Charles Brackett and Billy Wilder.

    Cast: Gloria Swanson (Norma Desmond), William Holden (Joe Gillis), Nancy Olson (Betty Schaefer), Erich von Stroheim (Max von Mayerling), Fred Clark

(Sheldrake), Cecil B. DeMille, Buster Keaton, Anna Q. Nilsson, H. B. Warner, Hedda Hopper, Ray Evans, Jay Livingston (themselves).

Union Station

1950. Paramount. *Director:* Rudolph Maté; *Producer:* Jules Schermer; *Screenplay:* Sydney Boehm, based on a story by Thomas Walsh.

    Cast: William Holden (William Calhoun), Nancy Olson (Joyce Willecombe), Barry Fitzgerald (Inspector Donnelly), Lyle Bettger (Joe Beacom), Jan Sterling (Marge Wrighter), Allene Roberts (Lorna Murchinson), Don Dunning (Gus Hudder).

Born Yesterday

1950. Columbia. *Director:* George Cukor; *Producer:* S. Sylvan Simon; *Screenplay:* Albert Mannheimer, based on the play by Garson Kanin.

    Cast: Judy Holliday (Billie Dawn), Broderick Crawford (Harry Brock), William Holden (Paul Verrall), Howard St. John (Jim Devery), Frank Otto (Eddie), Larry Oliver (Norval Hedges), Barbara Brown (Mrs. Hedges), Grandon Rhodes (Sanborn), Claire Carleton (Helen).

Force of Arms (AKA *A Girl for Joe*)

1951. Warner Bros. *Director:* Michael Curtiz; *Producer:* Anthony Veiller; *Screenplay:* Orin Jannings, based on the story *Italian Story* by Richard Tregaskis

    Cast: William Holden (Peterson), Nancy Olson (Lt. Eleanor McKay), Frank Lovejoy (Major Blackford), Gene Evans (Sgt. McFee), Dick Wesson (Sgt. Klein), Paul Picerni (Sheridan), Katherine Warren (Major Waldron).

Submarine Command

1952. Paramount. *Director:* John Farrow; *Producer:* Joseph Sistrom; *Story and Screenplay:* Jonathan Latimer.

    Cast: William Holden (Commander White), Nancy Olson (Carol), William Bendix (C.P.O. Boyer), Don Taylor (Lt. Peter Morris), Arthur Franz (Lt. Carlson), Peggy Webber (Alice Rice), Moroni Olsen (Admiral Joshua Rice), John Mitchum (Sailor).

Boots Malone

1952. Columbia. *Director:* William Dieterle; *Producer and Screenplay:* Milton Holmes.

    Cast: William Holden (Boots Malone), Johnny Stewart (The Kid), Stanley Clements (Stash Clements), Basil Ruysdael (Preacher Cole), Carl Benton Reid (John Williams), Ralph Dumke (Beckett), Ed Begley (Howard Whitehead), Ann Lee (Mrs. Gibson).

The Turning Point

1952. Paramount. *Director:* William Dieterle: *Producer:* Irving Asher: *Screenplay:* Warren Duff, based on a story by Horace McCoy.

Cast: William Holden (Jerry McKibbon), Edmond O'Brien (John Conroy), Alexis Smith (Amanda Waycross), Ed Begley (Eichelberger), Tom Tully (Matt Conroy), Don Porter (Joe Silbray), Don Dayton (Ackerman), Neville Brand (Red).

Stalag 17

1953. Paramount. *Director and Producer:* Billy Wilder; *Screenplay:* Billy Wilder, Edwin Blum, based on the play by Donald Bevan and Edmund Trzcinski.

Cast: William Holden (Sefton), Don Taylor (Lt. Dunbar), Otto Preminger (Oberst von Scherbach), Peter Graves (Price), Robert Strauss (Stosh), Harvey Lembeck (Harry), Neville Brand (Duke), Michael Moore (Manfredi), Robert Shawley (Blondie), Peter Baldwin (Johnson), William Pierson (Marko), Edmund Trczinski (Triz), Richard Beedle, John Mitchum (Prisoners).

The Moon Is Blue

1953. United Artists. *Director and Producer:* Otto Preminger; *Screenplay:* F. Hugh Herbert, based on his own play.

Cast: Maggie McNamara (Patty O'Neill), William Holden (Donald Gresham), David Niven (David Slater), Tom Tully (Mr. O'Neill), Dawn Addams (Cynthia Slater), Gregory Ratoff (Taxi Driver), Fortunio Bonanova (TV Singer).

Forever Female

1954. Paramount. *Director:* Irving Rapper; *Producer:* Pat Duggan; *Screenplay:* Julius J. Epstein, Philip G. Epstein, based on the play *Rosalind* by Sir James M. Barrie.

Cast: Ginger Rogers (Beatrice Page), William Holden (Stanley Krown), Paul Douglas (E. Harry Philips), George Reeves (George Courtland), James Gleason (Eddie Woods), Pat Crowley (Sally Carver), Jesse White (Willie Wolfe).

Escape from Fort Bravo

1954. MGM. *Director:* John Sturges; *Producer:* Nicholas Nayfack; *Screenplay:* Frank Fenton.

Cast: William Holden (Captain Roper), Eleanor Parker (Carla Forrester), John Forsythe (Captain John Marsh), William Demarest (Campbell), Polly Bergen (Alice Owens), William Campbell (Cabot Young), John Lupton (Bailey).

Executive Suite

1954. MGM. *Director:* Robert Wise; *Producer:* John Houseman; *Screenplay:* Ernest Lehman, based on the novel by Cameron Hawley.

Cast: William Holden (McDonald Walling), June Allyson (Mary Blemond Walling), Fredric March (Loren Phineas Shaw), Barbara Stanwyck (Julia O. Tredway), Walter Pidgeon (Frederick Y. Alderson), Shelley Winters (Eva Bardeman), Louis Calhern (George Nyle Caswell), Nina Foch (Erica Martin).

Sabrina

1954. Paramount. *Director and Producer:* Billy Wilder; *Screenplay:* Samuel Taylor,

Billy Wilder and Ernest Lehman, based on the play *Sabrina Fair* by Samuel Taylor.

Cast: Audrey Hepburn (Sabrina Fairchild), Humphrey Bogart (Linus Larrabee), William Holden (David Larrabee), Walter Hampden (Oliver Larrabee), John Williams (Thomas Fairchild), Martha Hyer (Elizabeth Tyson), Nella Walker (Maude Larrabee).

The Country Girl

1954. Paramount. *Director:* George Seaton; *Producer:* William Perlberg; *Screenplay:* George Seaton, based on a play by Clifford Odets.

Cast: Bing Crosby (Frank Elgin), Grace Kelly (Georgie Olga Elgin), William Holden (Bernie Dodd), Anthony Ross (Phil Cook), Gene Reynolds (Larry), Jacqueline Fontaine (Singer-Actress), Eddie Ryer (Ed), Robert Kent (Paul Unger).

The Bridges at Toko-Ri

1955. Paramount. *Director:* Mark Robson; *Producer:* William Perlberg, George Seaton; *Screenplay:* Valentine Davies, based on the novel by James A. Michener.

Cast: William Holden (Harry Brubaker), Grace Kelly (Nancy Brubaker), Fredric March (Admiral George Tarrant), Mickey Rooney (Mike Forney), Robert Strauss (Beer Barrel), Earl Holliman (Nestor Gamidge), Charles McGraw (Comdr. Wayne Lee).

Love Is a Many-Splendored Thing

1955. 20th Century–Fox. *Director:* Henry King; *Producer:* Buddy Adler, *Screenplay:* John Patrick, based on the novel *A Many-Splendored Thing* by Han Suyin.

Cast: Jennifer Jones (Han Suyin), William Holden (Mark Elliott), Torin Thatcher (Mr. Palmer-Jones), Murray Matheson (Dr. Tom), Jorja Curtwright (Suzanne), Isobel Elsom (Adeline Palmer-Jones), Richard Loo (Robert Hung), Soo Yong (Nora Hung), Angela Loo (Mei Loo).

Picnic

1955. Columbia. *Director:* Joshua Logan; *Producer:* Fred Kohlmar; *Screenplay:* Daniel Taradash, based on the play by William Inge.

Cast: William Holden (Hal Carter), Kim Novak (Madge Owens), Rosalind Russell (Rosemary Sydney), Susan Strasberg (Millie Owens), Cliff Robertson (Alan Benson), Betty Field (Flo Owens), Arthur O'Connell (Howard Bevans). Hellen Potts (Verna Felton), Linda Sue Breckenridge (Reta Shaw).

The Proud and Profane

1956. Paramount. *Director:* George Seaton; *Producer:* William Perlberg; *Screenplay:* George Seaton, based on the novel *The Magnificent Bastards* by Lucy Herndon Crockett.

Cast: William Holden (Lt. Col. Colin Black), Deborah Kerr (Lee Ashley), Thelma Ritter (Kate Connors), Dewey Martin (Eddie Wodcik), William Redfield

(Chaplain Holmes), Ward Wood (Sgt. Peckinpaugh), Ray Stricklyn (First Casualty).

Toward the Unknown

1956. Warner Bros. *Director and Producer:* Mervyn LeRoy; *Screenplay:* Beirne Lay Jr.

Cast: William Holden (Major Lincoln Bond), Lloyd Nolan (General Banner), Virginia Leith (Connie Mitchell), Charles McGraw (Colonel Mickey McKee), James Garner (Major Joe Craven), Murray Hamilton (Major Bromo Lee), Karen Steele (Polly Craven).

The Bridge on the River Kwai

1957. Columbia. *Director:* David Lean; *Producer:* Sam Spiegel; *Screenplay:* Pierre Boulle, based on his own novel.

Cast: William Holden (Shears), Alec Guinness (Colonel Nicholson), Jack Hawkins (Major Waden), Sessue Hayakawa (Colonel Saito), Geoffrey Horne (Lt. Joyce), James Donald (Dr. Clipton), Andre Morell (Colonel Green), Peter Williams (Captain Reeves), John Boxer (Major Hughes), Percy Herbert (Grogan), Harold Goodwin (Baker), Anne Sears (Nurse).

The Key

1958. Columbia. *Director:* Carol Reed; *Producer and Screenplay:* Carl Foreman, based on the novel *Stella* by Jan de Hartog.

Cast: Sophia Loren (Stella), William Holden (David Ross), Trevor Howard (Chris Ford), Oscar Homolka (Captain Van Dam), Bryan Forbes (Weaver), Kieron Moore (Kane), Bernard Lee (Wadlow), Beatrix Lehmann (Housekeeper), Michael Caine (Extra).

The Horse Soldiers

1959. United Artists. *Director:* John Ford; *Producer and Screenplay:* John Lee Mahin, Martin Rackin, based on a novel by Harold Sinclair.

Cast: John Wayne (Colonel Marlowe), William Holden (Mayor Kendall), Constance Towers (Hannah), Althea Gibson (Lukey), Hoot Gibson (Brown), Anna Lee (Mrs. Buford), Russell Simpson (Sheriff), Stan Jones (General U.S. Grant), Denver Pyle (Jackie Jo).

The World of Suzie Wong

1960. Paramount. *Director:* Richard Quine; *Producer:* Ray Stark; *Screenplay:* John Patrick, based on the novel by Richard Mason and on the play by Paul Osborn.

Cast: William Holden (Robert Lomax), Nancy Kwan (Suzie Wong), Sylvia Syms (Kay O'Neil), Michael Wilding (Ben), Laurence Naismith (Mr. O'Neil), Jacqueline Chan (Gwenny Lee), Andy Ho (Ah Tong), Bernard Cribbins (Otis), Yvonne Shima (Minnie Ho), Lier Hwang (Wendsday Lu).

Satan Never Sleeps

1962. 20th Century–Fox. *Director and Producer:* Leo McCarey; *Screenplay:* Claude Binyon, Leo McCarey, based on the novel *The China Story* by Pearl Buck

Cast: William Holden (Padre O'Banion), Clifton Webb (Father Bovard), France Nuyen (Siu Lan), Athene Seyler (Sister Agnes), Weaver Lee (Ho San), Martin Benson (Kuznietsky), Edith Sharpe (Sister Theresa).

The Counterfeit Traitor

1962. Paramount. *Director:* George Seaton; *Producer:* William Perlberg; *Screenplay:* George Seaton, based on a novel by Alexander Klein.

Cast: William Holden (Eric Erickson), Lilli Palmer (Marianne Mollendorf), Hugh Griffith (Collins), Erica Beer (Kalra Holtz), Eva Dahlbeck (Ingrid Erickson), Ernst Schroder (Baron Von Oldenbourg), Ulf Palme (Max Gumpel), Klaus Kinski (Kindler), Werner Peters (Bruno Ulrich).

The Lion

1962. 20th Century–Fox. *Director:* Jack Cardiff; *Producer:* Samuel G. Engel; *Screenplay:* Irene Kamp and Louis Kamp, based on a novel by Joseph Kessel.

Cast: William Holden (Robert Haywad), Capucine (Christine), Trevor Howard (John Bullitt), Pamela Franklin (Tina), Samuel Obiero Romboh (Kihoro), Paul Oduor (Oriunga), Zakee (Ol'Kalu), Zamba the Lion.

Paris When It Sizzles

1964. Paramount. *Director:* Richard Quine; *Producers:* George Axelrod, Richard Quine; *Screenplay:* George Axelrod, based on a story by Julien Duvivier and Henri Jeanson.

Cast: William Holden (Richard Benson), Audrey Hepburn (Gabrielle Simpson), Noël Coward (Alexander Meyerheimer), Grégoire Aslan (Police Inspector), Ramond Bussiers (Gangster), Tony Curtis, Marlene Dietrich, Mel Ferrer (Guest Stars).

The Seventh Dawn

1964. United Artists. *Director:* Lewis Gilbert; *Producer:* Charles K. Feldman; *Screenplay:* Karl Tunberg, based on the novel *The Durian Tree* by Michael Keon.

Cast: William Holden (Ferris), Susannah York (Candance), Capucine (Dhana), Tetsuro Tamba (Ng), Michael Goodliffe (Trumphey), Allan Cuthberson (Cavendish), Tony Price (Morley), Allan Wong (Colonel Hsai), Maurice Dehnam (Tarlton).

Alvarez Kelly

1966. Columbia. *Director:* Edward Dmytryk; *Producer:* Sol C. Siegel; *Screenplay:* Franklin Coen, Elliott Arnold, based on a story by Franklin Coen.

Cast: William Holden (Alvarez Kelly), Richard Widmark (Colonel Tom Rossiter), Janice Rule (Liz Pickering), Patrick O'Neal (Major Albert Stedman), Victoria Shaw (Charity Warwick), Donald Barry (Lt. Farrow).

Casino Royale

1967. Columbia. *Directors:* John Huston, Ken Hughes, Robert Parrish, Joseph McGrath, Val Guest; *Producers:* Charles K. Feldman, Jerry Bresler; *Screenplay:* Wolf Mankovitz, John Law, Michael Sayers, loosely based on the novel by Ian Fleming.

Cast: David Niven (Sir James Bond), Peter Sellers (Evelyn Tremble), Deborah Kerr (Agent Mimi/Lady Fiona McTarry), Ursula Andress (Vesper Lynd), Orson Welles (Le Chiffre), Joanna Pettet (Mata Bond), Woody Allen (Jimmy Bond), William Holden (Ransome), Charles Boyer (Le Grand), John Huston (McTarry), Jean-Paul Belmondo (French Legionnaire), Jacqueline Bisset (Miss Goodthings), Barbara Bouchet (Miss Moneypenny).

The Devil's Brigade

1968. United Artists. *Director:* Andrew V McLaglen; *Producer:* David L. Wolper; *Screenplay:* William Roberts, based on a novel by Robert H. Anderson.

Cast: William Holden (Lt. Col. Robert T. Frederick), Cliff Robertson (Major Alan Crown), Vince Edwards (Major Cliff Bricker), Michael Rennie (Lt. General Mark Clark), Dana Andrews (Brigadier General Walter Naylor), Patric Knowles (Admiral Lord Louis Mountbatten), Carroll O'Connor (Major General Hunter).

The Wild Bunch

1969. Warners–7 Arts. *Director:* Sam Peckinpah; *Producer:* Phil Feldman; *Screenplay:* Walon Green, Sam Peckinpah, based on a story by Walon Green and Roy N. Sickner.

Cast: William Holden (Pike Bishop), Robert Ryan (Deke Thornton), Edmond O'Brien (Freddie Sykes), Ernest Borgnine (Dutch Engstrom), Warren Oates (Lyle Gorch), Emilio Fernandez (Mapache), Bo Hopkins (Crazy Lee), Albert Dekker (Harrigan), Strother Martin (Coffer), Ben Johnson (Tector Gorch), Jaime Sanchez (Angel).

L'Arbre de Noël (AKA *The Christmas Tree*; AKA *When Wolves Cry*)

1969. Walter Reade–Continental. *Director:* Terence Young; *Producer:* Robert Dorfmann; *Screenplay:* Terence Young, based on the novel *L'arbre de Noel* by Michel Battaille.

Cast: William Holden (Laurent), Virna Lisi (Catherine), André Bourvil (Verdun), Brook Fuller (Pascal), Madeline Damien (Mariette), Friedrich Ledebur (Vernet), Mario Feliciani (The Doctor).

Wild Rovers

1971. MGM. *Director and Screenplay:* Blake Edwards; *Producer:* Ken Wales.

Cast: William Holden (Ross Bodine), Ryan O'Neal (Frank Post), Karl Malden (Walter Buckman), Lynn Carlin (Sada Billings), Tom Skerritt (John Buckman),

Leora Dana (Neil Buckman), Victor French (Sheriff), James Olson (Joe Billings), Rachel Roberts (Maybell).

The Revengers

1972. National General Pictures. *Director:* Daniel Man; *Producer:* Martin Rackin; *Screenplay:* Wendell Mayes, based on a story by Steven W. Carabatsos.

Cast: William Holden (John Benedict), Ernest Borgnine (Hoop), Susan Hayward (Elizabeth), Roger Hanin (Quiberon), Woody Strode (Job), Warren Vanders (Tarp), Raul Prieto (Warden) Jorge Luke (Chamaco), Rene Koldehoff (Zweig), Scott Holden (Lieutenant).

Breezy

1973. Universal. *Director:* Clint Eastwood; *Producer:* Robert Daley; *Screenplay:* Jo Heims.

Cast: William Holden (Frank Harmon), Kay Lenz (Breezy), Roger C. Carmel (Bob), Dennis Olivieri (Bruno), Marj Dusay (Betty Tobin), Eugene Peterson (Charlie), Joan Hotchkiss (Paula), Shelley Morrison (Nancy), Scott Holden (Veterinarian).

Open Season

1974. Columbia. *Director:* Peter Collinson; *Producer:* Jose S. Vicuna; *Screenplay:* David Osborn, Liz Charles Williams, loosely based on a short story by Richard Connell.

Cast: Peter Fonda (Ken), Cornelia Sharpe (Nancy), John Phillip Law (Greg), Richard Lynch (Art), Albert Mendoza (Martin), William Holden (Walkowski).

The Towering Inferno

1974. 20th Century–Fox–Warner Bros. *Director:* John Guillermin; *Producer:* Irwin Allen; *Screenplay:* Stirling Silliphant, loosely based on the novels *The Tower* by Richard Martin Stern and *The Glass Inferno* by Thomas N. Scortia and Frank M. Robinson.

Cast: Steve McQueen (Michael O'Hallorhan), Paul Newman (Dough Roberts), Faye Dunaway (Susan Franklin), William Holden (James Duncan), Fred Astaire (Harlee Claiborne), Richard Chamberlain (Roger Simmons), Jennifer Jones (Lisolette Mueller), Susan Blakely (Patty Simmons), O.J. Simpson (Jernigan), Robert Wagner (Dan Bigelow), Robert Vaughn (Senator Gary Parker), Susan Flannery (Lorrie), Scott Newman (Fireman).

Network

1976. MGM. *Director:* Sidney Lumet; *Producer:* Howard Gottfried; *Screenplay:* Paddy Chayefsky.

Cast: Peter Finch (Howard Beale), William Holden (Max Schumacher), Faye Dunaway (Diana Christensen), Ned Beatty (Arthur Jensen), Robert Duvall (Frank Hackett), Beatrice Straight (Louise Schumacher), Lee Richardson (Narrator).

Damien — Omen II

1978. 20th Century–Fox. *Director:* Don Taylor; *Producer and Screenplay:* Harvey Bernhard, based on characters created by David Seltzer.

Cast: William Holden (Richard Thorn), Lee Grant (Ann Thorn), Jonathan Scott-Taylor (Damien Thorn), Sylvia Sidney (Aunt Marion), Lew Ayres (Bill Atherton), Leo McKern (Bugenhagen), Lucas Donat (Mark Thorn).

Ashanti

1979. Columbia–EMI–Warner Bros. *Director:* Richard Fleischer; *Producer:* Georges-AlainVuille; *Screenplay:* Stephen Gelier, based on the novel *Ebano* by Albert Vasquez-Figueroa.

Cast: Michael Caine (Dr. David Linderby), Peter Ustinov (Suleiman), Beverly Johnson (Dr. Amansa Linderby), Kabir Bedi (Malike), Omar Sharif (Prince Hassan), Rex Harrison (Brian Walker), William Holden (Jim Sandell).

Fedora

1979. United Artists. *Director and Producer:* Billy Wilder; *Screenplay:* Billy Wilder, I.A.L. Diamond, based on a story by Thomas Tryon.

Cast: William Holden (Barry Detweiler), Marthe Keller (Fedora), José Ferrer (Dr. Vando), Hildegarde Knef (Countess Sobryanski), Mario Adorf (Hotel Manager), Frances Sternhagen (Miss Balfour), Stephen Collins (Barry Detweiler at 25), Henry Fonda, Michael York, Arlene Francis (Themselves).

Escape to Athena

1979. Associated Films. *Director:* George Pan Cosmatos; *Producers:* Jack Wiener, David Niven Jr.; *Screenplay:* Richard S. Lochte, Edward Anhalt, based on an original story by George Pan Cosmatos and Lochte.

Cast: Roger Moore (Major Otto Hecht), Telly Savalas (Zeno), David Niven (Professor Blake), Claudia Cardinale (Eleana), Richard Roundtree (Nat), Stefanie Powers (Dottie Del Mar), Sonny Bono (Bruno Rotelli), Elliott Gould (Charlie), William Holden (War Prisoner).

When Time Ran Out (AKA *The Day the World Ended*)

1980. Warner Bros.–Irwin Allen. *Director:* James Goldstone; *Producer:* Irwin Allen; *Screenplay:* Carl Foreman, Stirling Silliphant, loosely based on the novel *The Day the World Ended* by Max Morgan-Witts and Gordon Thomas.

Cast: Paul Newman (Hank Anderson), Jacqueline Bisset (Kay Kirby), William Holden (Shelby Gilmore), James Franciscus (Bob Spangler), Edward Albert (Brian), Red Buttons (Francis Fendly), Ernest Borgnine (Tom Conti), Valentina Cortese (Rose Valdez), Burgess Meredith (René Valdez), Barbara Carrera (Iolani), Veronica Hamel (Nikki Spangler), Pat Morita (Sam), Ava Readdy (Dolores).

The Earthling

1981. Filmways. *Director:* Peter Collinson; *Producer:* Elliot Schick; *Screenplay:* Larry Cotler.

Cast: William Holden (Patrick Foley), Ricky Schroder (Shawn Daley), Jack Thompson (Ross Daley), Olivia Hamnett (Bettina Daley), Alwyn Kurtz (Christian Neilson), Redmond Phillips (Bobby Burns), Willie Fennell (R.C.), Roy Barrett (Parnell), Pat Evison (Meg Neison).

S.O.B.

1981. Paramount. *Director and Screenplay:* Blake Edwards; *Producers:* Tony Adams, Blake Edwards.

Cast: Julie Andrews (Sally Miles), William Holden (Tim Culley), Richard Mulligan (Felix Farmer), Robert Preston (Dr. Irving Finegarten), Robert Webber (Ben Coogan), Robert Vaughn (David Blackman), Larry Hagman (Dick Benson), Marisa Berenson (Mavis), Shelley Winters (Eva Brown), Robert Loggia (Herb Maskowitz), Rosanna Arquette (Babs).

Documentaries, Television Films and Appearances, Radio Programs, and Music and Soundtracks

Documentaries Narrated by William Holden and Short Films

Wings Up (1943), a recruiting short film for the Army Air Corps.

Reconnaissance Pilot (1943), a short film for the Army Air Corps.

Give Then This Day (1953), a documentary for the American-Korean Foundation.

Report on Hong Kong (1961), a documentary on the city of Hong Kong.

Miyamoto Musashi (1954), a Japanese film by Hiroshi Inagaki; Holden is the narrator (uncredited) of the original 1955 U.S. release.

Nova: The Business of Extinction, (1977), PBS documentary on African endangered species.

Unconquered Worlds: Adventures at the Jade Sea, documentary for CBS (1969).

Mysteries of the Sea (1980).

Television Films

The Blue Knight

1973. NBC. *Director:* Robert Butler; *Producer:* Walter Coblenz; *Screenplay:* E. Jack Newman, based on the novel by Joseph Wambaugh.

Cast: William Holden (Bumper Morgan), Lee Remick (Cassie Walters), Joe Santos (Sergeant Cruz Segovia), Sam Elliott (Detective Clarkie Bronski), Anne Archer (Laila), David Moody (Marvin), Jamie Farr (Yasser Hafiz), Vic Tayback (Neil Grogan), Gloria LeRoy (Ruthie).

21 Hours at Munich

1976. ABC–Filmways. Picture. *Director:* William A. Graham; *Producers:* Frank von

Zerneck, Robert Greenwald; *Screenplay:* Edward Hume, Howard Fast, based on the book *The Blood of Israel* by Serge Groussard.

Cast: Franco Nero (Issa), William Holden (Police Chief Manfred Schreiber), Shirley Knight (Annaliese Graese), Anthony Quayle (General Zvi Zamir), Richard Basehart (Chancellor Willy Brandt), Noel Willman (Interior Minister Bruno Merk), Georg Marischka (Hans Dietrich Genscher), Elsa Quecke (Golda Meir).

Television Appearances

The Colgate Comedy Hour, NBC, 1954.
Operation Entertainment, NBC, 1954.
"Welcome, Stranger," *Lux Video Theatre,* CBS, February 9, 1954.
"Love Letters," *Lux Video Theatre,* NBC, January 20, 1955.
Bob Hope Buick Show, NBC, 1955.
Toast of the Town, CBS, 1955.
The Christophers: You Can Change the World, NBC, 1955.
Person to Persons, CBS, 1955.
I Love Lucy: L.A. at Last! (AKA *Hollywood at Last!*), CBS, 1955.
Producers Showcase: Dateline 2, NBC, 1955.
The Jack Benny Program, CBS, 1956.
What's My Line, CBS, 1956.
Academy Award Nominations, NBC, 1956.
The Perry Como Show, NBC, 1956.
"Now, Voyager," *Lux Video Theatre,* NBC, October 4, 1956.
The Steve Allen Show, NBC, 1957.
The Ed Sullivan Show, CBS, 1958.
The Merv Griffin Show, Syndicated, 1968.
The Merv Griffin Show, Syndicated, 1972.
The Dean Martin Show, NBC, 1973.
The Tonight Show Starring Johnny Carson, NBC, 1976.
The Mike Douglas Show, NBC, 1977.
Oscar's Best Actors, ABC, 1978.
Bing Crosby: His Life and Legend, ABC, 1978

Radio Programs

"Our Town," *Lux Radio Theatre,* CBS, May 6, 1940.
"Drink a Glass of Sassafras," *Screen Guild Theatre,* CBS, January 5, 1941.
"I Wanted Wings," *Lux Radio Theatre,* CBS, March 30, 1942.
Dear Adolph, NBC Network, July 26, 1942.
The Cavalcade of America: Name, Rank, Serial Number, January 8, 1945.
"Christmas Holiday," *Lux Radio Theatre,* CBS, March 17, 1945.
"Recon Pilot," *The Cavalcade of America,* CBS, May 28, 1945.
"Miss Susie Slagle's," *Lux Radio Theatre,* CBS, October 21, 1946.
"The Farmer Takes a Wife," *Theatre Guild on the Air,* ABC, February 2, 1947.
"Nancy Has an Accident," *The Smiths of Hollywood,* Syndicated, April 11, 1947.
"Song for a Long Road," *Family Theatre,* Syndicated, July 17, 1947.

Hollywood Fights Back, ABC, October 26, 1947.
"Dear Ruth," *Lux Radio Theatre*, CBS, April 26, 1948.
"Apartment for Peggy," *Lux Radio Theatre*, CBS, February 28, 1949.
"Dear Ruth," *Lux Radio Theatre*, CBS, December 5, 1949.
"The Firefly Lamp," *The Cavalcade of America*, CBS, April 25, 1950.
"Blood on the Trumpet," *Suspense*, CBS, November 9, 1950.
"Blow Ye Winds," *Theatre Guild on the Air*, ABC, November 10, 1950.
"Dear Wife," *Lux Radio Theatre*, CBS, February 19, 1951.
"Love Letters," *Lux Radio Theatre*, CBS, May 21, 1951.
"Report on the Jolly Death Riders," *Suspense*, CBS, August 27, 1951.
"Sunset Blvd.," *Lux Radio Theatre*, CBS, September 17, 1951.
"The Lost Weekend," *Theatre Guild on the Air*, ABC, December 9, 1951.
"The Men," *Lux Radio Theatre*, CBS, December 17, 1951.
"Union Station," *Lux Radio Theatre*, CBS, April 7, 1952.
"Submarine Command," *Lux Radio Theatre*, CBS, November 17, 1952.
"Appointment with Danger," *Lux Radio Theatre*, CBS, January 19, 1953.
"High Tor," *Lux Radio Theatre*, CBS, June 1, 1953.
"Needle in the Haystack," *Suspense*, CBS, November 9, 1953.
"Outer Limit," *Suspense*, CBS, February 15, 1954.

Music and Soundtracks

As I Hear It (1958), William Holden, Dramatic Themes from His Great Motion
  Pictures, Warner Bros., BS 1247.
William Holden Presents A Musical Touch from Far Away Places (1959), Warren
  Barker and His Orchestra, Warner Bros., B-1308

Chapter Notes

Chapter 1

1. Giuseppe Gilioli, *I magnifici di Hollywood: William Holden* (Milano: Editoriale Albero, 1982), p. 8.
2. Pauline Swanson, "Mr. Dynamite," *Photoplay*, January 1952, p. 75.
3. "The Conquest of Smiling Jim," *Time*, February 27, 1956, p. 64.
4. Frank S. Nugent, "Golden Holden," *Collier's*, June 2, 1951, p. 64.
5. Irene Kahn Atkins, *Arthur Jacobson* (Metuchen, NJ: Scarecrow Press, 1991), p. 112.
6. Richard Gehman, "Still the Golden Boy," *McCall's*, July 1962, p. 123.
7. Irene Kahn Atkins, *op. cit.*, p. 114.
8. Edwin Schallert, *Los Angeles Times*, February 21, 1939, p. 14.
9. "William Holden," *The New Yorker*, October 21, 1961, p. 113.

Chapter 2

1. Axel Madsen, *Stanwyck* (New York: HarperCollins, 1994), p. 165.
2. Beverly Linet, *Ladd. The Life, the Legend, the Legacy of Alan Ladd* (New York: Arbor House, 1979), p. 42.
3. John R. Franchey, "That's Holden for You," *Photoplay*, July 1940, p. 10.
4. Bob Thomas, *King Cohn* (New York: Putnam's, 1967), p. 156.
5. *Ibid.*
6. Kay Proctor, "Bill Holden Lady Luck's Protege," *Screen Book Magazine*, July 1939, p. 87.
7. James Reid, "Gilding Golden Boy," *Silver Screen*, October 1939, p. 61.

8. Axel Madsen, *op. cit.*, p. 166.
9. Al Di Orio, *Barbara Stanwyck* (New York: Coward-McCann, 1983), p. 115.
10. Jane Ellen Wayne, *Stanwyck* (New York: Arbor House, 1985), p. 79.
11. Ella Smith, *Starring Miss Barbara Stanwyck* (New York: Crown, 1974), p. 128.
12. Lillian Ross and Helen Ross, *The Player. A Profile of an Art* (New York: Limelight Editions, 1984), p. 118
13. Al Di Orio, *op. cit.*, p. 115
14. Thomas M. Pryor, "Golden Boy Come to Town," *New York Times*, August 27, 1939.
15. Lillian Ross and Helen Ross, *op. cit.*, p. 118.
16. Pauline Swanson, *op. cit.*, p. 76.
17. Lewis Yablonsky, *George Raft* (New York: McGraw-Hill, 1974), pp. 137–38.
18. A.M. Sperber and Eric Lax, *Bogart* (New York: Morrow, 1997), p. 103.
19. Gene Feldman and Suzanne Winter, *William Holden. The Golden Boy*, 1989, videocassette.
20. Bosley Crowther, "The Screen," *New York Times*, June 11, 1940, p. 25.
21. Ed Sikov, *On Sunset Boulevard. The Life and Times of Billy Wilder* (New York: Hyperion, 1998), pp. 150–51.
22. John Oller, *Jean Arthur: The Actress That Nobody Knew* (New York: Limelight Editions, 2004), p. 121.
23. Liza Wilson, "Bill Holden. He Lives With Danger," *The American Weekly*, December 8, 1957, p. 14.
24. Thomas Brady, "High-Jinks in Hollywood," *New York Times*, August 18, 1940.
25. Theodore Strass, "At the Music

Hall," *New York Times*, February 7, 1941, p. 23.

26. Thomas Brady, *op. cit.*

27. James Robert Parish and Don E. Stanke, *The All-Americans* (New Rochelle, NY: Arlington House, 1977), p. 147.

28. Gene Feldman and Suzanne Winter, *op. cit.*

29. Bob Thomas, *op. cit.*, pp. 215–16.

30. Mart Martin, *Did He or Didn't He?* (New York: Citadel Press, 2000), p. 83.

Chapter 3

1. Kahn Atkins, *op. cit.*, p. 115.

2. Georges Baume, *Vedettes sans maquillage* (Paris: La Table Ronde, 1954), p. 125.

3. Dorothy Lamour, *My Side of the Road* (Englewood Cliffs, NJ: Prentice-Hall, 1980), p. 98.

4. *Ibid.*, pp. 109–10.

5. Bob Thomas, *Golden Boy. The Untold Story of William Holden* (New York: St. Martin's Press, 1983), p. 43.

6. Robert LaGuardia and Gene Arceri, *Red. The Tempestuous Life of Susan Hayward* (New York: Macmillan, 1985), pp. 43–44.

7. Bob Thomas, *King Cohn* (New York: Putnam's, 1967), p. 232.

8. Arthur Laurents, *Original Story By. A Memoir of Broadway and Hollywood* (New York: Knopf, 2000), p. 32.

9. James Robert Parish and Don E. Stanke, *op. cit.*, p. 150.

10. Hank Greenberg, *Hank Greenberg: The Story of My Life* (New York: Benchman Press, 2001), p. 143.

11. Kay Sullivan, "Hollywood's Firecracker," *Parade*, 1950, p. 17.

12. James Robert Parish and Don E. Stanke, *op. cit.*, p. 150.

13. Giuseppe Gilioli, *op. cit.*, p. 32.

Chapter 4

1. Axel Madsen, *op. cit.*, p. 243.

2. Gene Feldman and Susan Winter, *op. cit.*

3. Lee Server, *Robert Mitchum: Baby I Don't Care* (New York: St. Martin's Press, 2001), p. 143.

4. Joan Wester Anderson, *Forever Young. The Authorized Biography of Loretta Young* (Allen Texas: Thomas More, 2000), pp. 159–60.

5. Lee Server, *op. cit.*, p. 144.

6. "The New Pictures," *Time*, September 27, 1948.

7. Barbara Leaming, *If This Was Happiness. A Biography of Rita Hayworth* (New York: Viking, 1989), p. 172.

8. David Chierichetti, *George Seaton*, (Beverly Hills: Louis B. Mayer/American Film Institute, 1975), pp. 117–18.

9. *Ibid.*

10. John L. Scott, "Bill Holden's a Hit Both in Film and Family Roles," *Los Angeles Times*, January 16, 1949, D, p. 1.

11. *Ibid.*

12. Bob Thomas, *op. cit.*, p. 101.

13. John L. Scott, *op. cit.*, p. 1.

14. Bob Thomas, *King Cohn* (New York: Putnam's, 1967), p. 255.

15. Coyne Steven Sanders and Tom Gilbert, *Desilu. The Story of Lucille Ball and Desi Arnaz* (New York: Morrow, 1993), p. 16.

16. Bob Thomas, *King Cohn, op. cit.*, p. 305.

17. Bernard Drew, "Where Has Everybody Gone?," *American Film*, vol. II n. 4, February 1977, p. 54.

18. Boyd Magers and Michael G. Fitzgerald, *Western Women* (Jefferson NC: McFarland, 1999), pp. 97–98.

Chapter 5

1. Cameron Crowe, *Conversation with Wilder* (New York: Knopf, 1999), p. 47.

2. *Ibid.*

3. Gloria Swanson, *Swanson on Swanson* (New York: Random House, 1980), p. 480.

4. Sam Staggs, *Close-up on Sunset Boulevard* (New York: St. Martin's Press, 2002), p. 72.

5. *Ibid.*, p. 63.

6. *Ibid.*, p. 72.

7. *The Making of Sunset Boulevard*, Paramount Homevideo, 2002.

8. Gloria Swanson, *op. cit.*, p. 482.

9. Maurice Zolotow, *Billy Wilder in Hollywood* (London: W.H. Allen, 1977), p. 249.

10. Howard Thompson, "Hollywood Hurrahs by Holden," *New York Times*, August 13, 1950.

11. Sam Staggs, *op. cit.*, pp. 92–93.

12. Thomas M. Pryor, "The Screen," *New York Times*, August 11, 1950, p. 15.

13. Hellmuth Karasek, *Billy Wilder. Un viennese a Hollywood* (Milano: Mondadori, 1993), p. 389.

14. Bob Thomas, *op. cit.*, p. 65.

15. *Ibid.*, pp. 82–83.

16. *Ibid.*, p. 64.

17. Hellmuth Karasek, *op. cit.*, 388.

18. Anne Edwards, *The Corporate Years* (New York: Morrow, 1990), p. 421.

19. Howard Thompson, *op. cit.*

20. Bernard Drew, "Where Has Everybody Gone," *American Film*, February 1977, p. 54.

21. Patrick McGilligan, *Alfred Hitchcock: A Life in Darkness and Light* (New York: Regan Books, 2003), p. 451.

22. Robert Emmet Long, *George Cukor Interviews* (Jackson, MS: University Press of Mississippi, 2001), p. 107.

23. Gary Carey, *Judy Holliday. An Intimate Story* (New York: Seaview Books, 1982), p. 110.

24. Jane Otten, "Capital Location," *New York Times*, June 25, 1950.

25. Bob Thomas, *King Cohn,* pp. 304–05.

Chapter 6

1. Frank S. Nugent, *op. cit.*, p. 64.

2. Ed Sikov, *op. cit.*, p. 336.

3. Hellmuth Karasek, *op. cit.*, p. 299.

4. Maurice Zolotow, *op. cit.,* p. 243.

5. Bob Thomas, *op. cit.*, pp. 80–81.

6. *Ibid.*, p. 147.

7. Cameron Crowe, *op. cit.*, p. 304.

8. Axel Madsen, *Billy Wilder* (London: Secker & Warburg, 1968), p. 96.

9. Ronald Reagan, *Where's the Rest of Me?* (New York: Duell, Sloan and Pearce, 1965), p. 237.

10. Bill Adler, *Ronnie and Nancy. A Very Special Love Story* (New York: Crown, 1985), p. 92.

11. Axel Madsen, *op. cit.*, p. 94.

12. James Robert Parish and Don E. Stanke, *op. cit.,* p. 161.

13. Maurice Zolotow, *op. cit.,* pp. 282–283.

14. Hellmuth Karasek, *op. cit.*, p. 389.

15. Leonard J. Leff and Jerold L. Simmons, *The Dame in the Kimono* (New York: Grove Weidenfeld, 1990), p. 192.

16. Willi Frischauer, *Behind the Scenes of Otto Preminger* (New York: Morrow, 1974), p. 128.

17. *Ibid.*

18. Ginger Rogers, *Ginger. My Story* (New York: HarperCollins, 1991), p. 308.

19. Doug McClelland, *Eleanor Parker. Woman of a Thousand Faces* (Metuchen, NJ: Scarecrow Press, 1989), p. 15.

20. Sergio Leeman, *Robert Wise on His Films* (Los Angeles: Silman-James Press, 1995), p. 123.

21. Ella Smith, *op. cit.,* p. 248.

22. Shelley Winters, *Shelley Also Known as Shirley* (New York: Morrow, 1980), pp. 238–39.

23. Bob Thomas, *op. cit.*, p. 256.

24. Bob Hope, *I Owe Russia $1200* (New York: Doubleday, 1963), pp. 53–55.

Chapter 7

1. Hellmuth Karasek, *op. cit.*, p. 388.

2. Ian Woodward, *Audrey Hepburn* (New York: St. Martin's Press, 1984), pp. 116–17.

3. *Ibid.*, p. 119.

4. Martha Hyer Wallis, *Finding My Way* (San Francisco: HarperSanFrancisco, 1990), p. 49.

5. *Behind the Scenes of Sabrina*, DVD Documentary, Paramount Pictures, 2005.

6. Stephen Humphrey Bogart. *Bogart. In Search of My Father,* (New York: Dutton, 1995) p. 179.

7. Maurice Zolotow, *op. cit.,* p. 252.

8. Alexander Walker, *Audrey* (New York: St. Martin's Press, 1994), p. 89.

9. Bob Paris, *Audrey Hepburn* (New York: Putnam's, 1996), p. 94.

10. Bob Thomas, *op. cit.*, p. 104.

11. Irene Kahn Atkins, *op. cit.*, p. 195.

12. Sarah Bradford, *Princess Grace* (New York: Stein and Day, 1984), p. 86.

13. Robert Lacey, *Grace* (New York: Putnam's, 1994), p. 157.

14. James Spada, *Grace. The Secret Lives of a Princess* (New York: Doubleday, 1988), pp. 86–87.

15. David Chierichetti, *op. cit.*, p. 155.

16. James Spada, *op. cit.*, p. 93.

17. Robert Lacey, *op. cit.*, pp. 157–58.

18. Wendy Leigh, *True Grace* (London: JR Books, 2007), p. 82.

19. Robert Lacey, *op. cit.*, p. 160.

20. Jeannie Sakol and Caroline Latham, *About Grace. An Intimate Notebook* (Chicago: Contemporary Books, 1995), p. 95.

Chapter 8

1. Edward Z. Epstein, *Portrait of Jennifer. A Biography of Jennifer Jones* (New York: Simon & Schuster, 1995), p. 321.
2. J.R. Parish, *op. cit.*, p. 164.
3. Bob Thomas, *op. cit.*, p. 111.
4. Joshua Logan, *Movie Stars, Real People and Me* (New York: Delacorte Press, 1978), p. 7.
5. *Ibid.*, 8.
6. Peter Harry Brown, *Kim Novak: Reluctant Goddess* (New York: St. Martin's Press, 1986), p. 88.
7. Tom Olivier, "Why Holden Laughed When He 'Went to Bed' with Faye," *Photoplay*, May 1977.
8. Joshua Logan, *op. cit.*, p. 12.
9. Rosalind Russell, *Life Is a Banquet* (New York: Random House, 1977), p. 187.
10. Joshua Logan, *op. cit.*, p. 18.
11. Peter Harry Brown, *op. cit.*, p. 93.
12. David Chierichetti, *op. cit.*, p. 163.
13. Eric Braun, *Deborah Kerr* (New York: St. Martin's Press, 1978), p. 153.
14. Richard Dyer McCann, "*Toward the Unknown* Salutes Jets," *The Christian Science Monitor*, August 14, 1956, p. 4.
15. George Carpozi, Jr., *That's Hollywood. Volume One. The Matinee Idols* (New York: Manor Books, 1978), p. 212.
16. Alvin H, Marill, *op. cit.*, p. 458.

Chapter 9

1. Natasha Fraser-Cavassoni, *Sam Spiegel* (New York: Simon & Schuster, 2003), p. 186.
2. *Ibid.*
3. *Ibid.*, p. 187.
4. Piers Paul Read, *Alec Guinness. The Authorized Biography* (New York: Simon & Schuster, 2003), p. 293.
5. Stephen M. Silverman, *David Lean* (New York: Harry N. Abrahams, 1992), p. 124.
6. Kevin Brownlow, *David Lean* (London: Richard Cohen Books, 1996), p. 366.
7. Piers Paul Read, *op. cit.*, p. 291.
8. Stephen M. Silverman, *op. cit.*, p. 122.
9. Sandra Lean, *David Lean. An Intimate Portrait* (New York: Universe Publishing, 2001), p. 75.
10. Jack Hawkins, *Anything for a Quiet Life* (New York: Stein and Day, 1974), pp. 111–12.

11. Gary O'Connor, *Alec Guinness: A Life* (New York: Applause, 2002), p. 324.
12. "William Holden Talks About … the Film I'll Never Forget," *National Enquirer*, January 21, 1973.
13. George Haddad-Garcia, "William Holden. One of the Most Enduring Stars," *Hollywood Studio Magazine*, March 1982, p. 13.
14. A.E. Hotchner, *Sophia Living and Loving. Her Own Story* (New York: Morrow, 1979), p. 136.
15. *Ibid.* p. 137.
16. Donal Zec, *Sophia. An Intimate Biography* (London: W.H. Allen, 1975), pp. 129–30.
17. *Ibid.* p. 128.
18. Alan Levy, *Forever Sophia* (New York: St. Martin's Press, 1986), p. 49.
19. Donal Zec, *op. cit.*, pp. 130–31.
20. Tony Crawley, *The Films of Sophia Loren* (London: LSP Books, 1974), p. 97.
21. Michael Munn, *Trevor Howard. The Man Behind the Myth* (New York: New American Library, 2005), p. 198.
22. Donald Zec, *op. cit.*, pp. 133–34.
23. Marialivia Serini, "Parigi mi ha trasformata," *L'Espresso*, September 27, 1959.

Chapter 10

1. Michael Munn, *John Wayne. The Man Behind the Myth* (New York: New American Library, 2005), p. 198.
2. Will Holtzman, *op. cit.*, p. 123.
3. Scott Eyman, *Print the Legend. The Life and Times of John Ford* (New York: Simon & Schuster, 1999), p. 470.
4. Michael Munn, *op. cit.*, p. 199.
5. Randy Roberts and James S. Olson, *John Wayne American* (New York: Free Press, 1995), p. 587.
6. Phyllis Battelle, "Bill's One and Only Wife," *New York Journal-American*, December 2, 1958.
7. Lawrence J. Quirk, *The Complete Films of William Holden* (Secaucus, New Jersey: Citadel Press, 1986), pp. 29–30.
8. Alvin H. Marill, *op .cit.*, p. 459.
9. Giuseppe Gilioli, *op. cit.*, p. 44.
10. Joe Hyams, "Bwana Bill Holden Was Scared," *Herald Tribune*, March 10, 1959.
11. *Ibid.*
12. J.R. Parish, *op. cit.*, p. 168.
13. "William Holden Helps Build Afri-

can School," *Los Angeles Times*, November 25, 1960, p. 15.

14. Lilli Palmer, *Change Lobsters — and Dance* (New York: Macmillan, 1975), p. 299.

15. J.R. Parish, *op. cit.*, p. 169.

16. Archer Winsten, "*Satan Never Sleeps*," *New York Post*, February 22, 1962, p. 13.

17. Will Holtzman, *op. cit.*, p. 127.

18. Murray Schumach, "3 Unions to Picket 'Runaway' Actors," *New York Times*, May 26, 1962, p. 13.

19. Will Holtzman, *op. cit.*, p. 129.

Chapter 11

1. Michael Munn, *op. cit.*, pp. 88–89.

2. Bob Thomas, *op. cit*, p. 143.

3. Diana Maychick, *Audrey Hepburn. An Intimate Portrait* (New York: Birch Lane Press, 1993), p. 174.

4. Bernard Drew, *op. cit.*, p. 56.

5. David Hofstede, *Audrey Hepburn. A Bio-Bibliography* (Westport, CT: Greenwood Press, 1994), pp. 107–08.

6. Warren G. Harris, *op. cit.*, p.190.

7. Graham Payn and Sheridan Morley, *The Noël Coward Diaries* (New York: Da Capo Press, 1982), p. 514.

8. Bob Willoughby, *Hollywood: A Journey Through the Stars* (New York: Assouline, 2001), p. 190.

9. Bob Paris, *op. cit.*, p. 184.

10. Boze Hadleigh, *Hollywood Lesbians* (New York: Barricade Books, 1994), p. 231.

11. Bob Paris, *op. cit.*, p. 319.

12. Bob Thomas, *op. cit*, p. 152.

13. Patrick McGilligan, *Backstory 2. Interviews with Screenwriters of the 1940s and 1950s* (Berkley, CA: University of California Press, 1991), p. 327.

14. Edward Dmytryk, *It's a Hell of a Life but Not a Bad Living* (New York: Times Books, 1978), pp. 272–73.

15. *Ibid.*

16. Peter Bart, "Holden: All-American Boy?," *New York Times*, December 12, 1965, p. 13.

17. Florabel Muir, "Hollywood," *Daily News*, April 5, 1967.

18. Gene Feldman and Suzette Winter, *op. cit.*

19. Alan Chester, "'Real' Africa Filmed," *The Evening News*, September 9, 1968, p. 14.

Chapter 12

1. David Weddle, *If They Move...Kill 'Em* (New York: Grove Press, 1994), pp. 319–20.

2. *Ibid.*, p. 328.

3. *Ibid.*, p. 326.

4. Paul Seydor, *The Wild Bunch: An Album in Montage*, DVD Warner Bros., 1996.

5. *Ibid.*

6. Marshall Fine, *The Life and the Films of Sam Peckinpah* (New York: Donald I. Fine, 1994), p. 134.

7. Edd Byrnes, "*Kookie" No More* (New York: Barricade Books, 1996), p. 143.

8. Ernest Borgnine, *Ernie. The Autobiography* (New York: Citadel Press, 2008), p. 164.

9. Roderick Mann, "'Wild' Bill Holden in Defence of Violence," *Sunday Express*, June 29, 1969.

10. Bob Thomas, *op. cit.*, p. 175.

11. Roderick Mann, *op. cit.*

12. William Murray, "Ryan Has the Whole Country Cry'n," *New York Times*, March 7, 1971, sec. D, p. 11.

13. Bob Lardine, "Holden Died from Fall," *The News*, November 18, 1981, p. 17.

14. Paul Gardner, "Directors Protest Studio Film Cuts," *New York Times*, April 19, 1972. p. 36.

15. Robert LaGuardia and Gene Arceri, *op. cit.*, p. 177.

16. George Haddad-Garcia, *op. cit.*, p. 13.

17. J.R. Parish, *op. cit.*, p. 174.

18. Douglas Thompson, *Clint Eastwood. Riding High* (Chicago: Contemporary Books, 1992), p. 113.

19. Richard Schickel, *op. cit.*, p. 295.

20. Archer Winsten, "Rages & Outrages," *New York Post*, June 19, 1972, p. 24.

21. Nora Sayre, "*Open Season*; A Film of a Dull Sadism at Neighborhoods," *New York Times*, November 2, 1974, p. 6.

22. Sidney Skolsky, "Tintypes: William Holden," *New York Post*, October 12, 1974, p. 42.

23. George Haddad-Garcia, *op. cit.*, p. 12.

24. Edward Z. Epstein, *op. cit.*, p. 425.

25. Guy Flatley, "At the Movies," *New York Times*, November 12, 1976.

Chapter 13

1. Jack Hicks, "He Helped Make Me Back into a Human Being, " *TV Guide*, August 20, 1983, p. 15.
2. *Ibid.*
3. Barbara Wilkins, "Couples," *People,* April 11, 1977, p. 5.
4. Rex Reed, "Holden: Movies Have Grown Up. So Have I," *Sunday News*, November 21, 1976, p. 5.
5. Patty Ivins, *William Holden. An Untamed Spirit* (New York: A&E Documentary, 1996).
6. Edd Byrnes, *op. cit.,* p. 143.
7. Joe Nicholson, "N.Y. Lawyer Knifed on a Peking Street," *New York Post,* September 19, 1977, p. 5.
8. Gene Feldman and Suzette Winter, *op. cit.*
9. Barbra Paskin, "The Terrifying Message of *Network*," *Film Review,* July 1977, p. 36.
10. Elaine Dundy, *Finch Bloody Finch* (New York: Holt, Rinehart and Winston, 1980), p. 324.
11. *Ibid.*
12. Faye Dunaway, *Looking for Gatsby. My Life* (New York: Simon & Schuster, 1995), p. 298.
13. Guy Flatley, *op. cit.*
14. Faye Dunaway, *op. cit.,* p. 301.
15. Stephen M. Silverman, "For William Holden, the *Omen* Is Devil of a Film," *New York Post,* July 7, 1978, p. 82.
16. Arthur Bell, "Bell Tells," *The Village Voice,* June 12, 1978, p. 33.
17. Ed Sikov, *op. cit.,* p. 554.
18. Kevin Lally, *Wilder Times. The Life of Billy Wilder* (New York: Henry Holt, 1996), p. 404.
19. Stephen M. Silverman, *op. cit.,* p. 82.
20. Ernest Borgnine, *op. cit.,* pp. 220–21.

Chapter 14

1. John Austin, *Hollywood's Unsolved Mysteries* (New York: Shapolsky Publishers, 1990), p. 111.
2. Laurence J. Quirk, *op. cit.,* pp. 281–82.
3. Gene Feldman and Suzette Winter, *op. cit.*
4. George Hadden Garcia, *op. cit.,* pp. 12–13.
5. Wally Burke, "Bill's Pals Scotch Reports of Marriage," *New York Post,* November 20, 1981.
6. John Austin, *op. cit.,* p. 109.
7. Jack Jones and Nancy Graham, "Holden Died from Blood Loss," *L.A. Times,* November 18, 1981, p. B3.
8. Keith Love and Dale Pollock, "Manner of Holden's Death Troubles Friends, Fans," *L.A. Times,* November 19, 1981, p. SD3.
9. Stephen Farber, "Wilder: A Cynic Ahead His Time," *New York Times,* December 6, 1981, p. 21.
10. Myrna Oliver, "Holden's Will Provokes Squabble," *L.A. Times,* July 29, 1982, p. D3.
11. Hellmuth Karasek, *op. cit.,* p. 389.

Bibliography

Anderson, Joan Wester. *Forever Young: The Authorized Biography of Loretta Young.* Allen, TX: Thomas More, 2000.

Aristarco, Guido. *Il mito dell'attore.* Bari: Edizioni Dedalo, 1983.

Atkins, Irene Kahn. *Arthur Jacobson.* Metuchen, NJ: Scarecrow, 1991.

Austin, John. *Hollywood's Unsolved Mysteries.* New York: Shapolsky, 1990.

Barbour, Alan G. *Humphrey Bogart.* New York: Pyramid, 1973.

Base, Ron. *Starring Roles.* London: Little, Brown, 1994.

Baume, Georges. *Vedettes sans maquillage.* Paris: La Table Ronde, 1954.

Behelmer, Rudy. *Memo from David O. Selznick.* New York: Modern Library, 2000.

Bogart, Stephen Humphrey. *Bogart: In Search of My Father.* New York: Dutton, 1995.

Bookbinder, Robert. *The Films of Bing Crosby.* Secaucus, NJ: Citadel Press, 1977.

Borgnine, Ernest. *Ernie: The Autobiography.* New York: Citadel Press, 2008.

Boyer, Jay. *Sidney Lumet.* New York: Twayne, 1993.

Bradford, Sarah. *Princess Grace.* New York: Stein & Day, 1984.

Braun, Eric. *Deborah Kerr.* New York: St. Martin's Press, 1978.

Brode, Douglas. *The Films of the Fifties.* Secaucus, NJ: Citadel Press, 1976.

_____. *The Films of the Sixties.* Secaucus, NJ: Citadel Press, 1980.

Brown, Peter Harey. *Kim Novak: Reluctant Goddess.* New York: St. Martin's Press, 1986.

Brownlow, Kevin. *David Lean.* London: Richard Cohen, 1996.

Byrnes, Edd. *"Kookie" No More.* New York: Barricade Books, 1996.

Carey, Gary. *Judy Holliday: An Intimate Life Story.* New York: Seaview Books, 1982.

Carpozi, George, Jr. *That's Hollywood. Volume One, The Matinee Idols.* New York: Manor, 1978.

Carrier, Jeffrey. *Jennifer Jones: A Bio-Bibliography.* Westport, CT: Greenwood Press, 1990.

Castello, Giulio Cesare. *William Holden.* Milano: Sedit, 1956.

Cavassoni Fraser, Natasha. *Sam Spiegel.* New York: Simon & Schuster, 2003.

Chierichetti, David. *George Seaton.* Beverly Hills: Louis B. Mayer/American Film Institute, 1975.

Cohan, Steven. *Masked Men: Masculinity and the Movies in the Fifties.* Bloomington: Indiana University Press, 1997.

Coppedge, Walter. *Henry King's America.* Metuchen, NJ: Scarecrow, 1986.

Crawley, Tony. *The Films of Sophia Loren.* London: LSP Books, 1974.

Crowe, Cameron. *Conversation with Billy Wilder.* New York: Knopf, 1999.

Darrid, Diana Douglas. *In the Wings.* New York: Barricade Books, 1999.

Day, Barry. *Coward on Film: The Cinema of Noël Coward.* Lanham, MD: Scarecrow, 2005.

Dickens, Homer. *The Films of Barbara Stanwyck.* Secaucus, NJ: Citadel Press, 1984.

Di Orio, Al. *Barbara Stanwyck.* New York: Coward McCann, 1983.

Dmytryk, Edward. *It's a Hell of a Life but Not a Bad Living.* New York: Times
Books, 1978.

Dunaway, Faye. *Looking for Gatsby: My Life.* New York: Simon & Schuster, 1995.

Dundy, Elaine. *Finch Bloody Finch: A Life of Peter Finch.* New York: Holt, Rinehart and Winston, 1980.

Edwards, Anne. *Early Reagan: The Rise to Power.* New York: Morrow, 1990.

Englund, Steven. *Grace of Monaco.* New York: Doubleday, 1984.

Epstein, Edward Z. *Portrait of Jennifer: A Biography of Jennifer Jones.* New York:
Simon & Schuster, 1995.

Evans, Peter William. *Carol Reed.* Manchester: Manchester University Press, 2005.

Eyman, Scott. *Print the Legend: The Life and Times of John Ford.* New York: Simon
& Schuster, 1999.

Fagen, Herb. *The Encyclopedia of the Westerns.* New York: Facts on File, 2003.

Fallaci, Oriana. *I sette peccati di Hollywood.* Milano: Longanesi, 1958.

Faris, Jocelyn. *Ginger Rogers: A Bio-Bibliography.* Westport, CT: Greenwood Press,
1994.

Fine, Marshall. *Bloody Sam: The Life and Films of Sam Peckinpah.* New York: Donald I. Fine, 1991.

Forbes, Bryan. *A Divided Life.* London: Heinemann, 1992.

Fowler, Karin J. *Anne Baxter: A Bio-Bibliography.* Westport, CT: Greenwood Press,
1991.

Frischauer, Willi. *Behind the Scenes of Otto Preminger.* New York: Morrow, 1974.

Gaines Holden, Virginia. *Growing Up with William Holden.* Westlake Village,
CA: StrateGems, 2007.

Gandini, Leonardo. *Billy Wilder.* Genova: Le Mani, 1999.

Gehring Wes D. *Leo McCarey.* Lanham, MD: Scarecrow, 2005.

Greenberg, Hank. *Hank Greenberg: The Story of My Life.* New York: Benchman
Press, 2001.

Hadleigh, Boze. *Hollywood Lesbians.* New York: Barricade Books, 1994.

Harris, Warren G. *Audrey Hepburn.* New York: Simon & Schuster, 1994.

_____. *Sophia Loren.* New York: Simon & Schuster, 1989.

Hawkins, Jack. *Anything for a Quiet Life.* New York: Stein & Day, 1974.

Helfer, Toni Ringo. *The Gentle Jungle.* Provo: Bringham Young University Press,
1980.

Hofstede, David. *Audrey Hepburn: A Bio-Bibliography.* Westport, CT: Greenwood
Press, 1994.

Holston, Kim R. *Richard Widmark: A Bio-Bibliography.* Westport, CT: Greenwood Press, 1990.

_____. *Susan Hayward: Her Films and Life*. Jefferson, NC: McFarland, 2002.
Holtzman, Will. *Judy Holliday*. New York: Putnam, 1982.
_____. *William Holden*. New York: Pyramid, 1976.
Hope, Bob. *I Owe Russia $1200*. New York: Doubleday, 1963.
Hotchner, A. E. *Sophia Living and Loving: Her Own Story*. New York: Morrow, 1979.
Jarlett, Franklin. *Robert Ryan: A Biography and a Critical Filmography*. Jefferson, NC: McFarland, 1990.
Karasek, Hellmuth. *Billy Wilder: Un viennese a Hollywood*. Milano: Mondadori, 1993.
Keaney, Michael F. *Film Noir Guide*. Jefferson, NC: McFarland, 2002.
Knight, Vivienne. *Trevor Howard: A Gentleman and a Player*. New York: Beaufort Books, 1987.
Lacey, Robert. *Grace*. New York: Putnam, 1994.
LaGuardia, Robert, and Gene Arcery. *Red: The Tempestuous Life of Susan Hayward*. New York: Macmillan, 1985
Lally, Kevin. *Wilder Times: The Life of Billy Wilder*. New York: Henry Holt, 1996.
Lamour, Dorothy. *My Side of the Road*. Englewood Cliffs, NJ: Prentice-Hall, 1980.
Landesman, Fred. *The John Wayne Filmography*. Jefferson, NC: McFarland, 2004.
Laurents, Arthur. *Original Story By: A Memoir of Broadway and Hollywood*. New York: Knopf, 2000.
Leaming, Barbara. *If This Was Happiness: A Biography of Rita Hayworth*. New York: Viking, 1989.
Lean, Sandra. *David Lean: An Intimate Portrait*. New York: Universe Publishing, 2001.
Leemann, Sergio. *Robert Wise on His Films: From Editing Room to Director's Chair*. Los Angeles: Silman-James Press, 1995.
Leff, Leonard J., and Jerold L. Simmons. *The Dame in the Kimono*. New York: Grove Weidenfeld, 1991.
Leigh, Wendy Leigh. *True Grace*. London: JR Books, 2007.
Lenning, Arthur. *Stroheim*. Lexington: University Press of Kentucky, 2000.
Levy, Alan. *Forever Sophia*. New York: St. Martin's Press, 1986.
Levy, Emanuel. *George Cukor, Master of Elegance*. New York: Morrow, 1994.
Linet, Beverly. *Ladd: The Life, the Legend, the Legacy of Alan Ladd*. New York: Arbor House, 1979.
Logan, Joshua. *Josh: My Up and Down, In and Out Life*. New York: Delacorte Press, 1976.
_____. *Movie Stars, Real People and Me*. New York: Delacorte Press, 1978.
Long, Robert Emmet. *George Cukor Interviews*. Jackson: University Press of Mississippi, 2001.
Longobardi, Mario. *Più stelle che in cielo*. Roma: Gremese, 2003.
Lord, Graham. *Niv: The Authorised Biography of David Niven*. London: Orion, 2003.
Love, Damien. *Robert Mitchum: Solid Dad Crazy*. London: B.T. Batsford, 2002.
Luhr, William, and Peter Lehman. *Blake Edwards*. Athens: Ohio University Press, 1981.
_____, and _____. *Returning to the Scene: Blake Edwards Volume 2*. Athens: Ohio University Press, 1989.
Macnamara, Paul. *Those Were the Days, My Friend*. Lanham, MD: Scarecrow, 1993.

Madsen, Axel. *Billy Wilder*. London: Secker & Warburg, 1968.

_____. *Stanwyck*. New York: HarperCollins, 1994.

Magers, Boyd, and Michael G. Fitzgerald. *Western Women*. Jefferson, NC: McFarland, 1999.

Martin, Mart. *Did He or Didn't He?* New York: Citadel Press, 2000.

Masi, Stefano. *Sophia Loren*. Roma: Gremese, 2001.

Maxford, Howard. *David Lean*. London: Batsford, 2000.

Maychick, Diana. *Audrey Hepburn: An Intimate Portrait*. New York: Birch Lane Press, 1993.

McBride, Joseph. *Searching for John Ford*. New York: St. Martin's Press, 1999.

McClelland, Doug. *Eleanor Parker: A Woman of a Thousand Faces*. Metuchen, NJ: Scarecrow, 1989.

McGilligan, Patrick. *Alfred Hitchcock: A Life in Darkness and Light*. New York: Regan, 2003.

_____. *Backstory 2. Interviews with Screenwriters of the 1940s and 1950s*. Berkeley: University of California Press, 1991.

_____. *Clint: The Life and Legend*. New York: St. Martin's Press, 2002.

Milne, Tom. *Rouben Mamoulian*. Bloomington: Indiana University Press, 1970.

Moreno, Eduardo. *The Films of Susan Hayward*. Secaucus, NJ: Citadel Press, 1979.

Morley, Sheridan. *Audrey Hepburn: A Celebration*. London: Pavilion, 1993.

_____. *The Other Side of the Moon*. New York: Harper & Row, 1985.

Munn, Michael. *John Wayne: The Man Behind the Myth*. New York: New American Library, 2005.

_____. *Trevor Howard: The Man and His Films*. Chelsea, MI: Scarborough House, 1990.

Nass, Herbert E. *Wills of the Rich and Famous*. London: Robson Books, 1991.

Niccoli, Vieri. *Tutto esaurito*. Napoli: Filema Edizioni, 1977.

Niven, David. *The Moon's a Balloon*. New York: Putnam, 1972.

Noguchi, Thomas T. *Coroner*. New York: Simon & Schuster, 1983.

O'Connor, Gary. *Alec Guinness: A Life*. New York: Applause, 2002.

Oller, John. *Jean Arthur: The Actress That Nobody Knew*. New York: Limelight Editions, 2004.

Palmer, Lilli. *Change Lobsters — and Dance: An Autobiography*. New York: Macmillan, 1975.

Paris, Barry. *Audrey Hepburn*. New York: Putnam, 1996.

Parish, James Robert, and Don E. Stanke. *The All-Americans*. New Rochelle, NY: Arlington House, 1977.

Payn, Graham, and Sheridan Morley. *The Noël Coward Diaries*. New York: Da Capo Press, 1982.

Pettigrew, Terence. *Trevor Howard: A Personal Biography*. London: Peter Owen, 2001.

Phillips, Gene. *George Cukor*. Boston: Twayne, 1982.

Pierce, Arthur. *Jean Arthur: A Bio-Bibliography*. Westport, CT: Greenwood Press, 1990.

Pirolini, Alessandro. *Rouben Mamoulian*. Milano: Il Castoro, 1999.

Poague, Leland. *The Hollywood Professionals. Vol. 7*. San Diego: A.S. Barnes, 1998.

Quirk, Lawrence J. *The Complete Films of William Holden*. Secaucus, NJ: Citadel Press, 1986.

_____. *The Films of Fredric March*. Secaucus, NJ: Citadel Press, 1971.
_____. *Paul Newman*. Dallas: Taylor, 1996.
Read, Piers Paul. *Alec Guinness: The Authorized Biography*. New York: Simon & Schuster, 2003.
Reagan, Ronald. *Where's the Rest of Me?* New York: Sloan and Pearce, 1965.
Reed, Rex. *Valentines & Vitriol*. New York: Delacorte Press, 1977.
Rivadue, Barry. *Lee Remick: A Bio-Bibliography*. Westport, CT: Greenwood Press, 1995.
Rogers, Ginger. *Ginger: My Story*. New York: HarperCollins, 1991.
Roberts, Randy, and James S. Olson. *John Wayne: American*. New York: Free Press, 1995.
Ross, Lillian, and Helen Ross. *The Player: The Profile of an Art*. New York: Limelight Editions, 1984.
Russell, Rosalind. *Life Is a Banquet*. New York: Random House, 1977.
Russell Taylor, John. *Alec Guinness: A Celebration*. Boston: Little, Brown, 1984.
Sakol, Jeannie, and Caroline Latham. *About Grace: An Intimate Notebook*. Chicago: Contemporary Books, 1993.
Sanders Coyne, Steven, and Tom Gilbert. *Desilu: The Story of Lucille Ball and Desi Arnaz*. New York: Morrow, 1993.
Sandford, Christopher. *McQueen: The Biography*. London: HarperCollins, 2001.
Schary, Dore. *Heyday: An Autobiography*. Boston: Little, Brown, 1979.
Schickel, Richard. *Clint Eastwood: A Biography*. New York: Knopf, 1996.
Server, Lee. *Robert Mitchum: Baby, I Don't Care*. New York: St. Martin's Press, 2001.
Sesti, Mario. *David Lean*. Milano: Il Castoro, 1988.
Sikov, Ed. *On Sunset Boulevard: The Life and Times of Billy Wilder*. New York: Hyperion, 1998.
Silver, Alain, and James Ursini. *David Lean and His Films*. Los Angeles: Silman-James Press, 1991.
Silverman, Stephen M. *David Lean*. New York: Harry N. Abrams, 1992.
Sinclair, Andrew. *John Ford*. New York: Dial Press 1979.
Smith, Ella. *Starring Miss Barbara Stanwyck*. New York: Crown, 1974.
Spada, James. *Grace: The Secret Lives of a Princess*. New York: Doubleday, 1987.
Sperber, A.M., and Eric Lax. *Bogart*. New York: Morrow, 1997.
Staggs, Sam. *Close-Up on Sunset Boulevard*. New York: St. Martin's Press, 2002.
Strasberg, Susan. *Bittersweet*. New York: Putnam, 1980.
Stricklyn, Ray. *Angels & Demons*. Los Angeles: Belle Publishing, 1999.
Swanson, Gloria. *Swanson on Swanson*. New York: Random House, 1980.
Taraborrelli, Randy. *Once Upon a Time: Behind the Fairy Tale of Princess Grace and Prince Rainier*. New York: Warner Books, 2003.
Thomas, Bob. *Golden Boy: The Untold Story of William Holden*. New York: St. Martin's Press, 1983.
_____. *King Cohn*. New York: Putnam's, 1967.
Thompson, Charles. *Bing: The Authorized Biography*. New York: David McKay, 1975.
Thompson, Douglas. *Clint Eastwood Riding High*. Chicago: Contemporary Books, 1992.
Thompson, Verita. *Bogie and Me*. New York: St. Martin's Press, 1982.

Von Gunden, Kenneth. *Alec Guinness: The Films.* Jefferson, NC: McFarland, 1999.

Walker, Alexander. *Audrey Hepburn: Her Real Story.* New York: St. Martin's Press, 1994.

Wallis Hyer, Martha. *Finding My Way.* San Francisco: HarperSanFrancisco, 1990.

Wapshott, Nicholas. *Carol Reed: A Biography.* New York: Knopf, 1994.

Wayne, Aissa. *John Wayne: My Father.* New York: Random House, 1991.

Wayne, Jane Ellen. *Grace Kelly's Men.* New York: St. Martin's Press, 1991.

_____. *Stanwyck.* New York: Arbor House, 1985.

Wayne, Pilar. *John Wayne: My Life with the Duke.* New York: McGraw-Hill, 1987.

Weddle, David. *If They Move ... Kill 'Em! The Life and Times of Sam Peckinpah.* New York: Grove Press, 1994.

Willoughby, Bob. *Hollywood a Journey Through the Stars.* New York: Assouline, 2001.

Winters, Shelley. *Shelley Also Known as Shirley.* New York: Morrow, 1980.

Wise, James E., and Paul Wilderson III. *Stars in Khaki.* Annapolis, MD: Naval Institute Press, 2000.

Woodward, Ian. *Audrey Hepburn.* New York: St. Martin's Press, 1984.

Yablonsky, Lewis. *George Raft.* New York: McGraw-Hill, 1974.

York, Michael. *Accidentally on Purpose: An Autobiography.* New York: Simon & Schuster, 1991.

Zec, Donald. *Put the Knife in Gently: Memoirs of a Life with Legends.* London: Robson Books, 2003.

_____. *Sophia: An Intimate Biography.* London: W. H. Allen, 1975.

Zolotow, Maurice. *Billy Wilder in Hollywood.* London: W.H. Allen, 1977.

Index

197